HIGHER EDUCATION FINANCING
IN EAST AND SOUTHERN AFRICA

Edited by Pundy Pillay

© 2010 Centre for Higher Education Transformation (CHET)

All rights reserved.

No part of this publication may be reproduced, stored in a retrieval system or transmitted in any form, or by any means, without the prior permission of the publisher.

Published for CHET
by African Minds, 4 Eccleston Place, Somerset West, 7130, South Africa

ISBN: 978-1-920355-33-3

Layout and printing: COMPRESS.dsl, South Africa
www.compressdsl.com

Distributed by African Minds
4 Eccleston Place, Somerset West, 7130, South Africa
info@africanminds.co.za
www.africanminds.co.za

For orders from outside Africa, excluding North America:
African Books Collective
orders@africanbookscollective.com
www.africanbookscollective.com

For orders from North America:
Michigan State University Press
msupress@msu.edu
http://msupress.msu.edu/

CONTENTS

1. Introduction 1
Pundy Pillay

2. Botswana 7
Happy Siphambe

3. Kenya 29
Wycliffe Otieno

4. Lesotho 63
Pundy Pillay

5. Mauritius 81
Praveen Mohadeb

6. Mozambique 103
Arlindo Chilundo

7. Namibia 123
Jonathan Adongo

8. South Africa 153
Pundy Pillay

9. Tanzania 173
Johnson M Ishengoma

10. Uganda 195
Nakanyike Musisi and Florence Mayega

11. Good practices, possible lessons and remaining challenges 223
Pundy Pillay

About the authors 233
References 234

Acknowledgements

The authors gratefully acknowledge financial support provided by the Ford Foundation in Johannesburg.

Special thanks are due also to Dr John Butler-Adam, Ford Foundation; the Centre for Higher Education Transformation (CHET), Cape Town; and the Sizanang Centre for Research and Development, Pretoria, which coordinated the research.

Chapter 1
INTRODUCTION

Pundy Pillay

The Development Context

This multi-country study of higher education financing includes three East African states (Kenya, Tanzania and Uganda), five countries in southern Africa (Botswana, Lesotho, Mozambique, Namibia and South Africa), and an Indian Ocean island state (Mauritius).

The countries in this sample of case studies vary considerably in terms of their size and development status. As Table 1.1 shows, there are four extremely small countries in terms of population (Botswana, Lesotho, Mauritius and Namibia) and five medium-sized countries, with South Africa being the largest of the five with 49 million people.

Table 1.1 provides information about these countries' development status as measured using United Nations Development Programme's (UNDP's) Human Development Index (HDI). The HDI is a composite index derived from three measures: income or GDP per capita; education (adult literacy, and the combined gross enrolment ratio for primary, secondary and tertiary education); and life expectancy. In its *2009 Human Development Report*, the UNDP derived the HDI for 182 countries which were categorised as very high, high, medium or low HDI countries. The countries with the highest HDIs were Norway and Australia, and the first category included all the Western European countries, the USA, some Asian countries (Singapore and Hong Kong) and, interestingly, Barbados.

Of the nine country case studies in this volume, Mauritius was ranked as a high HDI country (ranking 81). Botswana (125), Namibia (128), South Africa (129), Kenya (147), Tanzania (151), Lesotho (156) and Uganda (157) were ranked as medium HDI countries; and Mozambique (172) was ranked as a low HDI country. Table 1.1 shows the HDI values which range from 0.804 for Mauritius to 0.402 for Mozambique. Norway ranked at number one had an HDI value of 0.971 (UNDP 2009).

Table 1.1 also shows the Human Poverty Index (HPI), the ranking of countries in terms of their levels of poverty, with the country being ranked number one having the least poverty. Amongst the nine countries included as case studies in this volume, Mauritius was ranked the highest at 45 out of the 135 countries on the HPI. It is clear that there is a close correlation between the value of the HDI and the extent of poverty, with Mozambique having the highest incidence of poverty at 46.8% at a HPI ranking of 127 out of 135 countries.

Table 1.1: Population and the Human Development Index by Country

COUNTRY	POPULATION (M)	HDI RANKING	HDI VALUE	HPI RANKING	HPI VALUE (%)
Botswana	1.9	125	0.694	81	22.9
Kenya	37.8	147	0.541	92	29.5
Lesotho	2.0	156	0.514	106	34.3
Mauritius	1.3	81	0.804	45	9.5
Mozambique	21.9	172	0.402	127	46.8
Namibia	2.1	128	0.686	70	17.1
South Africa	49.2	129	0.683	85	25.4
Tanzania	41.3	151	0.530	93	30.0
Uganda	30.6	157	0.514	91	28.8

Source: UNDP, 2009. The average HDI ranking for sub-Saharan Africa is 0.514; for South Asia it is 0.612; and for Latin America and the Caribbean, 0.821. The Human Poverty Index (HPI) value indicates the extent of poverty.

In terms of income per capita measures, four countries in the sample have attained middle income status – these are Botswana, Mauritius, Namibia and South Africa. The other five countries are regarded as low income in terms of this measure.

In summary, the nine countries vary considerably in terms of their population size and their development status as reflected, for example, by their respective HDIs, HPIs and income per capita.

Higher Education: Access, Equity and Financing

The challenges in education in general, and higher education in particular, in sub-Saharan Africa (SSA) are well-known. These relate in the main to inadequate access particularly at the secondary and tertiary levels, poor quality of provision, low levels of efficiency as reflected in high drop-out and repetition rates, and inequity in access and the distribution of resources along gender, regional (urban versus rural) and socio-economic lines.

Obtaining a measure of access and equity is difficult in Africa given data and definitional challenges. In some countries (such as Botswana and Egypt) higher or tertiary education refers to all post-school or post-secondary education. In South Africa, on the other hand, higher education refers only to university education. In this regard, comparing gross enrolment ratios might be inappropriate. For example, South Africa's Gross Enrolment Ratio (GER) for higher education is around 15–16% while that for Egypt and Mauritius (both covering all post-school education) are respectively 30% and 34%.

Notwithstanding this definitional problem, it is evident that participation in higher education in SSA is low in both absolute and relative terms. Of 23 SSA countries for which data are available, only Mauritius, Nigeria and South Africa have a GER in double figures (Pillay 2008; Adedeji & Pillay 2009). Among these 23 countries the GER ranges from 0.4% in Malawi to 34% in Mauritius.

Moreover, participation rates in SSA are substantially lower (5–6% in 2005) than the average for both developing (17% in 2005) and industrialised (66%) countries (UNESCO 2008).

In addition to low participation rates, access to higher education is highly inequitable. There are three important determinants of inequity: gender; socio-economic status and region.

Almost all SSA countries with the exception of Mauritius, Nigeria and South Africa, have significantly lower participation rates. Where women have managed to enter higher education in SSA countries, their participation is often concentrated in so-called traditional women's disciplines such as the humanities and education, rather than in commerce, engineering and science.

Second, access is often dependent on socio-economic status. In most SSA countries, enrolment at universities is dominated by students from the highest income categories. Often, public funding mechanisms act to exacerbate such inequities by providing free higher education to the 'best' students who invariably come from the wealthiest households and the top secondary schools.

Third, participation in higher education is often skewed in favour of urban students. Students from rural households face enormous barriers to gaining access to higher education in general, and the better quality higher education institutions in particular.

The public commitment to higher education by most countries in eastern and southern Africa is relatively high (as a percentage of national income), particularly in countries such as Kenya, Lesotho and Namibia. For the countries considered in this volume, average expenditure on higher education as a percentage of national income was around 4.6% in 2005 compared to 4.5% for developing countries as a whole, and 5.5% for industrialised countries (OECD 2006). However, public spending on higher education as a proportion of the education budget varies substantially amongst countries in this volume.

In SSA, as in many developing countries, there are often several reasons for low expenditure on higher education. First, there may be inadequate expenditure on education in general, as a percentage of the government's budget. Second, where education expenditure may be considered to be adequate or reasonable, there are often considerable political pressures to ensure that the schooling sector gets the dominant share of the public sector's commitment to education. Third, in a situation of serious resource constraints, there is often keen inter-sectoral competition for financial resources from sectors such as health, housing and social welfare. Finally, the case for increased higher education financing has not been helped by the low prioritisation of this sector by many African governments. The value of higher education for economic growth and broader social and sustainable development has not yet been fully recognised by African governments (Pillay 2008).

Overview

This nine-country study explores trends in financing policies paying particular attention to the nature and extent of public sector funding of higher education, the growth of private financing (including both household financing and the growth of private higher education institutions) and the changing mix of financing instruments that these countries are developing in response to public sector financial constraints.

Siphambe's chapter on Botswana shows that education expenditure as a proportion of gross domestic product in that country is relatively high at around 9%, but the proportion of the education budget allocated to higher education is relatively low at 12.5%. Public higher education in Botswana has effectively been free for a long time. Interesting features of the Botswana system include the recent establishment of a new university on a public–private partnership basis and the fact that government-funded scholarships are provided also to students in private higher education institutions. The loan/grant scheme is notionally linked to human resource needs with financial incentives linked to relative scarcity. However, until recently, the loan scheme has been ineffective (in not addressing scarce human resources needs) and inefficient (because of poor cost recovery).

INTRODUCTION 5

In Chapter 3, Otieno provides a detailed analysis of higher education financing in Kenya showing how the system in that country has evolved to the present situation characterised by a 'dual-track' system within public higher education, and the accelerated growth of private higher education. Otieno draws attention to the patterns of state funding at the public universities and provides a useful critique of the 'unit cost' system currently in use in Kenya. This chapter also provides a detailed description of the student loan scheme, one of two effective schemes currently operating in SSA (the other being in South Africa). Finally, Otieno proposes a new funding framework to enhance efficiency, equity and effectiveness.

The chapter on Lesotho by Pillay shows the high level of government expenditure (around 40% of the education budget) on tertiary education by this tiny, landlocked country. Government funds students through a loan/bursary scheme but the loans are actually grants as no recovery has taken place. However, some plans initiated by the Ministry of Finance are now under way to implement an effective loan recovery scheme. In addition, there is a high level of bursary expenditure on students outside the country. This is understable from the viewpoint of developing scarce human resources for the country. However, anecdotal evidence suggests that only a small proportion of students return to the country on graduation.

Mohadeb's description of the Mauritian system shows a system clearly differentiated into its public and private components. In this system, government covers only about a quarter of all higher education expenditure. An interesting feature of the public funding framework is the existence of a differentiated government funding model. For example, the University of Mauritius provides free undergraduate education while at the University of Technology, students pay fees (but not full cost). More than half of the funding for higher education derives from private households and goes to international institutions both inside and outside the country.

In Chapter 6 on Mozambique, Chilundo shows first the high percentage of the education budget devoted to higher education, at around 40%. A feature of the system is the high level of dependence on donor funding. There is minimal cost sharing in the system and government funds institutions on the basis of inputs (student numbers) only. The pattern of funding suggests a high degree of inefficiency and inequity. Innovative features of the system include the funding of quality improvement initiatives in both public and private higher education institutions, and provincial (rural) scholarships to address equity.

Adongo's chapter on Namibia describes a system receiving a relatively high level of resources yet is characterised by high unit costs and general systemic inefficiency. There are no clear criteria for allocating funds and the gap between institutional requests for funds and actual allocations is large. The national loan scheme benefits relatively few students. However, cost sharing in the form of tuition fees has been introduced.

The South African case study by Pillay describes a higher education financing system which is probably the most advanced in SSA. Key features of the system include a fairly serious public commitment to funding; an effective student loan scheme; a close link between systemic and institutional planning on the one hand and funding on the other; substantial cost sharing; and a funding formula which contributes to achieving the objectives of the higher education sector. Nevertheless, serious challenges persist with regard to quality, efficiency and inter-institutional equity.

In Chapter 9 on Tanzania, Ishengoma describes a system in which government is the dominant player with respect to funding. As in Mozambique, there is significant donor involvement in the higher education sector. There is limited cost sharing with loans being provided to students in both public and private institutions. Until 2007, no attempts were made to recover these loans. Recurrent funding is based on capitation grants and unit costs. Capital funding in the form of grants and loans are made available to public and private institutions through a parastatal, the Tanzania Education Authority.

Musisi and Mayega provide a detailed description of the higher education system and the manner of its financing in Uganda. A thorough analysis is undertaken of the trends in financing over time for the various components of the tertiary education system including universities, technical institutions and teacher colleges. The analysis of the university system pays particular attention to the evolution of the 'dual-track' system and the growth of private institutions. In addition, an extended comparative analysis is undertaken of the country's 'flagship' institution, Makerere University, and Kyambogo University, including enrolment patterns, funding trends and unit costs. Finally, the authors provide a set of options for more a effective system of higher education financing by describing the respective roles of the state, private sector and donors.

The concluding chapter draws attention to the remaining challenges around the financing of higher education in this set of countries. In addition, some common themes, lessons and good practices are identified.

Chapter 2
BOTSWANA

Happy Siphambe

Overview of Higher Education

At independence in 1966 and for many years afterwards, the lack of skilled and educated Batswana was one of the most significant constraints to development. At independence, there were few schools and educated Batswana as a result of the neglect of education by the colonial government. The few schools that existed were a result of local and missionary initiatives. At independence, Botswana is believed to have had 40 Batswana who were university graduates and about 100 with a senior secondary certificate in a total population of slightly more than half a million people. All of the university graduates were trained outside the country, mainly in the Republic of South Africa (Harvey & Lewis 1990; Colclough & McCarthy 1980). Given the low level of human capital inherited from the colonial government, the newly independent Botswana Government had to invest heavily in education, but the skills shortages persisted for a long time mainly due to time lags inherent in education and rapid economic growth which, in turn, increased the demand for educated people (Harvey & Lewis 1990).

Most of these critical skills shortages were met by heavy importation of skilled labour, which was very expensive for the Botswana Government. Just two years prior to its independence, only 24 of the 184 administrative posts were held by Batswana; at lower levels, only 275 out of 623 posts in the technical, executive and secretarial grades were held by Batswana (Colclough & McCarthy 1980). It is this scarcity of human capital that informed the government's training policy since independence and has shaped the nature of education and training.

Higher education, in particular, was for most of the period after independence geared towards training of people for white collar jobs, with the hope that they would replace the expatriates. As a result technical, vocational and agricultural studies were seriously neglected. The Botswana College of Agriculture for instance, did not start offering degree programmes until the 1990s. The same is true of engineering and technology, which only started to be offered at degree level with the creation of the Faculty of Engineering and Technology in the 1990s.

Higher education in Botswana is grouped under what is called 'tertiary education', which refers to all education that requires the minimum entry requirement of a senior secondary education. These include certificates/diplomas, degrees and other advanced courses offered by the various institutions. Table 2.1 summarises the institutions that currently operate in the country.

Table 2.1: Higher Education Institutions in Botswana

NAME OF INSTITUTION	TYPE OF INSTITUTION	QUALIFICATION(S) OFFERED
1. University of Botswana	Public university	Certificates, diplomas and degrees
2. Molepolole College of Education	Public college	Diploma in Secondary Teaching
3. Tonota College of Education	Public college	Diploma in Secondary Teaching
4. Tlokweng Teacher's College	Public college	Certificates and diploma in Primary Teaching
5. Francistown Teacher's College	Public college	Certificates and diploma in Primary Teaching
6. Lobatse Teacher's College	Public college	Certificates and diploma in Primary Teaching
7. Serowe Teacher's College	Public college	Certificates and diploma in Primary Teaching
8. Botswana College of Agriculture	Public college	Originally offering certificates and diplomas but now degrees in Agriculture
9. Institutes of Health Sciences (currently 5)	Public institutions	Diploma in Nursing
10. Botswana Accountancy College	Public institution	Certificates, diplomas and professional accounting courses (CIMA, AAT, ACCA)
Private Institutions		
1. Limkomkin University of Arts and Technology	Private	
2. Ba Isago University College – a branch of UNISA (South Africa)	Private	
3. Academy of Business Management (ABM)	Private	
4. Gaborone Institute of Professional Studies (GIPS)	Private	
5. National Institute of Information Technology (NIIT)	Private	

The main provider of tertiary education programmes in the country has been the University of Botswana (UB) which was established in 1982 from being a campus of the then University of Botswana, Lesotho and Swaziland (UBLS) which was discontinued as such in 1975. The UBLS main campus was located in Maseru, Lesotho. The campus was itself originally a college of liberal arts of the University of South Africa (UNISA), which was geared towards preparing students for the Bachelor of Arts degree. However, in the 1950s the college had begun to experience problems of shortage of income, deteriorating ties with UNISA and restrictions on student admissions. Given the scarcity of places for higher education, the three high commission territories started negotiations with the Roman Catholic authorities responsible for the college to establish the college as an independent university run by the three countries. The autonomous campus was set up in 1963 in Lesotho and was to be fully funded by the three governments.

When they attained independence, the three countries began to take a closer look at their economic and human resource needs. This led to a series of academic planning reports, a major one being the Alexander Report of 1970 (University of Botswana 2007). The Report recommended the establishment of university campuses in each country and a unified development of higher education, and vocational and technical training. There were to be new campuses in Gaborone in Botswana and Kwaluseni in Swaziland. Funds were also obtained from major donors and the three governments to develop campuses in each of the countries. Following student unrest at Roma, Lesotho, and strained relations between UBLS administration and the Lesotho Government over implementation of the agreed plans, Lesotho withdrew the Roma campus and constituted it as the National University of Lesotho (NUL) in 1975. The collaboration had thus broken and students from Botswana and Swaziland were immediately withdrawn from the Roma campus. Botswana and Swaziland then set up the University of Botswana and Swaziland (UBS) with two constituent university campuses, one in Gaborone and another in Kwaluseni. The two campuses were planned to develop into two independent universities, which came to pass in 1982. The independent Universities of Botswana and Swaziland continued to cooperate in certain areas and exchange students for some time after the establishment of the two independent campuses.

Other major players in tertiary education in Botswana are the Colleges of Education offering diploma and certificate courses (currently six), Institutes of Health Sciences (five), Botswana Accountancy College (BAC), and Botswana College of Agriculture (BCA). The University of Botswana and the Colleges of Education report directly to the Ministry of Education, while the Institutes of Health Sciences report directly to the Ministry of Health, and BCA falls under the Ministry of Agriculture. In terms of governance, BCA is an associate institution of UB with separate governance under the Ministry of Agriculture, while the colleges of Education and the Institutes of Health Sciences are affiliated to UB for quality assurance and certification of programmes.

Botswana's tertiary education development has had two major phases. The first phase was a period prior to 2001 when most students were sponsored to study at the only public university (the University of Botswana), the Colleges of Education and National Health Institutes. A few students were sponsored to study at universities outside the country especially in areas that were not offered by the local university (these included Medicine, Engineering and other applied science subjects).

The Government of Botswana abolished National Service and was therefore faced with two streams of students, one coming from National Service and one just having completed their secondary education. To deal with the double intake, the government had to seek more places especially in South African universities. At that time there were no private universities operating in the country on a full scale.

The second phase is the current period, whose starting point is 2007. A major feature of this current period is the Government of Botswana decision to extend scholarships to students admitted to private institutions locally, which was not the case prior to 2007. Among the private institutions that are eligible are Limkomking University of Arts and Technology, Ba Isago University College, National Institute of Information Technology, Academy of Business Management, and Gaborone Institute of Professional Studies. Government subsidy takes the form of tuition paid by the government for the sponsored student and they do not enjoy any direct government funding.

Plans are at an advanced stage to start a second university, the Botswana International University of Science and Technology (BIUST), to be located in Palapye in the Central District of the country. This university is to be funded under a public–private partnership (PPP) but with a larger proportion of the capital development funding coming from government. This university together with the private providers is likely to increase access to tertiary education quite significantly.

Botswana has, over the past four decades, achieved very high economic growth which has enabled the country to move from being one of the poorest at independence to one with an upper middle income status. In the 30 years following independence, Botswana was the fastest growing economy in the world, outperforming the Southeast Asian 'Tiger' Economies (Singapore, Hong Kong, South Korea and Taiwan) with an average annual growth rate of over 10%. One of the major results of this phenomenal growth of the economy was a huge escalation of social expectations fueling the demand for tertiary education. Over the years, there has been evidence of excess demand for places in tertiary education locally, which saw a rapid increase in private tertiary education institutions as well as government sponsoring of students in tertiary education outside the country.

In trying to deal with some of the problems of coordination between UB and the need to introduce future competition between UB and other institutions, the Revised National Policy on Education (RNPE) proposed the formation of a Tertiary Education Council (TEC) whose main duties will be to promote and coordinate tertiary education and maintain standards of teaching, examination and research in tertiary institutions.

Other specific functions of the TEC as stipulated by the Act are to:

- Formulate policy on tertiary education and advise the government accordingly;
- Coordinate the long-term planning and overall development of tertiary education;
- Liaise with both the public and private sectors of the economy on all matters relating to human resources development and requirements; and
- Plan for the funding of tertiary education and research, including the recurrent and development needs of public tertiary institutions (TEC 2006).

Among the issues tackled by the TEC was the registration of new and existing tertiary institutions for accreditation and quality assurance purposes. The TEC is also in the process of developing a funding model for tertiary education institutions so that in future tertiary education institutions will be funded through the TEC rather than through their respective Ministries as is currently the case. The funding model is likely to take into consideration, inter alia, the discipline and the level of courses offered. Given dwindling public resources, it is unlikely that public funding will be extended to private universities, except in the form of sbisidised student fees as is currently the case.

Even though public institutions are mainly funded by government they are autonomous in terms of governance structures. In the University of Botswana for instance, the highest decision-making body is the University Council comprising representatives from government (Ministry of Finance and Development Planning, and Education), individuals from the private and parastatal sectors, and members of the university community. The head of the university is the Chancellor who is also the President of the country. Theoretically, the university has been autonomous in terms of its functions except when it comes to financial matters where the government usually has the final say. Remuneration of university staff for instance is linked to that of the public service. That linkage is in terms of the salary ranges and not on a job-to-job basis.

The private institutions have different governance structures that allow them greater autonomy especially as they are financially independent of government. For most of them, they are branches of the main universities located in their home countries. All they are required to do is meet requirements of the TEC in terms of quality of their programmes, staffing and physical resources.

The tertiary education policy that gives the TEC more powers in terms of control of higher education was approved in May 2008, and given that the TEC is still a fairly new body, it would be difficult to judge its effectiveness to date. It is also still in the process of building up its capacity to effectively carry out its mandate.

Planning in Education and Training

Given the shortage of skilled human resources and the need to rapidly 'localise' the various posts for the expanding economy, the government decided to plan using so-called 'manpower plans'. The main aim of these 'manpower plans' was to try and eliminate imbalances between the demand for and supply of human resources. The projections made provided useful information for training institutions, trainees, students, workers and employers regarding labour market supply and demand. The 'manpower plans' were prepared by the Employment Policy Unit (EPU) of the Ministry of Finance and Development Planning (MFDP) to help guide the economy in terms of education, training and demand for various skills. The forecasted numbers were then used for enrolment projections in higher education and as a basis for Ministry of Education planning and budgeting (Republic of Botswana 1993).

Five 'manpower plans' were developed between 1982 and 1987. From the outset, the 'manpower plans' were meant to cater mainly for the public service. As would be expected given the shortage of skilled labour, in the early years of Botswana's independence, there was an aggressive demand for the localisation of positions in the Public Service. To meet this demand, the government utilised almost every local university graduate emerging from the University of Botswana as well as from other universities outside the country. The private sector remained mainly 'not localised' for most of the early post-independence period, especially with regards to technical and other professional positions. This situation, although improved, has continued to this day. What has improved the situation over time is the ability of the private sector to attract and recruit qualified workers from the public sector, especially after 1990, when a Revised Incomes Policy was implemented. The policy for the period before then had tied the salaries of the private sector to the public sector on a job-to-job basis, and therefore the private sector could not use salaries to attract qualified and experienced civil servants.

Due to lack of human resources in EPU and a shift in employment policy focus, no 'manpower plans' were produced for more than ten years. Since the last 'manpower plan' in 1987, higher education enrolment planning was undertaken mainly made on an ad-hoc basis. In 2001, the Botswana Institute of Development Policy Analysis (BIDPA) was commissioned to produce the national 'manpower' projections. These projections were to be used for guiding training institutions in terms of courses to emphasise and identify priority areas of study for the Ministry of Education. However, these projections were not used for future planning even though some of the recommendations from this study have been implemented on a small scale, including tracer studies by training institutions. The University of Botswana for instance started its own plan for 2004–2009, which is in its last phase with projections based on estimates of population, other economic parameters, and availability of building space. The plan envisaged increasing enrolment of undergraduate students to 15 000 full-time students by 2009 (University of Botswana 2004).

In 2006 the country began a process of formulating a National Human Resources Development Strategy. The strategy recommended a move away from 'manpower' planning given the flaws in its approach to human resources development. Some of these flaws relate to the fact that it ignores substitution possibilities as well as the costs of educating and training one type of labour relative to another (MFDP 2006). The implementation of a new way of forecasting human resource demand and supply is in the process of being finalised, and future enrolment and budgets for training and the Ministry of Education will be guided by this new thinking. The demand side will be determined by current and projected employment needs while the supply side will need to take into consideration all the stages of education as well as issues of oversupply.

Participation and Access in Higher Education
As stated earlier, in response to the scarcity of skilled labour, and given the availability of revenues from diamond mining, the Government of Botswana began to expand schooling in the early 1970s both in terms of physical facilities and increases in enrolment. The education sector has always received the major share of both the development and recurrent budgets of government. As a result of these efforts there has been a large increase of graduates from tertiary education, some of whom are currently unable to find jobs in the labour market.

School enrolment at all levels increased considerably after independence. In 1975, 58% of the primary school-going-age children were enrolled, while that percentage had increased to 91% by 1991 and is currently at 100%. The percentage of school-age group enrolled in secondary education also increased remarkably from 7% in 1970 to 54 % in 1991 and is currently around 95% as a response to the country's goal of universal access to ten years of basic education by 2016 (Republic of Botswana/UN 2004). However, post-secondary (tertiary) enrolment increased only slightly from 1% in 1970 to 3% in 1991 (World Bank 1994: 217). This was because spaces for tertiary education were few given that there was only one university and a few Colleges of Education. Compared to most countries in the region for which data are available, the increase in enrolment in secondary education between 1970 and 1991 for Botswana was exceptional. For example, South Africa increased its enrolment from 30% to 54% over the same period, Zimbabwe from 4% to 13%, and Lesotho from 7% to 25% (World Bank 1994: 216–217).

Between 1997 and 2005, as a ratio of the total population, primary school enrolment was declining, while that of secondary education was rising. The decline in primary population was partly due to the impact of HIV/AIDS which significantly lowered the number of primary school-age students, as fertility rates were declining.

Table 2.2 shows the access rates to tertiary education for the population aged 18–24. The access rate has been rising over time, from 5% in 1997 to about 7.3% in 2005. Total access for tertiary education rose initially from 11.4% in 1997 to 14.6% in 2000/2001 before declining slightly to 11.3% in 2005.

Table 2.2: Student Enrolment (1997–2005)

INSTITUTION/YEAR	1997	1998	1999	2000	2001	2002	2003	2004	2005
University of Botswana	8 284	8 965	10 160	11 876	12 286	12 783	15 425	15 725	15 710
Botswana College of Agriculture	392	392	392	604	801	849	820	853	858
Colleges of Education	1 261	1 257	1 259	1 263	1 495	1 643	1 802	1 659	1 576
Institutes of Health Science	1 300	1 358	1 423	1 451	1 449	1 316	1 403	1 418	1 453
18–24 population	224 036	231 570	238 893	245 612	250 322	254 581	258 646	262 602	266 650
Access rate (%)	5.0	5.2	5.5	6.2	6.4	6.5	7.5	7.5	7.3

Source: TEC 2006

For the 18–24 age group, Botswana's tertiary education compares unfavourably with other countries in the region at similar levels of development. Within the region South Africa and Mauritius had enrolments of 15% and 19% respectively in 2005. Adding those sponsored outside Botswana does not improve the situation much. As Table 2.3 shows, this group increased from 394 in 1997 to 1 620 in

2005. Looking at the whole population in terms of people with post-secondary education, however, shows a tremendous improvement between 1991 and 2001. While the percentage of the population with post-secondary education was just 1.6% in 1981 and 3.2% in 1991, it increased dramatically to 18.9% by 2001. This was the result of enormous efforts from government in terms of expansion of school facilities, enrolment increases and consequent increases in the budget to the education sector.

Table 2.3: Government Outbound-Sponsored Students

YEAR	1997	1998	1999	2000	2001	2002	2003	2004	2005
Total	394	964	541	795	5 285	3 213	1 880	1 686	1 620

Source: TEC 2006

There are likely to be improvements in terms of access to tertiary education as a result of the new policy directions and intentions. The overall policy of the TEC is to move the country towards a knowledge-based society. As part of that move towards making Botswana's development knowledge-based, the TEC proposes to increase access to tertiary education to 17% by 2016 and to 20% by 2020. This will require a major expansion of the current institutions. This process will be facilitated by the proposed Botswana International University of Science and Technology (BIUST), the construction of which will start within the National Development Plan 9 period (2005–2009).

There is also pressure for tertiary education to expand to accommodate the increasing number of graduates from secondary education. With universal access to junior education having been achieved, there is now pressure to increase access from junior to senior secondary, which has increased from about 50% at the beginning of the millennium to close to 70% by 2007. Plans are to achieve 100% transition rate from junior secondary to senior secondary within NDP 10 which will be starting in 2009. Botswana is also in the process of implementing a Human Resource Development strategy, which is anchored on lifelong learning. All these factors will lead to an increased demand for tertiary education, which, if accommodated, will increase access and would likely lead the country to achieving access rates that are commensurate with its middle income status.

In terms of access to postgraduate training, Botswana still has a very small proportion of total enrolment, even though it has risen slightly, from 2.8% in 1997 to about 5.5% of total enrolment in 2005 (Table 2.4). In the 2006/2007 academic year, the University of Botswana had an enrolment of 16 239, of which 946 (5.8%) were enrolled in master's degrees and only 44 (0.3%) were enrolled in MPhil/PhD degrees (UB Strategic Plan 2008). Out of the eight faculties at the University of Botswana, only three faculties currently offer MPhil/PhD degrees.

In terms of enrolment by discipline, the highest levels of enrolment are in the Humanities and Social Sciences at about 37%, followed by Education and Business at 28% and 26% respectively in 2005. Science had the lowest enrolment at about 9% in 2005.

Table 2.4: Enrolment at Graduate Level

ENROLMENT	1997	1998	1999	2000	2001	2002	2003	2004	2005
Post-Secondary tertiary	9 957	10 614	11 811	13 531	14 582	15 275	18 047	18 237	18 144
Graduate	283	347	419	498	571	700	769	779	993
Graduate % of total	2.8	3.3	3.5	3.7	3.9	4.6	4.3	4.3	5.5

Source: CSO 2008

Table 2.5: Enrolment by Discipline

FACULTY/YEAR	1997	1998	1999	2000	2001	2002	2003	2004	2005
Business	1 309	1 404	1 624	1 145	1 771	1 540	1 898	2 250	2 354
Education	1 518	1 624	1 755	1 828	2 057	2 242	2 572	2 680	2 535
Humanities & Social Science	1 313	1 333	1 560	1 976	2 188	2 720	3 361	3 277	3 296
Sciences	571	566	589	624	701	710	783	750	778
Total	4 711	4 927	5 528	5 573	6 717	7 212	8 614	8 957	8 963

Source: TEC 2006 Table 6

In terms of access to higher education by gender, Botswana has reached gender equity as women generally constitute a higher percentage of total enrolment. This ratio has been quite stable at 53% of the total enrolment being female. As shown in Table 2.6, males are proportionally more in only two of the faculties – Science and Engineering.

Table 2.6: Enrolment at University of Botswana by Gender (2006)

FACULTY	TOTAL	FEMALE	% FEMALE
Business	1 799	1 079	60
CCE	2 317	1 488	64
Education	2 748	1 629	59
Engineering	1 381	193	14
Humanities	2 997	1 916	64
Science	1 606	438	27
Social sciences	2 390	1 403	59

Source: UB Factbook 2006

Education Expenditure and Financing

Education Expenditure
Most of education, except private primary and secondary education, is funded by the government. Therefore the budget going to education from the total government budget has been substantial. A significant proportion of both the development budget and recurrent budgets is allocated to the education sector.

Generally government expenditure on education has been increasing over time. The budget is based on per unit costs, which were based on the generated enrolment figures in the 'manpower plans'. For the other years, general estimates were used.

For the fiscal periods between 1980 and 1990, the government was allocating between 17 and 19% of total annual national budget to education, a figure that is high in international and regional terms.

Expenditure allocated to education rose from 19% in 1979 to about 25.2% of the total government budget in 2005/2006. The budget item with the biggest increase is the recurrent budget which rose from 23% in 1979 to about 29% in 2005/2006. Development expenditure to education, however, has been declining over time, falling from 15% of total development budget in 1979 to about 14% in the 2005/2006 fiscal year. Education expenditure as a percentage of total GDP rose from 7.3% of GDP in 1993/1994 to a peak of 10% of GDP in 2001/2002 before beginning to decline to 9% of GDP in 2005/2006. The peak in 2001/2002 is partly due to the expenditure towards an almost double intake as government abolished National Service that particular year leading to two streams of students having to be sponsored for tertiary education. A significant number of them were aslo sponsored at South African universities. The education GDP ratio is comparable by the standards of a developing country but a little bit lower than that expected for a middle income country. Akanbi (2007) for instance shows that for the whole of Africa education expenditure as a percentage of GDP has been about 10% between 1996 and 2004. Given Botswana's relative success in terms of output and revenue one would have expected the country to have achieved a relatively higher share of the expenditure. This is, however, understandable given that there were some major competing challenges that also required more government resources, including HIV/AIDS.

Financing of Higher Education
Many countries did not prioritise higher education because it was considered to lead to income inequality and provided lower social rates of return than other education levels. Higher education often exacerbates income inequality because it

is mainly accessible to children from relatively rich families who are able to afford school fees for secondary education. As a result of this thinking, the proportion of budgets allocated to higher education was for most developing countries less than 10% of the total budget.

Historically, Botswana has consistently spent more than 10% although that figure has declined from 15.6% in 1995 to 10.9% in 2005. This latter figure may be a bit of an understatement given that part of the education budget falls under the different ministries for in-service training, particularly the Department of Public Service Management (DPSM) and the Ministry of Health (for the Institute of Health Sciences). A part of the budget for higher education also falls under the general post-secondary budget.

One can conclude that Botswana has done better than most developing countries in terms of allocation of resources towards higher education. However, access rates still remain low, which may be indicative of the high per unit costs of education. Most of the expansion after the abolition of National Service in 2001 was accommodated by expenditure on sending students to universities outside the country, especially South Africa, since the University of Botswana did not have the capacity to absorb the expanded output.

Education in Botswana is mainly financed by the Government of Botswana. After independence school fees were charged at primary and secondary levels of education. During the late 1970s, the government became increasingly aware of equity issues in education as evidence was clearly showing that a number of students were unable to complete some levels of education due to financial constraints. In line with its universal education for all goal, the government abolished school fees, first at primary school (in 1978) and later for secondary school (in 1989). Due to financial constraints and, the government has since 2006 implemented cost sharing in secondary education. Primary education continues to be free.

Higher education in Botswana has always been paid for by the government via a loan which was granted provided that the graduate would contribute 5% of initial gross salary for each year of sponsorship. Those who went into other government tertiary institutions operating under the respective ministries other than the universities got 100% funding with no requirement to pay back the loan.

Apart from the fact that the government contribution to students for university education did not cover the full costs of training, a more serious problem was that a majority of the graduates were not contributing, and repayment and recovery of the loans was extremely low. The coordination between the employers and Bursaries Department was poor, making it difficult to find out who was contributing or to trace graduates (Republic of Botswana 1991).

Following the recommendations of the Presidential Commission on the Revised National Policy on Incomes, Employment, Prices and Profits of 1990, the bursary system was re-organised into a loan/grant system. This was provided to every citizen who qualified to go to university to study for a course of his/her choice. The loan/grant scheme for higher education students was introduced in 1995. Loans are payable on a sliding scale. Students studying in subject areas that are deemed to be in short supply are awarded a 100% grant. Loan beneficiaries are required to pay loans within a stipulated period after training, and the loans are interest free. The loan/grant is based on the human resource needs of the different sectors of the economy and is aimed at assisting the economy in terms of giving students an incentive to follow the areas in which skills are considered to be scarce while also providing cost recovery from higher education.

There are five categories of loans. Category 1 comprises those areas considered to be experiencing a critical shortage of the human resources and include the science and technical fields. These include Medicine, Dentistry, Engineering, Professional Accounting and Actuarial Studies. This category is awarded a 100% grant on both tuition and maintenance costs. Students contribute in terms of being required to take up employment in Botswana for a specified period of time. Category 2 comprises areas with human resource shortages because programmes were unattractive to students in the past. These include subjects such as Economics, Statistics, Town Planning, Chemistry and Agricultural Science. Subjects of study in this category attract 100% grant on tuition costs and 50% loan on maintenance. Graduates contribute in terms of service for a specified period plus repayment of 50% loan on maintenance. Category 3 is for those subjects needed to encourage local capacity to increase supply of qualified human resources to satisfy the market or balance demand and supply. Examples of these are Law, Public Administration, Journalism, Social Work, BSC (general) and Psychology. Students in this category have a 100% grant on tuition costs, 100% loan on maintenance costs. Graduates contribute in terms of service for a specified period plus repayment of 50% loan on tuition costs and 100% maintenance costs. Category 4 applies to programmes that benefit the society and economy but are less of a priority. These include Sociology, Philosophy, Museum Studies, Physical Education and Archaeology. Graduates have a similar degree of cost recovery to Category 3 in that they are to contribute in terms of service for a specified period plus repayment of 50% loan on tuition costs and 100% maintenance costs. Category 5 is for programmes largely benefiting individuals. These include Hair Dressing, Cosmetology, Photography, Modelling, Interior Design, and Performing Arts. Cost recovery is in terms of service in Botswana for a specified of time and repayment of 100% loan on both tuition and maintenance costs (Ministry of Education [MOE] 2004).

Since the inception of the loan/grant system, a total of 96 813 students have been sponsored in different tertiary education institutions. As Table 2.7 shows, a majority of the students prior to 2001 were sponsored in Botswana, particularly to the University of Botswana and the Colleges of Education and Institutes of Health Sciences. In 2001, which is when National Service was abolished, government had to deal with placing the two streams by increasing enrolment to South African universities. There were almost 5 000 students sponsored by the Government of Botswana to study at various South African universities in that year. Excluding South Africa, Malaysia has the largest group of students from Botswana, with the intake for 2007 having been 987 students. Another significant change in terms of sponsorship was in 2007 when government for the first time sponsored students to the private institutions within the country. As a result, as shown in Table 2.7, enrolment in the country increased by more than three times from about 5 500 students to 15 450 students. Given that the private sector normally responds much faster to demand, the change is likely to increase access to education within a very short period of time. Several of the new private universities for instance, are expanding their facilities to be able to absorb more students into their programmes.

Table 2.7: Student Placement Trend

YEAR	1995	1996	1997	1998	1999	2000	2001	2002	2003	2004	2005	2006	2007
Botswana	1 320	3 283	3 698	3 784	4 374	5 556	6 054	6 232	6 495	5 953	5 490	5 511	15 451
South Africa	2	20	36	196	177	399	4782	3304	1765	1605	1664	1563	1 373
Other countries	173	294	381	818	402	415	662	448	404	403	345	648	1 333
Total	1 495	3 597	4 115	4 798	4 953	6 370	11 498	9 984	8 664	7 961	7 499	7 722	18 157

Source: Ministry of Education

To date, however, the scheme has had limited success in increasing outputs of students in priority areas. Between 1997 and 2005, the total number of students sponsored was 28 672, with 22 796 of them (80%) having been sponsored to the University of Botswana. As Figure 2.1 shows, the majority of them were in Category 2 at 64%. Category 1 was second with 22% while the least preferred Category 5 had only 0.3% of the total students sponsored. The picture is similar in 2007. The majority of those sponsored by Government in 2007 were in Category 2 at 54%. Category 1 only makes about 12% which is even lower than the proportion of total students in that category sponsored between 1997 and

Figure 2.1: Student Sponsorship by Category (2007)

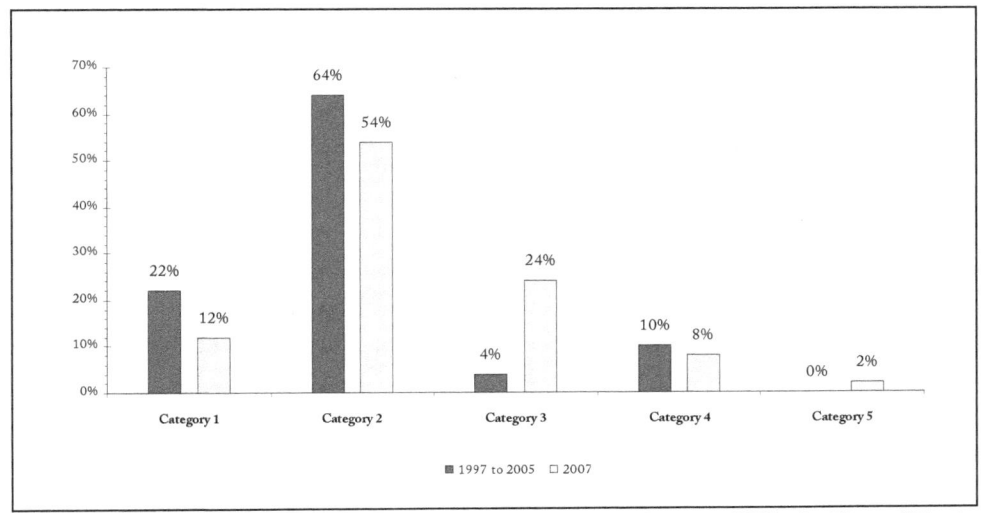

Source: Department of Student Placement and Welfare data, Ministry of Education

2005. Average yearly costs per student are quite high for external placement, the lowest being in the region for countries like Namibia, Lesotho and South Africa. For other countries, the expenditure is almost eight times that of University of Botswana, the highest being the UK at BWP 297 000 per year per student.

The implication for cost effectiveness is that Botswana will need to increase access to higher education locally rather than rely on external placement. There are efforts in that direction as discussed earlier, which entail sponsoring students to local private institutions. Costs at these institutions, including the private ones, are between BWP 20 000 and BWP 30 000 per student annually. Other efforts include starting some of the priority programmes at the University of Botswana and the upcoming new Botswana International University of Science and Technology. University of Botswana has for instance opened a Faculty of Health Sciences which will host medical studies and other health-related studies. This will go a long way in terms of increasing access to higher education at cost-effective levels. The loan/grant scheme was to be reviewed in 2008 in order to address some of the problems experienced since its implementation in 1995. Among the issues to be addressed are sustainability, alignment to the country's human resource needs, enforcement of the loan agreement, and recovery of loans from beneficiaries, as well as exploring effective administration and management of the scheme.

Apart from the lack of effective means to attract students in the priority areas (e.g. Category 1) the loan/grant system has a problem of low loan repayment rates mainly because of poor information on graduates. Given the tightness of the labour market for graduates (at least up until recently), it may be that the net advantages of studying what are generally perceived to be difficult subject areas (especially Science and Engineering) are not sufficient relative to other degree courses.

Equity in Higher Education Expenditure

There are no data on access to education in Botswana by income level to be able to assess the extent to which public expenditure on higher education is equitable. However, given the generous eligibility criterion for accessing financing for higher education as well as the fact that the lower levels of education have been free, it is very likely that Botswana's public expenditure on education benefits children from rich families as much as it benefits children from poor families. There are, however, a few children who may not be benefiting because they are unable to access lower education levels due to hidden costs of education that have been prevailing even after education was made free. There is anecdotal evidence to the effect that children from remote areas are unable to complete lower levels of education due to the cost of uniforms, feeding fees and distance to schools.

Appropriate Financing Models

In this section, the current financing model for Botswana is analysed, as well as the parameters that influenced its design. An appropriate financing model is proposed for Botswana given the country's socio-economic conditions and the need to make public expenditure cost effective and sustainable in the long term.

The Current Financing Model and Parameters for a Future Funding Model
Initially the Ministry of Education through its Bursary Department had a bursary scheme which emphasised training for the government sector. As a token of appreciation, beneficiaries were to contribute 5% of their initial salary for each year that they were being educated. They were also bonded to work for the Government of Botswana for a period of not less than their period of study. Following the 1990 Presidential Commission on the Revised National Policy on Income, Employment, Profits and Prices, the Ministry of Education introduced the grant/loan scheme (in 1995). A major problem with the financing model has been the lack of cost recovery as loans remain unpaid due to lack of information and unemployment of some of the graduates. The Department of Student

Placement and Welfare (DSPW) also has inadequate capacity and resources to trace or track the beneficiaries once they finish their studies. There is also lack of information from the demand side of the labour market as well as unavailability of a national human resources database.

Given limited public resources for higher education, there is an urgent need to make the loan scheme more sustainable through increasing repayment. This situation is compounded by the fact that cost recovery is not very effective as most graduates are unable to repay their loans and yet the numbers of eligible Batswana for loans/grants is increasing.

Empirical evidence also indicates that the private benefits to tertiary education are increasing, indicating the need for beneficiaries and/or their parents to contribute more to their education. As Table 2.8 shows, the private rates of return to higher education have increased from 11% to 24% between 1993/1994 and 2002/2003. There is therefore a need to review the current loan/grant system with a view to making it more sustainable and effective. This has necessitated the Government of Botswana to commission a study to review the grant/loan sponsorship scheme. This review will examine all the relevant factors: for example reviewing the scheme in its current form and reporting on its financial and economic sustainability; designing an appropriate, efficient and effective financial aid scheme that will result in a sustainable sponsorship fund; and aligning the scheme to the country's human resource needs and emerging global needs.

Table 2.8: Private Rates of Return to Education in Botswana (1993/1994–2002/2003)

EDUCATION LEVEL	PRIMARY	LOWER SECONDARY	UPPER SECONDARY	TERTIARY
Rate of return – 1993/1994 data	7	26	36	11
Rate of return – 2002/2003 data	9	15	8	24

Source: Siphambe 2008

Graduate training is currently not funded by government except through the Department of Public Service Management as part of a training programme for the government departments. Government has recently agreed to fund graduate programmes in a similar manner to the undergraduate programmes. Details of the funding model are yet to be worked out.

The review of the loan/grant system will have to benefit from the international experience in terms of making it effective. There are issues relating to the autonomy of the institution responsible for financial aid. There are indications that the fact that the DSPW is a department under the Ministry of Education constrains it in terms of its mandate given that it does not have the necessary resources. In several countries such as Australia and the UK, the institution responsible for disbursement of loans is an autonomous institution (Bray 1998). For some countries such as India, subsidised education loans are mainly available from national banks. There are also models where the disbursing body is separated from the collecting body to allow for each to implement its mandate effectively. Some of the functions of collecting loans due for repayment are outsourced to private companies who are known to be more effective in loan recovery (Shantakumar 1992). These are all options that will need to inform the future of the Botswana loan/grant system.

Proposed Financing Model

In designing an appropriate financing model for Botswana, a number of issues have to be taken into consideration. The first consideration is that of the principle of equity. Even though the equity issue does not seem to be problematic as discussed earlier, international experience has indicated that a higher proportion of university graduates come from richer families. Moreover, the poor are known to be reluctant to take loans especially if the loan amount is too large and is to be paid over a long period of time. While the bias should gradually be towards loans and away from grants, there is a need to make sure the loan does not act as a major deterrent to accessing higher education by children from poorer families.

The second issue relates to the expenditure argument. With the anticipated increase in access to tertiary education as per the currently approved tertiary education policy, public education is likely to increase significantly, posing a big burden on public expenditure which has to be rationalised and prioritised relative to other areas of socio-economic development. There is a need even within the education sector to increase expenditure for primary, secondary and vocational education as the country strives to address the education quality issues at those levels. Given the need to reduce costs in the long term and dwindling resources, the financing model that is suitable for Botswana would be one that is biased towards loans rather than grants. Given economic circumstances and the resource constraints, the continuation of the current loan/grant system is proposed with some modifications to make it more effective. In particular, the loan/grant currently in operation will need to be reformed to make sure that graduates can make a contribution to the higher education sector from which they have benefited.

Given the high and increasing private rates of return to higher education, biasing the scheme towards loans is in order especially for children from richer families as it will encourage the participation of parents in funding their children's education in the long run and therefore partially reduce the burden on the state for tertiary education funding. That, however, has to be balanced with equity issues to make sure that no able student from a poorer family is denied access to tertiary education on grounds of lack of finance. Given that cost recovery has started to be implemented at secondary school level since 2006, and that children from poorer backgrounds have been identified and given exemption, these same records will be useful to continue to identify them for higher education financing.

Another important area that needs to be explored in terms of financing of higher education is the involvement of the private sector in higher education financing. Currently, apart from a few scholarships offered by companies like Debswana, the private sector's involvement in the financing of higher education is negligible. Past efforts, however, show that they are capable of getting involved in financing higher education if efforts are made to involve them. They have for instance been involved in sponsoring prizes for best performing students and have been quite active in fundraising for the University of Botswana Foundation, which so far has been able to raise substantial amounts of money to sponsor graduate students at the University of Botswana. Through issues such as tax rebates on deductions for provision of training, the private sector in Botswana can be made to be more involved in higher education training. There is need to work out linkages and benefits that will ensure that the private sector is more actively involved.

Conclusions and Recommendations

Botswana has made tremendous efforts in terms of increasing access to higher education through increasing facilities in local institutions as well as placing students in institutions outside the country. Access to higher education, however, remains low as the country has until recently had only one university (the University of Botswana) offering undergraduate and postgraduate degrees. This was supplemented by enrolment in Colleges of Education and Institutes of Health Sciences that offered certificate and diploma courses. Efforts are being made to increase access to higher education as part of the tertiary education policy of moving the country towards a knowledge-based society. Plans are to increase access of 18–24-year-olds to 20% by 2020 through expanding the University of Botswana, building a second university and sponsoring students in the local private tertiary education institutions, which, until 2007, were not supported in terms of having students sponsored by the government. As a result, government expenditure on tertiary education has been increasing significantly and is likely to increase in line with the new tertiary education policy approved by Parliament this year. Gender equality has been achieved over time even though there are disparities in some of the disciplines especially science-based courses and engineering and technology. Even though data are not available on the equity aspects of expenditure, there is evidence that education expenditure does benefit children from poor families as much as it does for the rich given that primary and secondary education were until recently free.

Public financing of higher education has been relatively high as reflected in the high percentage of expenditure going to the education sector, and to tertiary education in particular. Almost all the financing of higher education has been undertaken by government with very negligible participation of the private sector. Initial financing was through a bursary system that required graduates to contribute 5% of their initial gross salary for the period equivalent to the period of study. Since 1995 this financing mechanism was changed to a loan/grant scheme that allows for a higher grant in those areas considered to be critical for the country's development. However, the loan/grant system has not brought the desired results in terms of attracting more students to the courses that are prioritised (e.g. Category 1 courses). Moreover, the evidence points to limited success in these programmes due to limited space within the local institution and the fact that per unit costs of external placement especially outside the region have been relatively high.

Education spending seems to have been more equitable given that more children from poor families are able to access higher education through the generous loan/grant scheme. Access has been facilitated because of high progression from lower levels as education has been free at the primary and secondary levels.

The following recommendations are made in the case of Botswana:

- There is a need to increase access to higher education through further expansion of University of Botswana, and allowing the private institutions to expand their programmes and intake through support in the form of scholarships for qualifying students. There is, however, a need to be cost effective as revenues are not enough to meet all the increasing social demands for government spending.
- The current administration of the loan/grant scheme is not sustainable given that cost recovery is very low. There is therefore a need to come up with ways and means of making the scheme more cost effective especially in terms of ensuring better cost recovery.
- Given the high private returns to tertiary education, there is a need to

shift more financing to individuals and their families through loans rather than grants. However, this should take into account equity considerations to avoid excluding students from poorer families.
- The inclusion of private providers has to be dealt with carefully as they may escalate the default in payment through expanding access even to those who are not capable of completing the programmes. This they could do as a way of attracting more funding from government through scholarships. There may be a need to devise penalties to deal with the adverse selection problem of private providers and to make them more accountable in their admissions.
- The private sector is currently making negligible contributions to financing of higher education. Efforts should be made to make it more involved through such instruments as taxation. They could for instance have tax-deductible benefits for every student they finance in higher education.
- The TEC will in future have a bigger role in terms of monitoring and making sure that standards are met. It will therefore be necessary to properly resource it to be able to deliver on its mandate. However, the entry of more providers may provide an environment for fair pricing if competition is enhanced.

Chapter 3
KENYA

Wycliffe Otieno

Historical Background

The development of higher education in Kenya cannot be discussed in isolation from the history of Kenya, as it owes its origins to colonial efforts at establishing a common system of education for East Africa. These origins can be traced from 1921 with the opening of a technical school on Makerere Hill in Kampala, Uganda. A year later, the school was renamed Makerere College and offered technical education for those who sat for the Cambridge School Certificate (CSC) examinations. Following the recommendations of the Earl De La Warr Report in 1937, the college started offering diploma courses in Medicine, Agriculture, Education and Veterinary Sciences (Bogonko 1992). In 1949, it was elevated to University College status following the recommendations of the Asquith Report four years earlier. It was consequently renamed the University College of East Africa and offered University of London degrees. As the only university-level institution in the region, it admitted students from the three East African colonies. In 1956, another college, the Royal Technical College of East Africa, was opened in Nairobi, Kenya, to offer diplomas in technical and commercial education for the whole of East Africa. In 1958, the government appointed a committee headed by J F Lockwood which recommended the establishment of a Federal University of East Africa. However, this did not come about until 1963 when the University of East Africa was inaugurated with two constituent colleges in Nairobi and Dar es Salaam. The parent university in Makerere offered Medicine and Agriculture with Dar es Salaam offering Law, while Nairobi offered Engineering, Veterinary Medicine and Architecture.

In 1968, the Working Party on Higher Education in East Africa was set up and it recommended the elevation of each college to full university status by 1970. Consequently, on 25 March 1970, the University of East Africa was dissolved and three independent universities, namely Makerere University Kampala (MUK), the University of Dar es Salaam (UDSM) and the University of Nairobi (UoN) were inaugurated. This marked the beginning of the independent development of university education in each of the three countries. In Kenya, the government proclaimed the establishment of the University of Nairobi through an Act of Parliament the same year. The dissolution of the University of East Africa was thus an opportunity for the independent states to fully regulate the development of higher education through enacting the relevant policies including financing. Thus, Kenya had its first fully-fledged university. In 1972, Kenyatta College, which had hitherto been a diploma teacher training centre, became a constituent college of the UoN before being elevated to full university status in 1985, one year after the setting up of the second university, Moi, in 1984. Other universities established subsequently include: Egerton University in 1987, Jomo Kenyatta University of Agriculture and Technology (JKUAT) in 1994, Maseno University in 2000, and Masinde Muliro University of Science and Technology in 2006. In all, Kenya has a total of seven public and 18 private universities with varying levels of accreditation.

Evolution of Higher Education Policy

Imperatives of Highly Skilled Human Resources and 'Free' University Education
On the attainment of independence, the Kenyan Government immediately set up a commission of inquiry into the country's education system. Known as the Kenya Education Commission, under the chairmanship of Prof. Simeon Ominde, it is credited with providing the policy direction for the education sector. The commission was set up against the backdrop of colonial education policies that had severely discriminated against the education of the African segment of the population and the consequent need to train an African cadre of experts to staff the various facets of the economy in the new nation. Understandably therefore, the Commission gave prime consideration to higher education, and recommended that efforts be made to ensure that there was a trained and sufficient number of highly skilled human resources to take over the management of the country's affairs from the departing Europeans. This recommendation formed the pedestal on which higher education policy was hinged, at least for the first two decades of independence.

In order to achieve the goal of having enough highly skilled human resources, university education therefore became almost entirely free in terms of direct costs. As will be evident, four clear phases can be identified in the evolution of higher education financing policy in Kenya, with the policies adopted in each of these phases being invariably dictated by the immediate to long-term human resource needs, and the prevailing economic circumstances. This was the first phase, namely, that of highly subsidised higher education funding.

It should be noted that the recommendation of the education commission and the policy measures arising from it were taken at a time when the young nation did not have a fully fledged university of its own, the Federal University of East Africa for the three countries only having been inaugurated a year before in 1963. This meant that the number of students that could be admitted to higher education was limited. Moreover, the University College in Nairobi was only offering Engineering, Veterinary Medicine and Architecture. Those who wanted to undertake other courses such as Law had to go to the University College in Dar es Salaam while medical students had to be enrolled in Makerere in Uganda. Thus, the opportunities available were not only limited but lacked diversity in terms of the breadth of the curricula and programmes. In 1970, the University of East Africa was wound up and Makerere University, the University of Dar es Salaam and the University of Nairobi were inaugurated. This marked the beginning of the independent development of public university education in each of the three states.

In the meantime, private, mainly religious, provision of higher education also started during the colonial era. The first secular private university, the United States International University (USIU), was started in 1969. Upon the enactment of the Commission for Higher Education Act in 1985, private universities have grown in quick succession from an initial three in 1978 to the current 18 with varying levels of accreditation.

Initiation of Cost Transfers
A policy shift began in 1974 with the government's Third Development Plan. In the first decade, the government managed to train a significant number of people to take over the running of the economy. It also succeeded in offering basic education to the citizens thereby nearly satisfying the pervasive demand that characterised the period immediately after independence. In subsequent years, the university population increased while economic growth declined. From a real GDP growth rate of more than 8% annually in the 1963–1972 decade, the growth rate declined to 4% annually, and government income declined significantly (Wagacha & Ngugi 1999). The decline in economic growth was also triggered

by the oil price shock of 1973, a development that resulted in serious structural constraints in the economy. Together, these developments forced the government to rethink its strategy of financing university education. Provision of highly subsidised education was no longer feasible in the face of diminished resources. In 1974, the government introduced a student loan programme. Initially, there was strong resistance to its introduction, but the government managed to put it in place nevertheless. However, the loan programme performed abysmally. It was characterised by high subsidies, poor administration, lack of legal framework and, consequently, low repayments.

Reforming the Regulatory Regime: Enactment of Council of Higher Education
In the 1980s the need to create a legal regime to regulate the provision of university education by non-state providers was overwhelming. In 1985, the government enacted the Commission for Higher Education (CHE) Act with the express mandate to oversee the development of both public and private higher education, though it has ended up 'policing' the private rather than the public institutions.

A decade after the enactment of the CHE Act, the government released the Economic Reforms for 1996–1998: The Policy Framework Paper (Republic of Kenya 1996: 36) which articulated its position on liberalisation and measures to encourage greater private sector participation in the economy. On education, it underlined the need to 'put in place policies to encourage the participation of the private sector in the establishment and operation of educational institutions'. Overall, the measures adopted by the government from the late 1980s have created a policy environment for increased provision of higher education by private sector players. This has seen an increase in the number of private universities from three in 1978 to the current 18.

Introduction of Cost Sharing
The late 1980s marked yet another change in Kenya's education financing policy. The government officially 'introduced' a cost-sharing policy in 1988 via Sessional Paper No. 6. This marked the government's abolition of 'free' and highly subsidised education. At the university level, the institutionalisation of structural adjustment entailed an increased emphasis on user charges and budget rationalisation that saw the diversion of more resources to primary education because of the high social rates of return to this level and intensification of deferred cost-recovery measures at the university level.

The government introduced direct tuition fees in 1992 and abolished free meals with the introduction of the cafeteria system (known as 'Pay-As-You-

Eat'). Given its inability to fully finance university education, the government left the institutions to find ways of generating own income to supplement public funds. Limited government funding meant a restricted supply of places. Consequently, it adopted a policy of encouraging private sector participation in developing higher education. Indeed, the private higher education sub-sector had always existed, except that there was a vacuum in terms of a regulatory framework.

Private Higher Education and Privatisation of Public Universities
Partial public privatisation, or the introduction of private entry schemes in public universities, has stemmed from the tacit encouragement by the government of the public institutions' efforts to find innovative ways of expanding enrolment while generating own funds to supplement diminishing state support. All the public institutions have initiated several programmes going by various names such as Self Sponsored Programmes (SSPs), Module II and Alternative Degree Programmes (ADPs). These programmes are open to those who are not absorbed by the public universities in the regular programmes controlled by the Joint Admissions Board (JAB) as well as the working class who would want to further their education. By all accounts, the introduction of these programmes has resulted in a partial privatisation of public education. The private entry schemes are characterised by high tuition fees compared to regular programmes. For instance, while a regular bachelor's degree in Computer Science costs a total of KES 120 000 (US$ 1 538 – tuition and accommodation) per year, tuition alone in the Module II programmes costs upwards of KES 240 000 (US$ 3 077) per year.

An analysis of issues and trends in privatisation should take into account the purely private universities as well as the privatisation of public universities. Currie and Vidovich (2001) note that the ideological shift towards privatisation includes both increasing the provision of education services by for-profit and non-profit private organisations, and tendencies to marketisation within institutions that continue to be publicly funded and driven. While the development of private universities is not a new phenomenon, the privatisation of public institutions is a recent one and Kenya is not alone in both tendencies. Other regions such as Latin America have had a long history of private higher education institutions while the growth has also been fairly significant in Asia (Wongosothorn & Wang 1997). In Kenya, of the total of 18 private universities, 14 are religious-based institutions. Private institutions have an enrolment that is about 20% of the total university student population. Together, students who get little or no public funding (including those in Module II programmes in public universities) constitute over 40% of university enrolment in Kenya. This is a significant proportion and confirms the crucial role played by private institutions in expanding higher education access, contrary to Altbach's (1999) assertion that students' inability to pay and lack of capital will result in a slower growth of private higher education in the continent as opposed to the trend in other parts of the world.

The liberalisation of higher education in Kenya has thus seen a major reorientation of policy. Higher education is no longer merely geared towards the production of 'highly skilled' human resources as at independence, but is also seen in the wider context of the challenges facing human development in the rapidly increasingly technological and integrating world.

While public universities dominate in enrolment, their pace of numerical growth has been slow compared to the private universities. A number of public and private non-university higher education institutions have been set up at different times and in different parts of the country. Like universities, however, the concentration of these institutions tends to be in the urban and high-growth areas, with Nairobi dominating.

A major problem in the study of higher education in Kenya is an intense, disproportionate focus on the university sub-sector, such that not much is known about the non-university tertiary sub-sector. For example, in Kenya, the exact number of the non-public higher education institutions is not known.

Higher Education in the Current Policy Framework

Kenya is currently implementing a five-year education programme called the Kenya Education Sector Support Programme (KESSP). KESSP sets out a total of 23 investment programmes for implementation, of which university education is one investment programme. KESSP notes that the rapid expansion of university education has stretched the capacity of existing facilities with adverse effects on teaching and learning, morale of staff, research productivity and the intellectual climate in the public university sub-sector.

Some of the strategies are already being implemented. These include the development of a national skills training strategy and the elevation of national polytechnics to offer degree programmes. However, as argued later on in this chapter, the government is yet to address the high cost of technical education, which is one of the main barriers to increasing enrolment in technical institutions.

Institutions

To some degree, this chapter continues the trend described above of focusing extensively on universities. Two reasons explain this focus. First, this is where the funds are concentrated. Second, there is much more data available on the university sector.

Higher Education Institutions
Any study on articulation and differentiation in higher education would no doubt single out: (i) the university and non-university institutions; (ii) the academic and technical, training and research; (iii) the public and the private; and (iv) the non-profit versus the for-profit institutions. This is true for Kenya and all institutions fall into one or more of these four categories.

It is, however, important to add that, as in Kenya, institutions can be further grouped into three main categories, that is, institutions that: (i) provide higher education; (ii) regulate the provision of higher education; and (iii) finance higher education. Institutions in the latter two categories include the Commission for Higher Education (CHE) – the regulator and the Higher Education Loans Board (HELB) that provides loans, scholarships and bursaries.

Universities
Public universities receive direct state funding, though most have been able to launch private entry schemes through which they have been able to raise substantial revenue. Universities are autonomous and are independently managed by the university councils. Private universities raise funds from their own sources and do not receive any grants from the State. They have varying degrees of recognition. The highest degree of recognition is the award of charter. Others operate on the basis of letters of interim authority awaiting chartering. Those that existed before the enactment of the CHE Act and the promulgation of Universities Rules of 1989 fall in the 'Registered' category.

CHE is the state body that presides over quality assurance in private universities, awards interim letters of authority to new private universities and confirms them as chartered institutions. Although CHE's administrative mandate is functionally restricted to the regulation of private universities, statutorily the commission should also regulate the entire higher education system including public universities.

Table 3.1 presents the public and private universities in Kenya.

Non-University Higher Education Institutions
Closely related but distinctly apart from the university sector in Kenya are the

tertiary- and middle-level colleges offering various programmes. These include six diploma colleges for the training of non-graduate secondary school teachers, 20 teacher training colleges (TTCs) for primary school teachers, four national polytechnics, 17 institutes of technology and 20 technical training institutes (TTIs). There are also a number of private post-secondary education and training institutions whose precise numbers are not known. Non-graduate healthcare professionals (e.g. nurses and clinical officers) are trained in 11 medical training colleges (MTCs) in various parts of the country.

Table 3.1: Public and Private Universities in Kenya (2007)

PUBLIC UNIVERSITIES (7)	PRIVATE UNIVERSITIES: CHARTERED (7)
University of Nairobi (1970)	University of Eastern Africa, Baraton (1991)
Moi University (1984)	Catholic University of Eastern Africa (1992)
Kenyatta University (1985)	Daystar University (1994)
Egerton University (1987)	Scott Theological College (1997)
JKUAT (1994)	United States International University (1999)
Maseno University (2000)	Africa Nazarene University (2002)
Masinde Muliro (2007)	Kenya Methodist University (2006)
OTHER PRIVATE UNIVERSITIES	
Letters of Interim Authority (7)	**Certificate of Registration (6)**
Kabarak University (2000)	The East Africa School of Theology (1999)
Kiriri Women's University (2002)	Kenya Highlands Bible College (1999)
Aga Khan University (2002)	The Nairobi International School of Theology (1999)
Strathmore University (2002)	The Pan Africa Christian College (1999)
Great Lakes University of Kisumu (2006)	The Nairobi Evangelical Graduate School of Theology (1999)
Gretsa University (2006)	St. Paul's United Theological College
Kenya College of Accountancy (2007)	

Source: CHE

Number of Higher Education Institutions by Type of Location

There is a clear pattern in the location of universities in Kenya. The tendency seems to be to locate institutions in densely populated and economically active areas. In this case, Nairobi and central Kenya seem to be the preferred regions. Understandably, there are more institutions in the urban areas principally because these areas happen to be the national and regional economic hubs, are more heavily populated and have readily available infrastructure. Institutions based in the rural areas are a result of deliberate government policy. For instance, the location of Moi University in a rural area was a deliberate attempt by the government to minimise student unrest that had been experienced at the University of Nairobi. Other middle-level institutions including the MTCs, TTIs and TTCs are spread all over the country with most being found in rural or peri-urban locations.

Participation

The Government of Kenya has endeavoured to increase participation in higher education since independence. Even when there was only the Federal University of East Africa, enrolment of Kenyan students in overseas universities was pursued to ensure widened access to higher education.

University Enrolments

Students who qualify for post-secondary schooling either enrol in the regular programmes in the public universities, in the self-sponsored programmes in the public universities, at private universities, at the middle-level colleges including the national polytechnics, teacher training colleges (both certificate and diploma) or opt for university education overseas. The minimum qualification needed for university admission is a C+ pass. Despite more than 50 000 students qualifying for admission each year, not more than 10 000 get admission into the regular programme. As a result, a number of students qualify but are not admitted (see Table 3.2).

Table 3.2: Admission Trends at Public Universities in Kenya (2002/2003–2005/2006)

ACADEMIC YEAR	TOTAL FORM 4 ENROLMENT	NO. QUALIFIED (C+ AND ABOVE)	JOINT ADMISSIONS BOARD ADMISSIONS	% QUALIFIED ADMITTED	% OF FORM 4 ADMITTED
2002/2003	176 018	42 158	11 046	26.2	6.3%
2003/2004	186 939	42 721	10 791	25.3	5.8%
2004/2005	193 087	58 218	10 200	17.5	5.3%
2005/2006	209 276	68 030	10 000	14.7	4.8%

Source: Joint Admissions Board and Statistical Abstract 2006

Despite the limited direct intake, the population of university students has continued to grow (Table 3.3). Public universities dominate in enrolments, even though there are more private institutions. By 2004/2005, the six public universities had enrolled 91 541 students, while all the private universities (18) had enrolled 10 050 students.

The total enrolment of self-sponsored students (Module II) at UoN in 2004/2005 was more than the number of regular full-time students and also higher than enrolment in all private universities. Enrolments in the self-sponsored programmes are higher because many students are integrated (attend the same classes as regular students, as opposed to mainly evening and school-based study) in full-time study. What this confirms is that public universities have been able to expand their internal capacity much faster than the private universities. The part-time, private programmes are responsible for this increase, since there is stagnation in the number of regular students being enrolled in public universities.

It is evident from Table 3.3 that the private university share of total enrolments is currently only 11%, down from a high of 20% before the onset of privatisation (that is, self-sponsored students) in public universities (Otieno 2005). The rapid growth of the public sector universities, especially through Module II programmes, largely explains the reduced private university share. Public sector enrolments in 2004/2005 reflect an increase of 80.5% (or 16.1% annually) from 2000/2001. In contrast, private university growth was 18.4% (3.7% annually) over the same period. This growth pattern reflects the changing fortunes of public and private institutions. The privatisation gains by the former create hurdles for the latter. For the private universities, stringent accreditation requirements played a great role in initial growth, but less stringent regulation (or the lack of it), now largely explains the public surge.

Two more aspects of public and private provision stand out. First, though public universities remain public, more than half of the enrolments are in private entry schemes in these universities (Kiamba 2003). Second, there are more female students in the private than public universities. In the former, they constitute about 52% of enrolments whereas in the latter, they are only about 30% of the total student population.

Technical Education Enrolments
Technical education is popularly known as TIVET, referring to technical, industrial, vocational and entrepreneurship education and training. Technical education is offered at four national polytechnics (Kenya, Mombasa, Eldoret and Kisumu), 17 institutes of technology, 20 technical training institutes and the Kenya Technical Teacher Training College (KTTC). In addition to these, a number of government ministries also offer three-year professional training at diploma level for their middle-level human resource requirements. In addition,

there are several other private commercial technical institutions whose exact number is not known.

Enrolments at TIVET institutions have fluctuated between 2002/2003 and 2006/2007. Enrolments grew from 52 254 to 66 737 students between 2002/2003 and 2003/2004 only to decrease to 29 870 in 2005/2006. The decrease may be attributed to (i) abolition of production courses in these institutions; (ii) unaffordability due the high cost of technical education (estimated at KES 110 000 per year [MoE MPER 2007]) compared with the high poverty levels; (iii) lack of scholarships or any form of government support for those not able to pay; and (iv) diversification of courses offered in the institutions and relevance of the same to the labour market. In 2006/2007 females constituted 41% of enrolment.

Table 3.3: Student Enrolments in Kenyan Universities (2000/2001–2004/2005)

INSTITUTION	2000/2001		2001/2002		2002/2003		2003/2004		2004/2005	
	M	F	M	F	M	F	M	F	M	F
Nairobi	10 532	4 301	15 426	9 270	16 200	9 489	16 992	9 720	21 268	11 706
Full time	8 383	3 341	8 724	4 450	9 163	4 428	9 603	4 406	9 987	5 250
Part time	2 149	960	6 702	4 820	7 037	5 061	7 389	5 314	11 281	6 456
Kenyatta	5 943	4 010	6 831	4 984	10 737	4 998	10 753	5 023	11 252	4 803
Full time	4 510	3 019	5 384	3 983	4 972	3 329	5 221	3 495	4 313	2 887
Part time	1 433	991	1 447	1 001	5 765	1 669	5 532	1 528	6 939	1 916
Moi	4 753	3 766	5 469	3 869	6 274	4 549	5 804	4 643	6 796	5 214
Full time	4 046	3 163	4 066	3 179	4 086	3 195	4 107	3 211	4 304	3 195
Part time	707	603	1 403	690	2 188	1 354	1 697	1 432	2 492	2 019
Egerton	6 629	2 356	6 816	2 285	6 975	2 387	6 908	2 444	6 350	2 247
Full time	5 981	2 127	6 161	2 053	6 307	2 151	6 207	2 196	5 540	1 960
Part time	648	229	655	232	668	236	701	248	810	287
JKUAT	2 992	1 288	2 565	1 115	3 184	1 404	3 202	1 455	4 315	1 959
Full time	1 301	520	857	339	1 442	613	1 373	624	2 201	999
Part time	1 691	768	1 708	776	1 742	791	1 829	831	2 114	960
Maseno	2 596	1 538	2 530	1 518	3 505	2 130	3 428	2 179	3 413	2 168
Full time	1 994	1 155	1 922	1 132	2 885	1 736	2 777	1 765	2 660	1 690
Part time	602	383	608	386	620	394	651	414	753	478
Sub-total	33 445	17 259	39 637	23 041	46 875	24 957	47 087	25 464	53 394	28 097
PRIVATE UNIVERSITIES										
Private: accredited	3 093	4 050	3 122	4 089	3 476	4 163	3 650	4 371	3 796	4 546
Private: unaccredited	876	472	949	511	748	742	763	757	801	907
Sub-Total	3 969	4 522	4 071	4 600	4 224	4 905	4 413	5 128	4 597	5 453
Total	37 414	21 781	43 708	27 641	51 099	29 862	51 500	30 592	57 991	33 550
Grand Total	59 195		71 349		80 961		82 092		91 541	

Source: Ministry of Education

Two of the national polytechnics have been elevated to degree awarding institutions from 2007. The Italian Government has helped the upgrading process with staff retraining and upgrading of facilities. It has enabled the institutions to establish linkages with the Milan Polytechnic. The polytechnics account for a total of 37% of technical education enrolments.

Enrolments in Teacher Education
There are 28 primary teacher training colleges in the country, of which 20 are public; there are also three diploma teacher training colleges. Enrolment in 2006 in these teacher training colleges was just under 18 000 in 2006, with females making up 50.5% of enrolment. Teacher training colleges form an important avenue for those who desire to continue with post-secondary education but fail to secure admission in the universities and other technical education institutions. Notably, however, enrolment in these institutions has not risen as steadily as in other higher education institutions. For the five years under consideration, the highest increase in enrolment of 1 064 was recorded in 2003. Subsequently, admissions have increased by less than 300 students, with some years such as 2004 recording a decrease over the previous year's admissions.

Funding and Expenditure

The university education sub-sector in Kenya can be categorised into three distinct finance structures: publicly-financed, privately-financed and a mix of public–private finance. The financing structure is closely tied to institutional type and ownership. However, there is a systematic move by public institutions to tap private funds, while private institutions also endeavour to access public funds. In general, public institutions have more latitude in accessing private funds than do private institutions in appropriating public funds. Purely public funding for higher education is exemplified by the yearly government allocations to public universities. Traditionally, public universities have received generous funding from the government; these funds have constituted the major sources of income for these institutions.

Government Expenditure on Education
Education takes the bulk of the resources provided for the social sector (education, health and home affairs), accounting for up to 73% of the total social sector budget. As a proportion of total government budget, it is still significant at about 27% and equivalent to 6.4% of GDP.

Expenditure Analysis by Type

For the purpose of this chapter, analysis is restricted to a five-year period within the financial years 2002/2003 and 2006/2007. The education budget has been rising steadily over this period. It rose by 14% from KES 63 billion in 2002/2003 to KES 72 billion in 2003/2004. Between 2003/2004 and 2004/2005 the recurrent expenditure allocations rose from KES 72 billion to KES 80 billion representing a 11% increase. Allocations have continued to rise to peak at KES 99.8 billion by 2006/2007. In 2002/2003, education took up 29.6% of the total budget but this had fallen to 23.7% by 2006/2007.

Recurrent expenditure allocations have been rising steadily, increasing from KES 61 billion during 2002/2003 to KES 68 billion in 2003/2004, and to KES 86 billion in 2005/2006. Recurrent expenditures are substantially high, in all the allocations for the five-year period, comprising over 80% of the total MoE budget. On the other hand, development expenditure allocations have remained below the KES 10 billion mark.

Higher Education Spending

Over time, funding for higher education has been dictated by prevailing economic conditions and national commitments to meeting specific international targets at various levels of education. Invariably, external factors such as the position taken by multi-lateral agencies, notably the World Bank and the International Monetary Fund (IMF), have also had a major impact on higher education financing policy. These include capping enrolment levels, which itself affects the level of institutional funding. Traditionally, funding for university education had been based on the budget prepared by the universities; in 1995 this practice changed with the adoption of the unit cost formula.

Funding for higher education has increased marginally during the financial years under consideration. In 2002/2003, higher education expenditure took up 11.5% of the total MoE expenditure, rising to 13.8% in 2003/2004 and 16.4% in 2005/2006. This significant rise in the higher education expenditure is attributed to the increase in lecturer salaries and house allowances. The financial year 2006/2007 saw a substantial decline in higher education allocations in both volume and proportion. This was the result of a deliberate shift in policy to place greater focus on lower levels of education and new items such as quality assurance across the system.

Higher education spending as a proportion of GDP for the five years has averaged 0.88% while as a proportion of total education spending, it has averaged 13.74%. This latter figure is below the international and sub-Saharan African average of between 15 and 20%. The highest allocation occurred in 2004/2005 when the respective proportions were 1.06% and 16.1% while the lowest was 2002/2003 (11.7%), increasing gradually to peak at 16.10% during 2005/2006 before declining to 14.40% during 2006/2007.

Comparative MoE Budget Allocations by Levels of Education
Basic education remains the priority area of expenditure for the government, averaging 53% for the four years from 2002/2003 to 2005/2006, compared to 23% for secondary education and 12% for higher education. Given respective enrolments, roughly for every shilling the government spends on university education, it spends two shillings on secondary education and 4.50 cents on primary education. The government, however, spends substantially less at early childhood education, special education and technical education which recorded means of 0.13%, 0.23% and 1.78% respectively. Teacher education is also low at 0.43% for the four years. The low allocations to technical education result, in part, from relatively low student presence in these institutions which also results from low institutional capacities and the improved access to university education.

Spending on salaries at all levels of education averages 86%, though universities have the lowest proportion. State allocation to public universities comprises 80% of individual institution's wage bill – the universities are in turn required to raise 20% of their wage bills from their internal revenues.

Any efforts to make university education affordable to the majority of the poor households should therefore begin with a shift in allocations from recurrent expenditure on salaries to development expenditure in public universities in order expand capacity. Tangible efforts in this direction have only been seen in the freeze on new primary and secondary teacher employment. Although this measure prevents further rise in the ministry's wage bill, it does not rationalise the already high wage bill within the ministry. But these efforts have more or less been eroded with the huge increases in teacher salaries to be effected from 1 July 2007. It is estimated that the MoE will require an additional KES 9.4 billion to meet the new salaries. University lecturers are also to benefit from a 14% salary raise. The MoE's overall budget and, specifically, its recurrent budgets, are set to rise significantly.

Patterns of State Funding of Public Universities
State funding of universities is usually presented as a wholesome allocation that is worked out as a function of the total student population. From the assumed unit cost of KES 120 000, funding to individual institutions is arrived at by multiplying enrolment by KES 70 000. The balance of KES 50 000 is expected to be met by the student, either through a publicly funded loan and bursary

scheme or other private sources. On the basis of the above grant computations, a university with 10 000 students would get KES 700 million. However, actual allocations are hardly 100% of these estimates (in most instances less). The government grant is usually disbursed as a lump-sum allocation with no itemised budgetary specifications on expenditures; it is the individual institution that in turn decides on its allocations by cost item.

State funding constitutes the bulk of universities' income, representing anything between 50 and 90% of total institutional revenues. While the total revenues of smaller public universities are made up almost entirely of grant allocations from government, for bigger public universities (with higher student numbers) capitation grants constitute lower proportions of their total revenue. This observation arises in part from the fact that while the bigger public universities (e.g. UoN and KU) have capacities to accommodate more self-sponsored students, the smaller institutions (e.g. Maseno and MMUST) face spatial, locational and structural constraints in attracting significant numbers of self-sponsored students to raise substantial private revenues. Other factors that diminish the grant capitation as a proportion of total revenue include donor funding to the institutions. Income from Module II programmes constitutes an average of 15%, though the actual proportions vary significantly between institutions. The UoN has the highest proportion of its income being derived from the MII programmes at an average of 40%, while MMUST has the lowest at 7.7%.

The disproportionately low figures for Module II earnings on the official records of some universities could also be the result of deliberate under-declarations of earnings in anticipation of higher allocations from the government. This deduction draws from the fact that administrators of various institutions can 'lobby' for better state allocations based on their institutions' balance sheet 'deficit' levels and proximity to state power.

Financing Private Universities

There has been a phenomenal growth in the number of private universities, from just three in 1980 to 18 in 2007. This contrasts with only seven public universities in over 40 years. While public universities get direct funding from the state, private universities depend on endowments, tuition fees and direct funding from founders and sponsors. While public universities are highly subsidised by the state, private universities have to recover most of their costs from instruction and other services such as hostel accommodation. As expected, this has made these universities notably expensive compared to the public institutions. The only form of public funding for these universities comes in the form of student loans. However, this is notably small compared to the amounts received by public universities. Lack of public funding for private universities partly stems from the legal definition of public and private universities. According to the law, 'a "private university" means a university established with funds other than public funds', while 'a "public university" means a university maintained or assisted out of public funds' (Kenya 1985: 90).

Cost of Private University Education

In comparison to public universities, private universities charge relatively high fees. A study by Wesonga *et al.* (2003) noted that the cost of university education per student per year (tuition only) for the chartered institutions and those with letters of interim authority ranged from KES 117 760 (US$ 1 570) to KES 171 540 (US$ 2 287) per term/quarter/semester. However, they note that tuition charges levied by private universities reflect the prevailing recurrent costs incurred. If development expenses are factored in, the overall unit cost would be much higher.

Private university students pay tuition that is on average 11 times higher than that of students in governmentally supported programmes in public universities. The high fee levels are not due to any special courses offered, but due to the profit motive of these institutions, including the religious institutions, and also the fact that the public university education is heavily subsidised by the state.

An important question is whether the high fees in private universities are inhibiting access and equity. Moreover, access to higher education is already inequitable because the rich have a higher representation in secondary level education. In Kenya, the introduction of the Module II programmes in public universities has effectively introduced an element of cross-subsidisation with the income from these programmes being used to improve facilities that are shared by both the regular and Module II programmes. The private institutions therefore charge fees that not only reflect the actual cost of offering university education but they are also meant to generate surplus funds.

While the public university sector seems unable to enrol more students because of limited capacity (an argument which does not hold considering that the institutions limit admission in the regular programme but 'open' the self-sponsored programmes, making one wonder where the 'extra' capacity comes from), private universities are closed to many who aspire to higher education because of their inability to pay the higher fees. This means that the capacity in private universities is underutilised, much as maintaining low enrolment is in line with increasing teacher–student interaction, one of the methods presumed to 'assure' quality. It is also true that most private universities are driven by a profit motive, meaning that they have to strike a balance between maintaining a realistic number of students while attracting more funds through increasing enrolment. The extent to which the universities have succeeded in doing this has not been investigated so far and remains largely unknown.

Private Household Expenditure
University education does not exist in a vacuum, and the level of private household expenditure at this level closely relates to the broader financing policy of the government (that influences decisions on how much to spend on each level, short- and long-term national human resource needs, the size of the private sector and poverty levels).

Further analysis on household expenditure at both public and private higher education institutions reveals the differences. The cost to parents for public institutions varies between KES 62 250 and KES 195 250 and an average KES 276 558 for private institutions.

Unit Costs

The most realistic method for funding institutions of higher education is to base tuition fees and other items on the real cost of providing those services. Funding based on any other model introduces distortions which impact negatively on equity and quality of education. This argument forms the rationale for a unit cost-based system in financing.

Unit Costs in University Education in Kenya
Public university financing in Kenya has been based on the unit cost system. Currently, the government uses an assumed unit cost of KES 120 000 per year. Each university gets funds depending on enrolment levels. This funding formula is unreasonable for a number of reasons. First, it is generally low and, secondly, it assumes that the cost of producing a philosophy graduate is the same as that of producing a medical doctor or an engineer. The system thus introduces distortions in the financing of university education. Third, the costs were computed in 1995 and do not reflect the real current situation. It is clear that policy-makers need to rethink the funding formula to make it more realistic. Fourth, under the unit cost system, government's preoccupation is funding universities in terms of the number of students only and not in terms of university needs for infrastructure development. This explains why the volume of funding for capital development has gone down drastically. Universities no longer submit budgets based on planned projects but merely on projected enrolment.

Even though the unit cost of KES 120 000 is supposed to be the basis of funding universities in Kenya, an analysis of state allocations to universities over the last several years reveals that the government has not really adhered to this principle. Actual funding is mostly higher than the supposed unit cost. For instance, UoN was funded at the rate of KES 145 986 per student for 2004/2005, while Maseno's funding was equivalent to KES 114 024 per student for the same financial period. According to the unit cost formula, some universities such as JKUAT would appear to be over-funded by more than 100%. The UoN realised that the basis of government funding is inadequate and does not reflect the reality. The university commission a committee to study its programmes and come up with a new cost structure for its programmes that reflect staff, student and infrastructure costs. The report has since been shared with the government and the CHE to form the basis of further discussions on the review of current unit costs. Using an objective formula, the unit costs that the committee worked out are notably higher than what had been worked out by a committee in 2003. For example, the unit costs for an Economics degree was KES 270 000; for a Humanities degree KES 180 000, and for Medicine KES 360 000.

A fact worth noting is that the unit costs used as the basis for funding university education (including students) were computed in 1995. This is notwithstanding the increase in the maximum possible loan allocation by KES 10 000 from KES 42 000 to KES 52 000 in 2003. This in itself raises fundamental questions since funding per student is pegged at KES 120 000 with the government direct contribution still standing at KES 70 000. If the maximum possible loan of KES 55 000 and KES 8 000 direct student contribution (or bursary) are added, the figure stands at KES 133 000 and not the conventionally known KES 120 000.

The new clustering of programmes that introduces a new cluster of medical and related programmes seems more realistic in so far as it tries to apportion the cost components. It should be noted that the CHE also undertook a review of unit costs for public universities in 2004. According to the CHE, the differentiated unit cost would accomplish three objectives, namely: (i) ensure fairness in payment of tuition for the different degree programmes; (ii) enable universities to get adequate funds to carry out their mission of teaching and research; and (iii) enable the government to sponsor students in accordance with the development needs of the country. In implementing a differentiated unit cost per degree cluster, priority is given to scholarship and critical skills. While the regular programmes continue to be highly subsidised, the self-sponsored programmes more or less charge full costs close to these unit costs. However, the CHE recommendations are yet to see light of day, three years on. This is characteristic of the lack of necessary political will to implement proposed higher education policies, the same fate that met earlier attempts to revise the unit costs.

Unit Expenditures
According to the most recent analysis of the MoE (Kenya 2007), the primary:secondary:university financing ratio is 1:3:24 (compared to the rest of Africa [1:3:11], Latin America [1:2:4], East Asia [1:2:8] and the OECD countries [1:1.4:2]). The current ratios would seem to be a significant improvement from the 1990s, when the ratios were 1:4:42-46 (Abagi 1997; Weidman 2000). The change in policy with the implementation of free primary education, increases in secondary school bursary programme and the reduced state funding for public universities (e.g. the requirement that they meet 20% of salaries from internal sources) could explain these changes.

State Funding by Institution

Officially, three factors determine the level of institutional funding: enrolment; the 'strain' levels of available facilities that may necessitate expansion; the existence of stalled capital projects; and the expected levels of privately earned revenues in an institution. Unofficially, however, the level of funding is also influenced by how well the individual university vice-chancellors are able to negotiate with Treasury. Table 3.4 summarises institutional funding by category for the last five years.

It is clear from Table 3.4 that the University of Nairobi (UoN) is the largest consumer of the recurrent budgetary allocations to public universities. However, the university has not benefited from development fund allocations primarily because it has been generating substantial amounts of revenue from its parallel degree programmes with which it has been able to fund most of its capital project costs that include completion of stalled teaching and learning facilities.

Kenyatta University has not benefited from state allocations for development expenditure and this is because the institution has not had serious capacity constraints at accommodating its students in the teaching, learning and residential facilities.

Egerton University receives disproportionately high development expenditure funds, which are second only to those seen at Jomo Kenyatta University of Agriculture and Technology (JKUAT). These high allocations to Egerton are targeted at the completion of its many stalled capital projects that include teaching and learning facilities, and residential hostels.

Moi University's low development expenditure allocations draws from the fact that it is the only institution of higher learning to have started off as a fully fledged university, it has better developed infrastructure with very low levels of capacity strains.

JKUAT has had significantly high development expenditure allocations, particularly because it is a technology-based university with high-cost facilities.

Maseno University has had modest development budget allocations mainly because as a relatively young university it has serious facility deficiencies for student accommodation and other teaching and learning facilities.

Table 3.4: Institutional Funding 2002/2003–2006/2007 (KES million)

UNIVERSITY	CATEGORY	FINANCIAL YEAR				
		2002/2003	2003/2004	2004/2005	2005/2006	2006/2007
University of Nairobi	Recurrent	1 653.00	1 970.46	2 675.86	3 648.86	3 269.86
	Development	0	0	0	0	27.00
Kenyatta	Recurrent	863.30	876.60	1 266.23	1 266.23	1 558.11
	Development	0	0	0	0	30.00
Egerton	Recurrent	1 050.71	1 099.70	1 476.54	1 633.90	1 750.14
	Development	232.40	500.00	190.41	90.00	90.00
Moi	Recurrent	1 089.11	1 105.90	1 576.60	1 600.68	1 851.58
	Development	26.50	3.00	190.41	20.00	40.00
JKUAT	Recurrent	691.50	691.50	734.17	892.22	914.17
	Development	555.08	628.13	60.00	0	70.00
Maseno	Recurrent	390.60	478.00	655.00	905.00	763.00
	Development	7.00	45.20	65.00	39.98	50.00

All the universities have registered increases in recurrent expenditure for all years, with the exception of UoN and Maseno. UoN had a reduced funding for in 2006/2007 because of the huge income it derives from the self-sponsored programmes. However, Maseno records a very sharp decline in recurrent allocation, though its income from the self-sponsored programmes is the lowest in the public universities.

Student Financing Schemes

Student financing instruments include scholarships, student loans (by far the most popular), educational vouchers, work study programmes and a system of waivers (the most rare). In Kenya, the student loan programme is the most widespread, though largely limited to public university students. In a few cases, private universities have work study programmes but these are very limited in scope. A number of public universities started work study programmes but due to abuse, lack of funds and limited impact, they were largely abandoned.

Within public universities, there are two main schemes through which students finance their education depending on the student's mode of entry. The regular subsidised students get governmental support while self-sponsored students pay from private (student's or family's) sources. Taking into account state and private sector participation in higher education finance, the following emerge as the most distinct modes of higher education financing.

Full Government-Sponsored Scholarships
These are opportunities to pursue an all costs paid higher education course with funds drawn from the government departments or foreign donations for study opportunities within Kenya and abroad administered by the MoE. Such opportunities are rare and are shrouded in non-transparent administrative processes. Some of the scholarships are funded externally, or through bi-lateral and multi-lateral agreements. Examples include the Indo–Kenya scholarship programme, Sino–Kenya scholarships and Commonwealth scholarships.

Partial Government Funding
Partial government funding is an option where the government pays a given proportion of the assumed cost of the programme for an academic year and the student pays for the remaining portion directly from private sources or through a study loan from the Higher Education Loans Board (HELB) or both. In this mode, there are two types of beneficiaries.

- **Regularly admitted students in public universities.** For this stream, the assumed unit cost of the programmes is KES 120 000, the government through the exchequer provides an allocation to the hosting university which translates to about KES 70 000 per student. The student in turn sources about KES 50 000 from government-sponsored loans administered by HELB that gives up to a maximum of KES 55 000 plus a bursary of KES 8 000 (non-refundable) for a total of KES 63 000 to the student, the deviation between the total KES 63 000 (KES 55 000 + KES 8 000 Bursary) and KES 50 000 (of KES 13 000) is attributable to inflationary correction factor for the value of KES 50 000 that has been lost to inflation since these assumed costs were set in 1991.
- **Privately sponsored students in private universities.** Responding to the

pressure from the popular social demand for higher education, HELB opened the borrowing window to some of the needy students enrolled in private universities. Such allocations are sent directly to the host universities to cover tuition costs to the student.

Full Private Sponsorship
In this option, the costs of higher education are met fully from the students' private sources. This mode applies to two categories of students, i.e. privately sponsored students in public universities and students in private universities.

Private Sector-Supported Funding
In this arrangement, which is not common, students enrolled in higher education programmes either benefit from private sector bursaries or scholarships (e.g. the Rattansi Educational Trust bursaries to university students).

HELB-Backed Second Loan Window
This window is run by the board in collaboration with a commercial bank, the National Bank of Kenya (NBK), which allows students who can demonstrate ability to service their loans as they study to access funds for fees at a market interest rate of 15% per annum compared to the subsidised loans the HELB advances directly to the other students.

Extent of Grant and Loan Financing
While grant financing of university education in Kenya is channelled directly to the public universities, loan financing is administered in part by the university hosting the beneficiary where KES 16 000 out of the loan advanced to the applicant by HELB is disbursed directly to his/her institution. Depending on the total amount of loan awarded to an applicant, the remaining difference after the remission of KES 16 000 to the university is disbursed in two parts of equal halves at the start of each semester in an academic year.

Grant financing of university education in Kenya is restricted largely to public universities. While for some of the public universities (universities with incomplete or crucial capital projects), the grant would include finances for both recurrent and development costs, for the others (universities without on-going capital projects), allocations are restricted to the recurrent budget costs only. In most cases, the amount of recurrent budget finances allocated is meant to cover only the staff wage bills for the institutions.

Loan Financing of Higher Education

Loan financing of university education is government supported, where the state through the HELB provides regular students with means tested loans. The latest loan allocation stratifications by need level (for the 2006/2007 academic year) indicates that while those ranked most needy receive KES 55 000 in addition to a bursary of KES 8 000, the least needy applicants receive KES 35 000.

HELB disburses both undergraduate and postgraduate loans. Other forms of funding include bursaries and scholarships. The number of beneficiaries for undergraduate loans has increased from 34 776 in 2002/2003 to 39 802 beneficiaries in 2005/2006. The number of the beneficiaries for postgraduate loans increased from 389 in 2002/2003 to 591 in 2005/2006. HELB bursary disbursement benefited 14 591 beneficiaries in 2002/2003 and this increased to 15 500 in 2005/2006.

Categories of HELB Loan Beneficiaries within Public universities

There are two categories of HELB loan beneficiaries in public universities. The first comprises undergraduate students who are admitted under the government-sponsored module. The second category comprises postgraduate students who were past beneficiaries at undergraduate level but who have made efforts to repay all or part of their loans. From its inception in 1995, HELB's primary focus has been on undergraduate public university students. With improved recovery, HELB expanded its loan support coverage to include postgraduate students and privately sponsored but needy students in private universities.

In general, there has been a steady rise in the total amount of loans disbursed to both undergraduate and postgraduate students. In particular, the amount of loans disbursed to undergraduate students accounts for the largest proportion of the HELB's loan portfolio.

a) **Undergraduate Loans.** By the 2002/2003 academic year, total undergraduate loan disbursements had reached the KES 1 billion mark. In 2003/2004, there was a significant increase in total disbursements to KES 1.336 billion representing an increase of 22.2%. Total disbursements rose marginally to KES 1.458 billion in 2004/2005 followed by an increase of KES 224 million to KES 1.682 billion in 2005/2006.

b) **Postgraduate HELB Loan Beneficiaries.** The postgraduate loan beneficiary population of 389 in the 2002/2003 acadmic year was relatively low before rising significantly to 643 during the 2003/2004 academic year. However during the 2004/2005 academic year, the number of postgraduate beneficiaries declined to 431 before increasing again to 495 in 2005/2006 and further to 591 during the 2006/2007 academic year.

Total postgraduate loans disbursed during the 2002/2003 academic year amounted to KES 37 million increasing to around KES 60 million by 2006/2007. The increase can be attributed to both a rise in the number of students and an improvement in the HELB's past loan recovery rates boosting its funds.

Trends in Loan allocation by Strata

In relation to the number of applicants and those actually awarded loans, HELB loan coverage is appreciably high. Between 98% and 99% of total applicants in every institution receive the loan. A closer look at the allocation proportions over the five-year period under study presents a consistent trend in the proportions of loan allocation by strata. This consistency in the proportion of loan allocation by strata implies two possibilities: that either student distribution in all the public universities by socio-economic characteristics is nearly uniform or that the HELB loan allocation process is possibly not means tested but rather based on a pre-set normal distribution curve formula.

Loan Recovery Trends

Recovery rates were initially low but have increased significantly during the past decade. From around 4% in the late 1990s the recovery rate on loans increased to 17.6% by 2002/2003. In KES terms, recovery amounts have risen consistently to KES 1.03 billion in 2006/2007. HELB has been recovering on average KES 88.3 million more per year. At this rate, it should record double its current disbursements in ten years from recovery alone. In other words, at an average loan size of KES 43 556 in 2006/2007, HELB should be able to give loans to finance the education of an additional 20 273 students per year in the next decade. These are new students who benefit from increased recoveries.

The current good record and future prospects nevertheless mask serious challenges from sectors that have very low repayment rates. Trends in loan repayment point to higher repayments by sectors which are easy to track, such as the civil service, teaching and other quasi-public bodies/parastatals.

Cumulatively, teachers, government departments (civil service) and parastatals accounted for 76.75% of all those who were repaying their loans in 2002. Relatively large sectors such as manufacturing and financial institutions contributed less than 1%. Though these are not the biggest employers when compared to the public sector, the potential repayment from these sectors has not been realised. Wages in these sector are much higher than in the public sector on average and beneficiaries would not feel the impact of repayment as much as their counterparts in the public service. The low repayment from these and other sectors, coupled with the high salaries, justify reforming the Kenyan loan programme from being a purely conventional/mortgage scheme to a more hybrid one.[1] This will enable the HELB to recover loans in reasonable time taking care of value erosion, especially given the low interest rate of 4%.

Equity in Public Expenditure

Public spending on education in Kenya is highly inequitable. This inequity is apparent on several fronts. First, the government is spending significantly higher proportion of its resources on relatively few students. It was shown earlier on that for every university student, the government could actually educate 22 primary school pupils and four secondary school students.

Second, the proportion of students in higher education is highly skewed in favour of the rich. According to the Welfare Monitoring Survey (1997) and Deolaikar (1999) more than two- thirds of students in university education come from the richest and second richest quintile, while the very poor have a representation of only 7.5%. The implication is that at the university level, the public is subsidising the education of the rich.

Third, there is a high discrepancy between institutions both in the absolute amounts of funding and relative proportions. Some universities that have capital intensive programmes are funded at the same levels as those with purely Arts and Humanities programmes. The rationale for funding universities therefore introduces serious distortions.

Fourth, there is serious discrepancy between development and recurrent expenditure categories. This inevitably means that little is spent on areas that can improve the quality of education and enhance the capacity of institutions to increase enrolment.

Fifth, the student loan programme is inequitably distributed, with 80% of the loans being accessed by public university students to the detriment of the private self-sponsored, university students.

The general assumption is that parental contribution is limited to bridging the gap of KES 8 000 for those who fail to get a bursary of an equivalent amount. This, however, is a fallacy. Parental contribution in supplementing living expenses is unknown, but is assumed to vary substantially, given the different socio-economic status of students. Virtually all students have to supplement the loans given by HELB, more so for those who do not get full loan allocations. Even

---

1   We do not cite a specific authority here. The practice of private sector generally paying better salaries than the public sector in most African countries is a truism that barely needs defending. The exceptions where public salaries are higher than or comparable to the private are few in the continent (e.g. South Africa). In Kenya, PriceWaterhouseCoopers carries out annual surveys that reveal wide disparities between the public and private sector wages.

for those who do get full allocations, the need to supplement remains. Currently, the living component of the undergraduate loan is distributed between tuition, boarding, stationery and food.

Incidence of Expenditure by Household Income Category

Levels of household financing of higher education depend on a number of factors. These include: (i) whether the student is attending a public university through a governmentally sponsored position or is purely self-sponsored; and (ii) if the student is government sponsored, the amount of fees paid also depends on whether the student receives a HELB loan. As has been seen in the previous sections, purely self-sponsored students pay full market costs of the course they are pursuing which differs by programme.

The HELB loan allocation strata for the 2006/2007 academic year (Table 3.5) can be used as a fairly accurate proxy indicator for determining the level of direct private financing of university education from household sources by socio-economic status level.

Table 3.5: Estimated Household Expenditure by Income Category

STUDENT FAMILY SOCIO-ECONOMIC STATUS CLASSIFICATION	LOAN ALLOCATION	EXPECTED BURSARY ALLOCATION	EXPECTED TOP-UP FINANCES FROM PRIVATE SOURCES
Very needy to extremely needy	55 000	8 000	0
	50 000	7 000	6 000–13 000
Moderately needy	45 000	6 000	12 000–17 000
	40 000	5 000	18 000–23 000
Less needy/non-needy	35 000	4 000	24 000–30 000
	0	0	63 000+

Source: Johnstone & Marcucci 2007

Using the maximum amount of HELB allocations of KES 63 000 (full loan of KES 55 000 plus full bursary of KES 8 000) as the assumed amount that a student needs to secure from private sources, Table 3.5 shows the range of financing that individual students source privately over and above the loans awarded to them. While those students receiving full loans would be able to pay for tuition and other charges without falling back on family sources (at least for substantial sums), those students who do not receive any amounts have to source KES 63 000 or more from private sources.

A New Model for Financing Higher Education

Implications of Current Financing Patterns in Designing a Model
The transformation of the higher education financing framework in Kenya has been remarkable. From being exclusively state-funded, it exhibits an interesting mix of public–private financing. However, opportunities for harnessing private contributions have not been exploited fully.

Public funding itself raises important questions about the sufficiency of funding, the level of subsidy and its equity implications, the rationale for funding institutions and especially the difficulty in implementing a unit cost-based funding system.

Higher education certainly constitutes a significant proportion of overall state expenditure on education, though at 14% of overall state funding, it is lower than the international and sub-Sahara African average of 15–20%. There may be a real fear that as much as it is desirable, the adoption of real unit costs as a basis for funding institutions would increase the share of public resources devoted to education, as the state would have to fund institutions based on the new real unit costs. That the government is currently funding universities on bases that are clearly above the assumed unit cost demonstrates that this is possible. However, there is no doubt that such a move will drastically alter the balance of allocations to different levels of education. At a time when the government has derived much political capital from the free primary education programme, its focus now is consolidating the gains at primary level and the possibility of free (or at best affordable) secondary education.

With more than two-thirds of students in the universities coming from the richest and second richest income groups, university financing is regressive. With the student loan in place as it is currently, means testing and need analysis does not make much sense. Nevertheless, the loan programme is to be commended for significantly increasing recoveries and disbursing funds to more students, including those in the private universities. This is despite the fact that the loans do not cover a significant portion of their tuition fees, unlike in the public universities. The government has been reluctant to increase funding for the loans programme as part of the broader policy of increasing funding for basic education while leaving higher education to increasingly tap alternative sources of funding.

One option for higher education institutions, especially universities, is to build on the success of the self-sponsored programmes that have proved crucial in helping universities bridge the gap caused by reduced state allocations. There are, however, notable differences among universities, which raises questions on the future of those universities that are not able to raise revenue from these programmes.

From the foregoing, there is reason to be concerned about higher education financing, and a new framework must be put in place to correct the current inadequacies and inconsistencies, and address the new realities in higher education financing. Some of the challenges facing the sub-sector which necessitate a rethinking of the financing framework include dwindling state allocations, increasing enrolments, unrealistic unit costs, skewed representation of the social and economic groups in higher education, an increasing private higher education sub-sector, an expansion of private entry programmes in public universities, increasing pressure from the state for universities to meet a bigger proportion of their own budgets and a heavy household burden in financing secondary and technical education.

A fundamental consideration that should guide the formulation of a new financing framework is the extent to which higher education is a public or a private good. Economists, educators and sociologists are agreed that education is neither an exclusively private nor public good. Its provision by both the government and the private providers therefore becomes a necessity. However, there are difficult questions on the extent to which both the public and private sectors can continue financing higher education in Africa. For most governments whose resources are already constrained, overwhelming evidence that basic education has higher social rates of return makes focusing on that level morally and economically justifiable. The other question is as much one of economics as it is a moral one: can the state leave the provision of higher education entirely to the private sector? Leaving the provision of education to purely market forces is likely to result into uneven provision and access by different socio-economic groups. State intervention is necessary to guard collective social interest and ensure a balance, particularly for the under-privileged who may not be able to afford the market cost of private education.

In the current Kenyan system, public intervention either through direct provision or finance is also made necessary by the dearth of student aid programmes in most private higher education institutions and the resultant inability of these institutions to promote social mobility through provision of opportunity to bright and underprivileged students (Altbach 1999). The opening up of public institutions to private students is increasingly making higher education a commodity for the rich. The government should put in place mechanisms for cushioning the vulnerable by increasing its student aid programmes. This should mostly target an increased capitation of HELB and revising the means testing mechanism to ensure that only those who are financially needy are supported by public funds.

Institutions should also strive to tap external funds, especially for research, from international organisations. This could take the form of supporting specific projects or postgraduate studies in fields that are relevant to the organisations. Locally, linkage with the industry and the private sector is also an avenue that should be pursued. The institutions will have to convince the private sector that there are benefits in the partnerships being fostered, including involving the sector in the design and, if possible, implementation of programmes. It might be necessary to make relevant changes in the governance structures of these institutions to include representatives of the industry as opposed to the current set up with top-heavy government representation which brings little innovation in these institutions.

Given the wide disparity in access to higher education by the poor in Kenya, an overriding principle in designing a new model of financing higher education in Kenya should not only aim at increasing the participation of the private sector, but also cushion the poor against market policies that will mostly favour students from the rich backgrounds. The kind of financing regime envisaged in this scenario is one that will put means testing and need analysis at the core of its basis on who to fund for what programme and in which institution. This is the challenge facing most African governments, Kenya included.

Parameters for Designing a Financing Model
The necessity of designing a new model is premised on the need to improve the current system to ensure better, more efficient and effective provision of higher education. It should adequately address increasing access, assuring quality, maintaining relevance to the economy and facilitating the realisation of national human resource needs, among other major objectives. These concerns are not limited to Kenya, and are applicable to the rest of the continent. Kenya must design a model that is in harmony with its broader development objectives. In this regard, a new financing framework should facilitate the realisation of the main pillars on which the current policy framework is hinged. These are access, quality, retention and equity.

The preceding sections of this chapter have highlighted the theoretical issues in higher education financing as well as the reality of the Kenyan situation. These should form the broad basis for determining the kind of financing model that the country adopts. In summary, there are several considerations that must guide the development of a new model for financing higher education. These are briefly discussed below.

Mechanisms for Funding Institutions
Public funds can be channelled directly to institutions or indirectly through students. The current system is a mix of both: universities get direct government capitation but also access publicly funded loans from the HELB through students.

The main problem with the system is that it is not incentive driven. Institutions are sure to receive funding from the government based on enrolment levels and given the arbitrary unit cost of KES 120 000. The tuition component of student loans is also sent directly to the university where a student is enrolled, while students pay other direct charges such as boarding directly to the university.

Two possible changes could be made to the current system. The first is to route funds through a body such as the Commission for Higher Education, a research agency such as the Kenya National Academy for Sciences, or the Higher Education Loans Board. A second is to directly fund students, with institutions receiving no money from the government at all. Institutions will then have to compete for students. The advantage of this approach is that institutions have to be responsive to students and also price their courses appropriately. Students would also be at liberty to enrol for non-degree programmes in accredited colleges.

Type of Institutions to Fund

The government has traditionally funded universities more generously compared to non-university higher education institutions. This has given universities an undue advantage over their non-university competitors in the higher education sector. But even among universities, only public universities have benefited from public resources. In a new financing framework, the government has to decide whether public funds should continue to be appropriated by public institutions only, or whether both public and private institutions should benefit. Another decision is whether those that benefit should include all higher education institutions, or only universities or any higher education institution accredited by the CHE, local institutions or both local and international institutions (beyond the Kenyan border).

The proposals here recognise that one of the long-term goals of any financing instrument and the accompanying design should be to invigorate the financial health of the institutions and eventually enhance standards through improved provision of teaching and learning resources including libraries, laboratories, expanded space and internships and attachments for students.

Equity Considerations

Equity considerations in funding higher education must be given priority. From the data presented in this report and elsewhere (e.g. Otieno 2005), other equity issues that must be addressed in a new funding regime are:

- Uniform funding levels to students in an institution such as a university irrespective of discipline, gender or socio-economic status;

- Weighting funding by study area, i.e. some disciplines receiving higher value vouchers/more funds;
- A financing regime that weights students by socio-economic background, with poor students receiving higher value vouchers/more funds in relation to the richer students; and
- Positive discrimination on the basis of gender, so that women get more funds to facilitate their entry into specific programmes or simply increase their numbers across the board.

The Question of Public Support to Module I versus Module II Students
There have been suggestions that the current funding system is unfair to students in privately sponsored programmes (Module II) in public universities who may not necessarily come from the richer sections of the population. Given the increase in the number of privately sponsored students, however, the government has to decide whether public funds earmarked for the public universities will be limited to students in the Joint Admissiona Board admitted (Module I) track or both the Module I track and the Module II track.

The Efficiency and Effectiveness Criteria
A model for funding higher education must achieve the twin goals of enhancing institutional efficiency and effectiveness in the delivery of higher education. Higher education institutions have operated on the basis of tradition, with little incentive to reform, or lack of disincentive in not reforming. A new funding framework should induce reforms and embed efficiency in the running of institutions by putting in place a system of financial rewards for good management, responsiveness to the clientele (students), relevance of programmes and linkages with industry. One method for doing this is to discourage the current complacency in public universities where institutions are sure to get public funds irrespective of the nature of their programmes, wastage or frequent closures.

Extent of Grant and Loan Financing
It was pointed out that because of the insufficiency of student loans, most students have to supplement the loans with private resources. For the poor, it is important that the difference between the actual cost of education and state support should not be too wide as to result in their dropping out of higher education. The rich are in most cases able to cover any financial short-falls and do not face any problems. A financing framework must therefore be able to positively discriminate between the different socio-economic groups and the appropriate safety nets that can

effectively cushion the very poor. Full grants or scholarships to poor but bright students are justifiable. Especially for rural women, it may be necessary to put in place a mix of partial scholarships and generous loans.

The Right of Choice: Consumer Sovereignty
Studies in Kenya indicate that overall up to 44% of all students in universities consider themselves to be in the wrong programmes in the wrong universities. In some universities, the proportion is as high as 74% (Otieno 2005). The situation is brought about by the admission system that literally allocates students to universities and programmes if they do not meet the subject cluster requirements but have met minimum admission criteria set by the JAB. These students finance their studies through loans which they have to repay. By this very principle of having to repay their loans, a financing model should be flexible enough to allow students to choose where to invest their money. It should empower students to demand and pay for the right programmes in institutions of their choice.

The Interplay of State Intervention and Market Forces
The state has played a major role in the funding and regulation of higher education in Kenya since independence. One of the outcomes of this domination is unrealistic unit costs in university education. This chapter has argued that this has brought distortions in the pricing of degree programmes, and also resulted in notable inequities. How long the state should continue giving directions on the fee levels in the Module I programmes cannot be predicted. What is not in doubt is the need for a change in state policy so that degree programmes are priced taking into consideration actual costs of providing them (Aduol 2001). It is rightly argued that leaving education provision purely to the market can result in uneven provision and in locking out the poor. Market influence in the provision of social services has its benefits, including efficiency and client responsiveness. There should therefore be a reasonable balance between the degree of state intervention to protect the greater social good, and allowing market forces to influence the provision of education. As argued here, the government's role should be to decide how many students it can fund on a yearly basis using whatever instrument and then leave the universities to decide fee levels. Those universities that price themselves out of the market or provide programmes that are not in demand will have themselves to blame. Government funding should also be designed in a manner that induces efficiency and effectiveness in the service providers while at the same time empowering students as already emphasised earlier.

Given these considerations, the mode of design proposed for Kenya takes the form presented in Figure 3.1.

The Proposed Financing Model
Considering all the factors enumerated above, the current study proposes a hybrid model that incorporates scholarships, grants and loans (see Figure 3.1). The model takes into account socio-economic status and types of funding, and proposes a range of funding models from a 100% scholarship through grants, grant and loan combinations to full self-financing.

The checked cells in Figure 3.1 indicate eligibility for funding based on the specified criterion. Aspects that do not come out clearly in the model are the types of institutions to fund and which programmes to fund even in the public universities. One may expect that these features would conspicuously stand out in the model, and that one should be able to determine what facility is open to which students in what type of institution. Because there is less agreement on these issues, the model is deliberately vague on this aspect. The proposed model is one that cannot afford to be prescriptive.

The proposed model has three distinct features: (i) it gives prime consideration to the fields of study identified by the government as its priority areas of investment; (ii) it is discriminant; and (iii) following from (ii) above, equity is an important feature.

All students are first placed in expenditure quintiles – developed from a national survey and made available in documents such as the Welfare Monitoring Survey and the Integrated Household Budget Surveys. Female students are further broadly grouped into three socio-economic groups: poor, middle income and rich. The purpose of giving special consideration to women is to enhance their participation in higher education. All in all, students from poorer backgrounds get full scholarships and generous loans. It is clear that the mix of grants and loans end in level four. The remaining three levels see heavier reliance on loans and self-financing. The implications of this are two-fold. First, it limits the number that would access public funds earmarked for the operation of the voucher programme. Secondly, and stemming from the first, it enhances equity by ensuring a redistribution of educational access proportionately with the income level and gender, thus ensuring mobility of the disadvantaged in the society by facilitating their entry into careers that are considered lucrative.

The need for corrective measures cannot be overemphasised. In Kenya, as already severally stated, the richest 20% of the population receive 21% of the total public expenditure on education compared to 17% for the poorest 20%.

Figure 3.1: Proposed Framework for Financing Higher Education in Kenya

Facility	Criterion*	I. ALL STUDENTS' SOCIO-ECONOMIC STATUS BY EXPENDITURE QUINTILES															II. FEMALE STUDENTS BY SOCIO-ECONOMIC STATUS								
		POOREST			SECOND			THIRD			FOURTH			TOP			POOR			MIDDLE			RICH		
Study areas+		A	B	C	A	B	C	A	B	C	A	B	C	A	B	C	A	B	C	A	B	C	A	B	C
		Occupational Clusters: A = Science and Technology; B = Social Sciences; C = Arts and Humanities																							
1. Scholarship	= 100%	X															X	X	X						
2. GRANT + loan	80 + (20)		X		X																				
3. Grant + LOAN	40 + (60)			X		X	X													X	X				
4. Grant + self	50 + (0,y)							X														X			
5. Self + loan	0 + (50,y)								X	X															
6. SELF + loan	0 (y + 40)										X	X	X												
7. SELF ONLY	0 (yy)													X	X	X							X	X	X

Key:

CAPS   Represent heavier financing using respective instruments, while lower case indicates limited funding by type.

*   The numeral is the loan component of university education costs (for those qualifying after means testing) while 'y' is a vector of private outlays. This could be from own savings, commercial bank or Savings and Credit Cooperative Organisation (SACCO) loans or any form of funding from non-public sources.

+   This represents the broader categories into which study areas/disciplines could be clustered in order of priority. Thus, 'A' represents the highest priority area followed by 'B' and 'C'. The classification will depend wholly on the government as to what it considers its priority human resource needs. As indicated earlier, this would need to be done based on projected human resource needs in the short, medium and longer term, itself arising from a rigorous labour market analysis. This might appear to be restricting students to particular disciplines (and thus working against choice, the very goal that vouchers seek to promote). However, choice would still be possible at two levels: going for the same programme in any institution of preference or opting for alternative programme at the polytechnic or some other level, money having been placed in the hands of the students. It is generally assumed that the government's projections would not be at considerable variance with the expectations of students. The whole system allows for a certain degree of flexibility, assuming that there are some programmes undertaken for 'consumption' purposes and not necessarily for future employment.

Chapter 4
LESOTHO

Pundy Pillay

Introduction: The Education Sector

The Ministry of Education and Training (MoET) is responsible for the management, provision and regulation of education and training in Lesotho. The education sector consists of four years of pre-primary education (non-compulsory), seven years of primary education, five years of secondary education, and three to six years of tertiary education. Post-secondary education has two main strands: (i) higher education, and (ii) technical and vocational education and training. The National University of Lesotho is the only university, although there are close to 20 other tertiary-level public institutions and 15 private tertiary institutions (MoET 2005).

Table 4.1: Types and Number of Tertiary Education Institutions in Lesotho

TYPE	NUMBER
Publicly-funded universities	1
Publicly-funded teacher training colleges	1
Publicly-funded polytechnic	1
Other	14
Private tertiary institutions	15

The more global policy principle of the MoET, guided by the MDGs (Millennium Development Goals) and EFA (Education for All), is that basic education is an integral part of social and economic development, and that it is a fundamental human right. It is also seen as an essential pre-condition for mid-level employment and secondary and post-secondary education and training, which is expected to lead to practical skills and knowledge.

The share of the education sector in total government spending has been increasing steadily, with the sector claiming 30% of the government budget in 2005/2006. Lesotho's expenditure on education is much higher than the average for comparable sub-Saharan African countries.

The Southern African Development Commnity (SADC) Protocol on Education and Training has explicitly influenced national higher education policy and practice in that students from SADC are treated like home students in terms of paying fees. Science and technology has officially been identified as a priority area for higher education, according to the MoET. The value of higher education is noted in both the National Indicative Plan and Country Strategy Paper (2008–2013) as well as the Poverty Reduction Strategy (2005).

The Higher Education Act, 2004 provides for the regulation of higher education, for the establishment, composition and functions of a Council for Higher Education, for the governance and funding of public higher education institutions, for registration of private higher education institutions, and for quality assurance.

Structure of Higher Education

Higher education in Lesotho includes technical education, teacher training and university education. Lesotho has one tertiary-level technical education institution, the Lerotholi Polytechnic (LP), which offers both certificate and diploma courses.

The Lesotho College of Education (LCE) offers teacher training courses for primary and secondary school teachers, with a Diploma in Education (Primary) for certified teachers, a Diploma in Education (Secondary) and a Diploma in Technology Education. In 2002, the LCE began offering a Distance Teacher Education Programme for primary teachers who wished to improve their teaching qualifications while continuing to work. The LCE does not yet offer any degree courses for teachers. The National University of Lesotho (NUL) offers a Bachelor of Education degree which caters to undergraduates aspiring to be secondary school teachers.

NUL is the only public university and offers programmes leading to certificates, diplomas and degrees in Agriculture, Education, Humanities, Law, Social Sciences, and the Natural Sciences, and a few postgraduate programmes.

There are several higher education institutions outside the ambit of the MoET, specifically under the Ministries of Agriculture, Health, and Finance and Development Planning. These institutions are respectively the Lesotho

Agricultural College, the National Health Training College and the Centre for Accounting Studies.

Private higher education has seen significant growth mainly through distance education provided by South African institutions.

Table 4.2: Higher Education Institutions and Associated Ministries

MINISTRY	INSTITUTION
Education and Training	• National University of Lesotho • Lesotho College of Education • Lerotholi Polytechnic • Institute of Development Management • Lesotho Institute of Public Administration & Management • Machabeng College
Health	• National Health Training College • (Christian Health Association of Lesotho – not a higher education institution, but the mother organisation for the nursing schools established by the churches)
Agriculture	• Lesotho College of Agriculture
Finance & Development Planning	• Centre for Accounting Studies

Education Sector Strategic Plan (ESSP): 2005–2015

The MoET's Education Sector Strategic Plan (2005–2015) (ESSP) provides a comprehensive review of all the education sub-sectors including identifying the main policies and challenges. It is the government's position that higher education institutions have to rationalise the composition of their expenditures and explore complementary ways of enhancing their self-generated revenue base.

Increasing student enrolment in these institutions is to be given priority, and the ESSP provides some examples in this regard. The reconstruction and refurbishment of LCE student hostels has opened up opportunities for increased enrolment. Similarly, NUL, under its new management, has embarked on a cost-containment strategy that includes the exploration of opportunities for the diversification of its revenue base beyond government funding through, for example, income-generating projects such as research and new investments in real estate. The expansion of student hostels on the Roma campus would not only lead to enrolment expansion but also to the minimisation of physical insecurity for students (particularly females) who have to make sub-optimal accommodation arrangements outside campus in a generally rural environment.

In terms of the governance structure for higher education, the Higher Education Act envisages the provision of a legal framework for the regulation of higher education in Lesotho and specifically focuses on the establishment, governance and funding of a Council of Higher Education (CHE). This body has the following responsibilities:

- Monitoring and implementing of policy on higher education institutions;
- Advising the Minister on every aspect of higher education, including quality promotion and assurance; research; structure and planning of the higher education system; mechanisms for the allocation of public funds; appropriate incentives/sanctions; student bursaries; governance of the higher education institutions and systems;
- Through the Higher Education Quality Committee: promoting quality assurance; auditing QA mechanisms in higher education institutions; accrediting higher education programmes; monitoring and evaluating performance of academic programmes; and
- Publishing information on higher education developments on a regular basis and promoting access of students to higher education.

Apart from the establishment of the CHE, the Higher Education Act addresses governance and funding issues in relation to public and private higher education institutions as well as the provision of quality assurance in higher education.

The ESSP identified four sets of 'main policies' for the higher education subsector during the plan period 2005–2015:

1. Increased access (on an equitable basis) to higher education;
2. Improving the relevance of higher education to make it responsive to the demands of the labour market;
3. Improving efficiency in institutions of higher learning; and
4. Mainstreaming gender, HIV and AIDS in higher education curriculum and activities.

Associated with these main policies are the following critical challenges:

- Enhancing the quality of higher education through well-programmed and structured curriculum improvement;
- Improving the developmental relevance of higher education;
- Addressing the structural/infrastructure expansion of institutions to facilitate quality and a secure learning environment;
- Improving management efficiency and effectiveness;

- Expanding the involvement of the private sector in the provision of higher education programmes; and
- Enhancing ICT capacity and e-governance.

Access and Participation

As Table 4.3 shows, Lesotho has made some progress with regard to access at the primary and secondary levels. The gross enrolment at the tertiary level of 4% is very low and is largely the outcome of still poor access to secondary education, where the gross enrolment ratio was still lagging at 37% in 2006.

Table 4.3: Access by Education Sub-sector

	1999	2006
Gross enrolment: Pre-primary	21	18
Gross enrolment: Primary	102	114
Net enrolment: Primary	57	72
Gross enrolment: Secondary	31	37
Gross enrolment: Tertiary	2	4

Source: UNESCO 2009

Government Spending on Education

Lesotho spends a very large proportion of its government budget on education. Table 4.4 shows that education expenditure as a percentage of GDP reached 21% in 2002 and as a percentage of the government budget it was 26%. Both these figures are at the very highest levels in both the developing and industrialised contexts. Higher education is substantially financed by the government. The NUL for instance, gets about 90% of its funds from the state.

Table 4.4: Education Expenditure as % of GNP and Total Government Expenditure

	1999	2006
Education expenditure as % of GNP	10.2	10.8
Education expenditure as % of total government expenditure	26.0	30.0
Current expenditure as % of Education Budget	74.0	91.0

Source: UNESCO 2009

Government support for higher education institutions is given in the form of subventions to autonomous higher institutions. The NUL, along with LCE and LP, are Lesotho's three largest institutions of higher education. Table 4.5 details the allocation of the higher education budget but includes only those institutions falling directly under MoET as well as the loan/bursaries provided by the National Manpower Development Secretariat (NMDS) in the Ministry of Finance.

Table 4.5: Subventions to Higher Education Institutions, 2003/2004, 2006/2007 (LSM, million)

HIGHER EDUCATION INSTITUTION	2003/2004	2006/2007
IDM	1.92	2.10
NUL	117.00	121.00
LCE	17.00	21.00
LP	14.55	18.00
NMDS Tertiary Bursaries	201.30	Not available
Total	351.77	

Source: World Bank 2005. Note: NMDS – National Manpower Development Secretariat

Recurrent expenditures on higher education increased from 29% in 1998/1999 to 36% of the total in 2003/2004 and 37% in 2004/2005 – excluding LCE (under the Department of Teacher Education in the MoE) and LP (under the Department of Technical and Vocational Education). If higher education is defined to include all post-secondary institutions, thus including LCE and LP, the tertiary sector absorbs approximately 40% of the education budget. However, even this figure does not include government funding of higher education institutions falling under the Ministries of Agriculture, Finance and Health.

NMDS tertiary bursaries constitute the largest component under higher education recurrent expenditure. Even though this bursary is supposed to be a 'loan bursary', its recovery rate is so low that it is essentially a grant. The value of NMDS bursaries increased from LSM 65 million in 1998/1999 to LSM 300 million in 2005/2006.

The fact that the NMDS is administratively under the Ministry of Finance and Development Planning (MoFDP) has made it very difficult for MoET to monitor expenditure patterns, but it is still part of the education sector expenditure. A very high proportion of tertiary students receive the scholarship and, as long they pass examinations at the end of the academic year, scholarships are renewed automatically. For example, 5 247 students in NUL were provided with NMDS scholarships out of a total of about 7 000 students in 2003/2004 (World Bank 2005).

Table 4.6 shows the annual national budget amounts allocated to the MoE as a whole and the NMDS expenditures on loan bursaries. The table also shows that since 2001, NMDS actual expenditures have been in excess of its annual budget due to a high growth rate of student enrolment in tertiary institutions. Since students are already enrolled and registered with their respective tertiary education institutions, these financial commitments have to be funded rather than being postponed. This over-commitment is not just a once-off expenditure but rather a recurring problem for at least four consecutive years (2001–2004). Furthermore, the amounts involved are also very high, in excess of 50% of the allocated budget for the financial years 2003 and 2004.

Table 4.6: Budget Allocations and NMDS Over-commitments (LSM, million)

	NATIONAL BUDGET	EDUCATION BUDGET	NMDS ALLOCATION	NMDS ACTUAL EXPENDITURE	VARIANCE (%)
2000/2001	1 988	513.2	83.1	80.4	+2.6
2001/2002	2 098	551.5	114.1	122.0	-7.9
2002/2003	2 365	687.1	115.2	176.6	-61.4
2003/2004	2 703	747.8	195.0	249.8	-54.8
Growth rate	136%	144%	235%	311%	
Annual growth	34%	36%	59%	78%	

The current Loan Bursary Fund was established in 1978 by the Minister of Finance and Development Planning. It was envisaged that the loan bursary would constitute a revolving fund. This loan bursary scheme replaced the traditional scholarship award that used to be made to students as pure study grants or scholarships. It is designed for Basotho students who have been admitted to tertiary education institutions in Lesotho, South Africa or overseas. The old bonding system only required that students should serve the Government of Lesotho (GoL) or at least work in the country after completion of their studies.

The main funding sources for the loan bursary scheme consists of three components: firstly, the government appropriation from the annual consolidated budget; secondly, overseas donor assistance (ODA) for education and training grants; thirdly, student loan payments into the revolving fund after completion of their studies.

The loan bursary is available to all candidates who are eligible and who have obtained admission to a tertiary education institutions. The loan bursary is interest free. The obligation or the percentage of the loan bursary to be paid by the student is contingent upon successful completion of the course and upon employment in the Lesotho civil service.

Table 4.7 shows the allocation of bursaries by country and by institution within Lesotho. It is evident from this that a large proportion of loan/bursary funds accrue to Lesotho students studying in South Africa.

Table 4.7: NMDS Expenditure by Country and Institutions (LSM, million)

COUNTRY/INSTITUTION	2003/2004	2005/2006
South Africa	101.9	126.0
Lesotho		
NUL	85.0	87.0
CAS	3.5	1.5
Machabeng	1.7	1.1
Agricultural College	–	1.6
IDM	0.8	1.1
Lerotholi	–	4.8
Other local institutions	17.3*	1.2
Total – Lesotho	108.3	98.3
Other African universities	5.0	6.4
International universities	1.0	14.0
Post-primary	15.0	19.0

* Could have included amounts for Agricultural College and Lerotholi

Table 4.8 shows that the proportion between non-repayable grant and student loan components of the loan bursary is based upon a variety of factors and considerations.

Table 4.8: Criteria for Loan-Grant Bursaries

CATEGORY OF STUDENT	PAYABLE LOANS (%)	NON-PAYABLE LOANS (%)
Serving government or statutory bodies for 5 years after completion of studies	50	50
Working for private sector or parastatal after completion of studies	65	35
Obtaining outstanding performance and serving government for 5 years after completion of studies	40	60
Do not serve government after completion of studies	100	0
Fail to return to Lesotho after completion of studies	100	0

Repayment of the loan is expected to be made through equal monthly instalments. However, the recipients are also free to accelerate their loan repayments.

In 1997, while LSM 43 million of loans and grants were disbursed, only LSM 1 848 was recovered. In 1998, LSM 24 million was disbursed and only LSM 169 was recovered!

Technical and Vocational Education and Training (TVET)
Given Lesotho's unique geographic situation and limited employment opportunities, the government recognises the importance of adapting its training policies to produce workers with marketable skills that will make the trainees competitive in both the local and regional markets. The Department of Technical and Vocational Training of the MoET is the umbrella regulatory body that aims to improve the quality of delivery systems and mechanisms through curriculum development; inspection and assessment; accreditation of programmes and institutions; administration of trade tests to determine skills proficiency levels of workers; support in terms of provision of workshops and equipment, training of staff at TVET institutions and schools; and continuous assessment of skills needs.

At present, there are eight public TVET institutions. Six of these are church-owned but receive government budgetary support for teacher salaries. The Lerotholi Polytechnic assumed autonomy in 2002 and receives an annual subvention from the MoET. A number of private providers also exist in the field of TVET including providers of informal training and traditional apprenticeships.

Generally, the ministry recognises the existence of major challenges in TVET that have to be addressed during the strategic plan period 2005–2015 and beyond. In the ESSP document, the MoET has acknowledged the following factors that continue to compromise the realisation of the TVET mission:

- Trade Training Institutes (TTIs) are under-funded and under-performing;
- Lack of confidence by employers in TTI graduates, demonstrated in the low placement rates;
- Absence of planning for TVET in the form of national, industry or institutional skills development plans, through which skills requirements can be identified – this has resulted in training being largely supply-driven;
- Unregulated and stagnated apprenticeship scheme;
- Weak governance and management of TVET at national and institutional levels with private participation in the TVET Board being largely symbolic;
- Limited training tailored to the needs of small business and the informal sector;
- Weak quality assurance; and
- No TVET accreditation system.

Recognising these challenges, the government has challenged TVET institutions to seek alternative sources of revenue to complement state subventions. At present, the main TVET funders are:

- Government at the level of meeting salaries, bursaries to students, support towards examinations and inspection;
- Private sources;
- Student tuition and boarding fees;
- Income generating activities; and
- Donor support.

Higher Education Financing Challenges

Table 4.9, drawn from the ESSP, shows that the projected cost of higher education is expected to decline from LSM 515 million in 2005/2006 to LSM 492 million in 2014/2015. However, during the entire period of the ESSP, the government is expected to be able to fund, at best, only about two-thirds of the projected higher education budget.

Table 4.9: Projected cost of Higher Education According to the ESSP, 2005–2015

	2005/2006	2006/2007	2007/2008	2008/2009	2009/2010	2014/2015
Total cost of higher education	515 286	562 168	569 918	492 993	501 536	491 702
Available recurrent resources	299 870	304 198	308 776	313 486	318 430	323 818
Available GoL capital resources	17 145	6 074	6 414	6 735	7 071	7 778
Funding gap	198 270	251 897	254 729	172 773	176 034	160 105
% of ESSP funded	62	55	55	65	65	67
% of funding gap	38	45	45	35	35	33

Source: Lesotho Ministry of Education

The government is currently introducing priority fields for consideration of scholarships to study in South Africa. These include general postgraduate studies, along with Health Sciences, Engineering, Building Technology, Information Technology, and Tourism. It is also considering strengthening the recovery of certain bursaries (as loans) from the graduates. These are certainly positive steps forward.

However, given the currently relatively high level of government funding of higher education and known priorities in primary and secondary education as well as in non-formal education (e.g. adult literacy), it is not clear whether the

Government of Lesotho will be able to increase funding to higher education. (The ESSP data shown in Table 4.9 suggests that it cannot.) Thus higher education institutions will need to develop innovative mechanisms for increased funding from non-governmental sources. In addition, it is well known that the higher education system is highly inequitable providing disproportionate access to students from the higher socio-economic groups. A major challenge for the higher education institutions therefore relates to how access can be enhanced for those from socio-economically disadvantaged backgrounds. In this regard, NMDS using its merit-driven selection process does give those students from socio-economically disadvantaged backgrounds the opportunity to access higher education.

It is the government's position that higher education institutions have to rationalise the composition of their expenditures and explore complementary ways of enhancing their self-generated revenue base. Increasing student enrolment in these institutions shall be given priority in this regard. As noted earlier, the reconstruction and refurbishment of LCE student hostels has opened opportunities for increased enrolment. Similarly, NUL has embarked on a cost-containment strategy that includes the exploration of opportunities for the diversification of its revenue base beyond government funding through, for example, income-generating projects such as research and new investments in real estate.

A major cost driver in tertiary education is the construction of additional facilities. The provision of bursaries to additional students associated with increased enrolment is also significant, as is the increase in the subvention associated with higher student numbers.

While the award of bursaries for individual learners in higher education is to be reviewed with intent to strengthen cost sharing in higher education, the need to expand teacher education and in ICT, will require subsidies to tertiary learners. The funding gap of 35% and 33% for 2009/2010 and 2014/2015 respectively shown in the ESSP reflects a shortfall that will have to be addressed through cost-sharing and public–private partnership initiatives.

NMDS Loan Bursaries

Different governments of Lesotho have placed a high value on the need to develop skilled human resources as a basis for sustained economic development and improvement in the quality of life for all Basotho. They have also recognised that many Basotho are too poor to afford post-secondary education for their children. Even though others could finance their children through university, they were considered too few in number to make a significant difference to the overall scheme of things.

Based on these considerations, the government offered scholarships for various fields of study for students who performed well in the school-leaving examinations. These students were not required to pay back the cost of this funding support from the government until 1978.

With the Loan Act of 1978, the government established the NMDS under the Ministry of Development Planning to administer scholarships and bursaries. It also changed the policy and granted scholarships and bursaries as loans, which were to be recovered from the students when they completed their studies.

NMDS was to issue contracts to the students which were guaranteed by their parents or guardians. It was also to keep records and track these students, and recover the loans from those who had completed their studies. More importantly, NMDS was to submit to government annual statements in accordance with the Act. There was also to be a National Council that would advise the Minister on the students to be awarded bursaries and scholarships.

All students who received admission to NUL and other higher education institutions inside and outside the country were granted bursaries or scholarships through NMDS. The country could afford this because the numbers who qualified were few and the bursary loan recoveries were expected to be proportionally large and therefore reduce the annual costs borne by the fiscus.

Specifically, those who completed their studies and worked in the public service were required to pay back 50% of the total bursary, those who worked in the private sector in Lesotho were to repay 65%, while those who worked outside Lesotho were to repay 100%. Unfortunately, those repayments from outside the government never materialised.

Factors accounting for the failure of the NMDS scheme were as follows:

1. **Appointment of the Council.** The Council, which was to advise the Minister, was never established. NMDS performed all the functions envisaged for the Council. However, its performance has been less than optimal.
2. **Quality of NMDS staffing.** Although the responsibility given to NMDS by the Act is broad and complex, the quality and quantity of staff appointed was not commensurate to the task. Consequently, all the key functions of NMDS were poorly or never done at all.
3. **Weak administration and systems.** With inadequate staffing, the administration of NMDS was weak in managing relations with institutions; keeping adequate records of contracts; maintaining a list of graduates; tracking the movements of graduates through their families; ensuring timely loan recoveries and presenting annual results. Consequently, it has

been impossible to track down those students who have not repaid their loans.
4. **Priority fields of study.** The Ministry of Development Planning did not put to government a clear list of courses that must be given priority in the award of scholarships.
5. **Planning the amount to be spent on awards.** Because of the lack of proper planning and management of NMDS awards, government does not know how much it will spend on bursaries over the next five years and whether it can afford that level.
6. **Impact of more admissions in RSA post-1994** led to increasing costs for the Government of Lesotho.

New Policy on Loan Bursaries
The Ministry of Finance and Development Planning announced that for the 2003/2004 budget and subsequent years, priority would be given to students whose aim is to study disciplines identified by government as critical for achieving Lesotho's national vision – reducing poverty, creating jobs and improving the quality of life of people. These fields are: ICTs and Computer Sciences; Economics and Business Sciences; Education, particularly the teaching of Maths and Science; Agriculture and Environmental Sciences; Health Sciences; Engineering; Sciences; and Legal Studies.

Evaluation of the NMDS Loan/Recovery Fund
As noted earlier, one of the priority objectives for the Government of Lesotho is to provide 'Education for All' and in pursuit of this objective the government established a Loan Bursary Act of 1978 in an effort to design a 'Revolving Fund'. The NMDS was then tasked with the responsibility to administer the Loan Bursary Fund. It is estimated that more than 10 000 students have benefited from this loan bursary scheme since 1978 and it is also estimated that over LSM 80 million is outstanding in the form of unpaid student loans due to poor management of loan recovery.

Effectively, the NMDS has failed to implement the revolving fund concept as envisaged by the Act and as a result, the government budget allocation has been increasing every year without any complementary support from the fund. A study commissioned by the Ministry of Finance and Development Planning (MoFDP 2005) reviewed and analysed the NMDS capabilities to manage and administer loan bursaries and has confirmed that this institution does not have the competence to handle this responsibility. For instance, the study revealed that (i) there is a significant divergence between the records and figures provided by the Office of the Accountant General at Treasury and those provided by the NMDS – it is quite obvious that these figures leave much to be desired and as such cannot be regarded as reflecting the true status of affairs unless proper accounts are prepared and audited; and (ii) that even the number of students sponsored by NMDS since 1978 to date is not known with certainty. To this end, therefore, it was recommended that the function and responsibility of loan bursaries and the revolving fund management be withdrawn from the NMDS and be transferred to a financial institution which has ICT systems and capabilities to manage the fund.

The study recommended a separation of the functions and responsibilities between the Council, the Secretariat and a financial institution tasked to manage the revolving fund. It also recommended that the revolving fund scheme should be administered outside the government's Consolidated Fund, except for the complementary fixed portion contributed by government as seed money. It was envisaged that the aforesaid revolving fund will be administered by a specialised financial institution with financially qualified personnel, adequate systems of loan recovery and credible in terms of transparency and accountability. Such a financial institution would be complemented with the following legal instruments to enhance its efficiency:

- Separation of the loan bursary fund or the revolving funds from the NMDS and transfer of responsibility to a commercial financial institution to manage and collect outstanding loans.
- Government to consider an application of banking procedure to recover the outstanding student debts.
- The financial institution responsible for the management of the loan bursary and student loan recovery will have a more structured approach to credit control.
- Review the legal status of loan recovery. The legal instruments for student loan recovery should be strengthened to empower the financial institution to recover loans at source.
- Student debtors should be given a specified period within which they will make arrangements with the financial institution to repay their loans. Government consideration of a six-month amnesty for loan defaulters to repay their loans or negotiate their repayment schedules without a penalty.
- Improvement in the flow of information regarding student loans. With regard to student beneficiaries who had to leave the country to seek employment in South Africa or those who never returned to Lesotho

after completion of their studies, it has been noted that these people have a higher earning capacity and their ability to repay their loans is high. Yet they do not pay their loan bursaries because there are no sufficient facilities for them to do so as against their unwillingness to pay. It is therefore recommended that financial arrangements be made with banks in South Africa as a convenient vehicle for repayment of student loans.

It was suggested that a selected financial institution responsible for student collection should facilitate the student loan repayment process by opening an account with a specific bank in both Lesotho and South Africa, and should communicate this information to all the debtors so that they could deposit their monthly instalments. The bank would then transfer these funds to the GoL account after deduction of their service charge fees. In addition to the bank account, the Revolving Fund Management Unit could arrange with private sector employers in both Lesotho and South Africa to facilitate an automatic deduction from the salaries of their employees who have student loans. These deducted funds would then be transferred to the GoL account.

The Loan Bursary Act of 1978 provides for student loans based on the actual cost of education for each student beneficiary. It does not specify the actual value of the loan to be repaid by students when they complete their studies. However, the NMDS seems to have made an arbitrary decision to fix the value of everybody's loan bursary at the NUL irrespective of the country of study and the actual amounts paid for tertiary education of such a person. Furthermore, the Act specifies that students employed in the civil service should pay only 50% of the education grant. The study recommended that students should pay at least 100% of the cost of their education irrespective of the amounts and the country of study.

The study pointed out that one of the weaknesses of the system is that every applicant for a loan bursary is considered eligible, irrespective of the parents' ability to pay for the education of their children. There is no mechanism to determine affordability of parents and to identify needy students. Similarly, loan repayments do not take this condition into account. It is recommended that a means test for parents' affordability be introduced as a criterion for scholarship award.

The study explored various education financing models and presented options for the revolving fund. It reviews the major provisions of the current loan bursary scheme and observes that student loan recovery rates have been very low regardless of where such graduates are employed. Employment with government does not guarantee repayment.

The study concluded that the reasons for this high rate of default included the following:

1. There is no legislative mechanism for the recovery of loans despite the fact that students and their parents have signed a memorandum of agreement (MoA) with the government.
2. Employers in the private sector may not deduct loan commitments from the salaries of student debtor employees without authorisation or any legal instrument.
3. The NMDS authorities responsible for the approval of loan bursaries do not assess the income of parents or the ability of the prospective recipients to pay the loans. It is simply assumed that employment in government will earn the graduates enough income to pay the loans. It is also assumed that government jobs or vacancies are unlimited and will absorb all the graduates when they complete their studies.
4. Students applying for the loan bursary are not required to choose courses or university programmes on the basis of costs and benefits so that they could enhance their ability to pay. Yet the primary purpose of education grants or loans is to create incentives for the development of skilled human resources in areas of critical need and also to improve loan recovery.
5. The present loan bursary scheme does not provide incentives for students and their parents to work harder and pay off their loans as quickly as possible.
6. The 50% loan repayment, coupled with the fact that its value is fixed at NUL levels, seem to be arbitrarily derived and represents a mere token contribution to the cost of education. It is not based on a pre-determined amount of the future fund which will sustain the loan scheme.
7. The MoA between the government and students/parents appears to be unsecured and does not quantify the amounts the recipient is liable to pay on completion of his/her studies. Also, the terms and methods of repayment are not stated except to specify that the loan will be paid in equal instalments over a period of five years.
8. The NMDS does not have a specialised department or unit responsible for collection of loan repayments. The Secretariat also does not have personnel officers who possess a financial background, relevant qualifications and the experience to efficiently administer the student loans.
9. When the recipient of the loan resigns from the civil service job prior to the completion of the five-year bonded period, s/he becomes liable for immediate repayment of the outstanding bond. Yet there are no provisions or mechanisms for government to take steps to recover the outstanding amount of the bond. Defaulters are never prosecuted and,

even if such provisions were in place, the civil litigation burden would be too large, too costly and time consuming.

The study recommended two payment options:

Option 1 – Up-front payment of tuition and maintenance fees
The key recommendation based on equity for the financing of the cost of tertiary education is that payment of fees should be based on the individual student's ability to pay. In this regard, at the beginning of each semester, students will have two options as to how they pay their fees and other associated costs of education, namely the up-front payment and the deferred payment options. The student who can afford to pay his/her fees may choose the first option to pay the whole amount upfront and receive an incentive of 25% discount.

Option 2 – Deferred payment of fees
Students who cannot pay their fees upfront may make a partial upfront payment of a given minimum, say a quarter of the fees or more and receive a 25% discount on that amount, and then defer the remainder which will be treated as a loan. Alternatively, students may choose to defer the whole amount of education fees and this will be paid by government or from the revolving fund and the student will be debited with a loan to be repaid on the completion of his/her studies.

Students who choose the deferred payment option are not required to begin paying their loans until they have completed their studies and have secured employment either in the government civil service or with the private sector (within or outside the country). Payments from students are to be made in equal monthly instalments as agreed in the signed MoA between the beneficiary and the financial institution managing the student revolving fund.

In summary, the key features of higher education financing in Lesotho are as follows:

- The high level of government financing – almost 40% of the education budget;
- Government funds institutions and students through a loan/bursary scheme;
- Loans which up to recently were effectively grants are provided by the Ministry of Finance and Development Planning through the NMDS;
- Low recovery of loans thus far but plans have been put in place to reverse this position;

- In the recent past, there has been substantial over-expenditure on the budgetary allocations for loans; and
- There has been a high level of bursary expenditure on students outside the country.

The challenges for the Government of Lesotho, and specifically the Ministries of Education and Training, and Finance and Development Planning, are as follows:

- To reduce the proportion of the education budget going to higher education so that more resources can be made available to the primary and secondary sub-sectors;
- From an equity perspective, the need to broaden access at both these levels makes eminent sense;
- To make the loan/bursary scheme more efficient and equitable; and
- To introduce cost sharing in higher education especially for students who choose to study outside the country.

Chapter 5
MAURITIUS

Praveen Mohadeb

Introduction

Location and History
Mauritius is a small island state situated in the Indian Ocean at a distance of some 2 000 km from the east coast of Africa. Although the total land area is small (2 040 km^2), its exclusive economic zone is quite vast, covering some 1 700 000 km^2 of the Indian Ocean. In 2006 the population of Mauritius was estimated at just above 1.2 million. The French occupied the island from 1715 to 1810. In 1810 the British conquered the Island and it remained a British colony but ruled by proxy until its independence in 1968. It became a Republic in March 1992.

Economic Challenges
Since independence, Mauritius has experienced major structural transformation in its economy from an agricultural mono-crop (sugar cane) economy with high levels of unemployment and a low per capita income to a middle-income country with almost full employment. In spite of this, Mauritius remains vulnerable to external influences, given the openness of its economy. On the external front, Mauritius is being confronted by new challenges arising post-GATT, the creation of new economic blocks and competition from former socialist and other newly developing and reformed economies.

With globalisation, the domestic and international environment confronting Mauritius in the future will be much more competitive and demanding, requiring increased emphasis on quality, value added, flexibility and innovation. Major constraints have also emerged internally. A growing shortage of skilled labour, coupled with increased pressures for higher wages and salaries, thus eroding the competitiveness of the country's exports on the international market, and the resurgence of unemployment, threaten to reduce the growth momentum of the economy.

Government policy is therefore to encourage the manufacturing sector to further modernise its operations and diversify its activities to ensure that Mauritian products become more competitive quality-wise and price-wise in order to maintain and, if possible, increase its share in international markets and further develop the services sector. It is also the declared policy of the government to develop the ICT sector and to transform the economy into a knowledge economy making it a knowledge hub in the Indian Ocean Region. This strategy requires a more rational and optimal use of available resources, i.e. a steady and continuing growth in total factor productivity, including labour productivity, a new industrial culture, improved work ethics and rapid response capacity. The education system, especially higher education, needs to be re-orientated to respond more effectively to these challenges in order to modernise the economy.

Education in Pre-independent Mauritius

The early years of French colonisation were insignificant in terms of educational development. Under British rule after the 1948 constitutional reforms, elections were held on an extended franchise and political power was transferred from the descendants of the colonial powers to the resident majority. Having realised the importance of education for development, more so when Mauritius does not have any natural resources, the politicians became committed to the idea of national literacy. Measures were thus taken to increase the literacy rate among underprivileged groups.

Education in Post-independent Mauritius

During the post-independence period, education in Mauritius has become increasingly state-driven. Discrimination on the basis of race, colour and sex was eliminated. The newly born state concentrated on bringing education more in line with the development needs of the country – these needs relating mainly to improvements in the economic performance of the country.

A glance at the different national development plans since independence shows that all reforms in education had very similar objectives, mainly laying stress on broadening access, equality of opportunity, a diversified curriculum, promotion of science, technical and vocational education, improvement of the quality of education, and strengthening the management of education.

Provision of education in Mauritius is governed by the Education Act of 1957. Government provides the bulk of primary and secondary education, and part of tertiary education. However, private operators are also allowed to operate from pre-primary to vocational and higher education. Primary education has always been free in Mauritius. Secondary education became free, though not compulsory, for all students up to the age of 20 in 1977. It became compulsory up to age 16 in 2005. The government extended free education for the limited student capacity available domestically to the higher education sector in 1988.

The present system is a 6 + 5 + 2 one, with six years of primary schooling, five years of secondary leading to the 'O'-level studies/School Certificate and two years for 'A' level/Higher School Certificate. The six years of primary education culminates in the Certificate of Primary Education (CPE) examination, which serves as a selection mechanism for entry into secondary schools.

The Structure of the Education System

The overall structure of the Mauritian Education System indicating the academic track and the TVET (Technical, Vocational Education and Training) track, is shown in Figure 5.1.

The Flow of Students

The education system in Mauritius can be divided into three distinct parts, namely, primary, secondary and higher. An analysis of a hypothetical cohort of 1 000 students who joined Standard 1 in 1994 shows a survival rate of 97.8% at the end of the primary cycle. However, out of the 1 000 students, only 670 (67%) passed the CPE (Certificate of Primary Education), 310 (31%) the SC (Senior Certificate – Lower Secondary) and 135 (13.5%) the HSC (Higher School Certificate) in 2006 in their first attempt. This is illustrated in Figure 5.2.

In terms of efficiency it is interesting to note that according to the Master Plan for Education 1991 (p 16), based on promotion rates in 1990 and using a hypothetical cohort of 1 000 students, only 7.5% of the number of students joining Standard 1 would graduate at the HSC level. This rate was 13.5% in 2006.

Figure 5.1: Structure of the Mauritian Education System

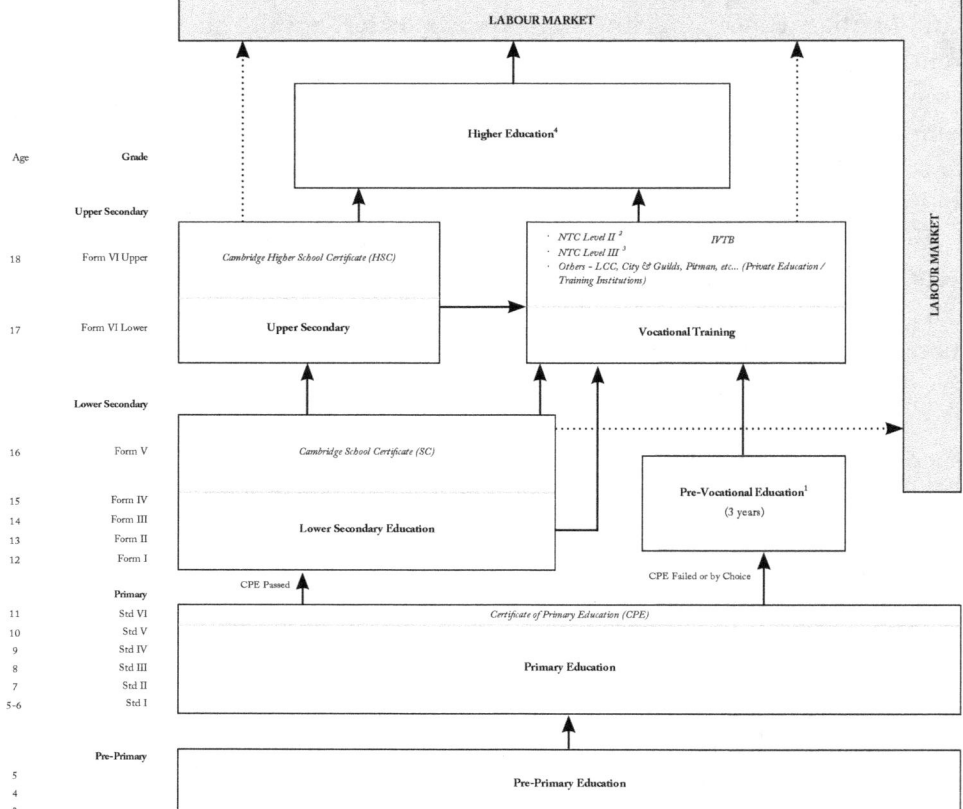

Notes

NTC – National Trade Certificate

IVTB – Industrial & Vocational Training Board

1. Pre-Vocational Education was launched in the 2000/2001 school-year and comprises predominantly students who failed CPE examinations; it is followed by the NTC Foundation Course
2. Requirements for NTC Level II vary between SC and HSC or NTC III
3. Requirements for NTC Level III vary between Form III and SC or NTC III Foundation Course (minimum age = 15)
4. Refers to Post A-Level/HSC

Figure 5.2: Flow of a Hypothetical Cohort Entering Standard I in 1994 and Reaching UVI in 2006

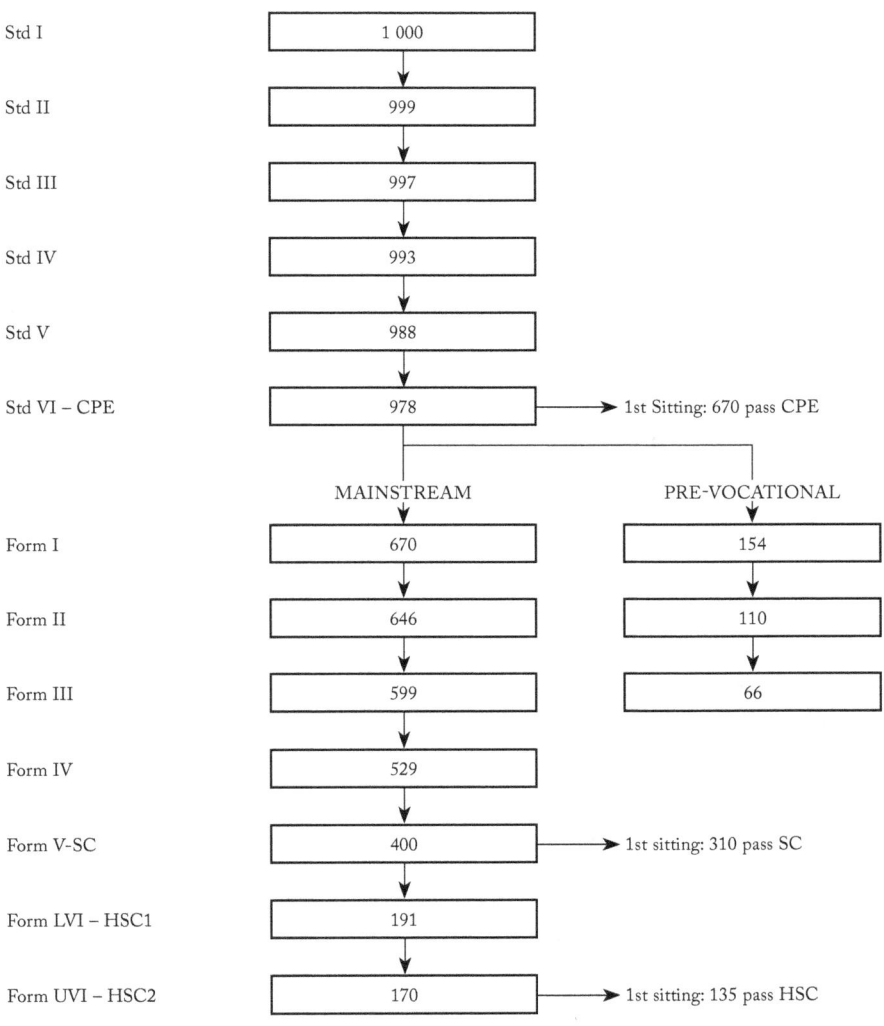

No. of CPE graduates = 825

No. of SC graduates = 570

No. of HSC graduates = 282

Education Expenditure

Total recurrent expenditure on education increased from MUR 3 907 million in 2000 to MUR 6 269 million in 2006, i.e. an increase of 60.5% for the period 2000–2006. However the share of the recurrent education budget compared to the total government expenditure decreased from 14.9% in 2000 to 13.2% in 2006. As a percentage of the gross domestic product, government expenditure on education decreased from 3.3% to 3.1%.

Details of government's recurrent expenditure in education for the years 2000 and 2006 are shown in Table 5.1.

In addition to government spending on education, expenditure is also incurred by the private sector, non-governmental organisations and parents (mainly for maintenance cost and fees for private tuition).

Capital expenditure allocated to higher education has been decreasing dramatically in recent years as a proportion of total expenditure. For instance, as a percentage of the higher education budget it fell from 18% in 2001/2002 to 3.5% in 2006/2007; in nominal rupee terms, it increased from MUR 561 million in 2001/2002 to MUR 822 million in 2004/2005, before declining to MUR 629 million in 2006/2007.

According to a study conducted under the auspices of the Association for the Development of Education in Africa and the Council for the Development of Social Science Research in Africa, the private costs of education in Mauritius were estimated at more than 10% of the government's recurrent outlay on education.

According to another study carried out by the Mauritius Institute of Education (Morisson 1997), the percentage of income spent on private tuition could range from 5% up to 83% (depending on the number of subjects taken, for up to five subjects at SC level and up to four subjects at HSC level). The conclusions of Morisson have to be read with caution as it would be unreasonable to expect that a household would spend 83% of its income on private tuition only. In fact, the income used in the study conducted by Morisson was 'declared' income. Many Mauritians have income from sources other than their salaries. Nevertheless it provides some indication of expenditure on education and specifically on private tuition by households.

At the higher education level, however, government spending accounts for some 25% of total expenditure in this sector.

Table 5.1: Government Recurrent Expenditure on Education by Sector (2000/2001–2006/2007)

	2000/2001[2]	2001/2002[2]	2002/2003[2]	2003/2004[2]	2004/2005[2]	2005/2006[2]	2006/2007[1]
	MUR m	MUR m	MUR m	MUR m	MUR m	MUR m	MUR m
Ministry of Education and Human Resources	3 807.9	4 038.5	4 478.6	5 160.5	5 611.4	6 003.0	6 101.4
Pre-primary	55.0	60.0	68.3	78.4	107.0	100.8	82.0
Primary	1 264.9	1 282.5	1 432.9	1 514.2	1 565.0	1 601.3	1 645.2
Secondary	1 472.0	1 610.6	1 815.7	2 308.1	2 579.3	2 644.4	2 641.6
Technical and Vocational	74.0	78.0	82.7	94.6	113.7	298.5	293.0
Higher	504.5	656.2	674.7	622.0	796.7	684.7	700.0
Others[3]	437.5	351.2	404.3	543.2	449.7	673.3	739.6
Island of Rodrigues				75.6	82.6	84.5	84.1
Other ministries[4]	98.9	235.1	404.4		146.7	10.6	83.0
Total government expenditure on education	3 906.8	4 273.6	4 883.0	5 236.1	5 840.7	6 098.1	6 268.5
% of expenditure by sectors							
Pre-primary	1.4%	1.4%	1.4%	1.5%	1.8%	1.7%	1.3%
Primary	32.4%	30.0%	29.3%	28.9%	26.8%	26.3%	26.2%
Secondary	37.7%	37.7%	37.2%	44.1%	44.2%	43.4%	42.1%
Technical and Vocational	1.9%	1.8%	1.7%	1.8%	1.9%	4.9%	4.7%
Higher	12.9%	15.4%	13.8%	11.9%	13.6%	11.2%	11.2%
Others	13.7%	13.7%	16.6%	11.8%	11.6%	12.6%	14.5%
	100.0%	100.0%	100.0%	100.0%	100.0%	100.0%	100.0%
GDP	120 290.0	132 146.0	142 484.0	157 394.0	175 542.0	185 355.0	205 359.0
Total government expenditure	26 252.0	27 996.0	33 529.0	36 880.0	40 564.0	45 354.0	47 628.0
% of education expenditure on GDP	3.25%	3.23%	3.43%	3.33%	3.33%	3.29%	3.05%
% of education expenditure on total government expenditure	14.88%	15.27%	14.56%	14.20%	14.40%	13.45%	13.16%
Expenditure on tertiary sector	504.5	656.2	674.7	622.0	796.7	684.7	700.0
% of expenditure on HE on GDP	0.42%	0.50%	0.47%	0.40%	0.45%	0.37%	0.34%
% of expenditure on HE on total government expenditure	1.92%	2.34%	2.01%	1.69%	1.96%	1.51%	1.47%
% of expenditure on HE on expenditure on education	12.91%	15.35%	13.82%	11.88%	13.64%	11.23%	11.17%

Notes:
1 – Provisional budget estimates
2 – Actual expenditure
3 – Includes administrative staff
4 – Includes Sea Training & MIH

Structure of Higher Education

History
The history of higher education can be traced back to the setting up of the School of Agriculture within the Department of Agriculture in 1914 which was integrated into the University of Mauritius when the latter was created in 1965. However, it was only in post-independent Mauritius that several public higher education institutions complementary to the University of Mauritius were created. Over the years the higher education sector has increasingly become diversified. Currently, it comprises a multiplicity of institutions: publicly-funded, local private, a branch campus of an overseas institution, one regional institution, and cross-border supply institutions.

Public Higher Education Institutions
The development of the higher education system really started after the establishment of the University of Mauritius (UoM) in 1965. The Mahatma Gandhi Institute (MGI) was set up in 1970 to promote Indian studies including the arts, followed by the Mauritius College of the Air (MCA) in 1971 with Education Media as its main responsibility, and the Mauritius Institute of Education (MIE) in 1973, responsible for teacher training and curriculum development. The University of Technology, Mauritius (UTM), was set up in 2000 to focus on demand-driven programmes. In 2002, the Rabindranath Tagore Institute was set up to further promote cultural education. In an attempt to increase access to higher education and promote lifelong learning and adult and continuing education, the Open University of Mauritius Act was passed in 2005. At the time of writing, this institution is in the process of being made operational.

Higher education in Mauritius is also provided by the following public institutions which are not under the purview of the Tertiary Education Commission:

- The Swami Dayanand Institute of Management;
- The Institut Superieur de Technologie;
- The Industrial and Vocational Training Board;
- The Mauritius Institute of Health;
- The School of Nursing; and
- The Council of Legal Education.

The Industrial and Vocational Training Board, which provides mainly vocational courses, also offers selected demand-driven post-secondary training programmes at the Diploma level in areas such as Tourism and Hospitality Management, Textile and Clothing, Information Technology, and Engineering.

The School of Nursing of the Ministry of Health and Quality of Life has the responsibility for providing the initial training for nurses. The Mauritius Institute of Health, also under the aegis of the Ministry of Health and Quality of Life, runs specialised training programmes for medical and paramedical personnel. The Council of Legal Education runs specific courses for barristers, notaries and attorneys.

Local Private Higher Education Institutions
In 2006, 32 private higher education institutions were registered with the Tertiary Education Commission offering a total of some 140 accredited programmes on a full-time, part-time and distance education basis at various levels (certificate, diploma, degree and masters) and professional levels (List of Registered Institutions and Accredited Programmes 2006). All the private institutions are for-profit institutions.

At present none of the private institutions has awarding powers. They run the programmes of overseas universities (except one which runs programmes of the UoM–SSRMC) through collaborative arrangements, in particular, from Australia, France, India, South Africa and the UK. The programmes are taught by academic staff recruited locally, and a few are taught by academic staff of the respective overseas institutions that come to Mauritius for short periods, in some cases several times a year.

Branch Campuses of Overseas Institutions: In collaboration with local private partners, a branch campus of an Indian university was set up in 2007.

Regional Institution: In 1999, the *Institut de la Francophonie pour L'Entrepreneuriat*, was set up following an earlier agreement signed between the then Ministry of Education and Scientific Research and the *Association des Universites Partiellement ou Entierement de Langue Francaise et l'Universite des Reseaux d'Expression Francaise*.

Cross-Border Supply: In 2006, there were some 50 overseas institutions and examination bodies providing courses and programmes through distance education and open learning mode. These institutions/bodies are based in the UK, South Africa, India, France/Reunion, Switzerland and the USA (TEC 2007). Several of the institutions also have collaborative arrangements with the local private institutions.

As stated earlier, the provision of higher education dates back to almost a century ago. The higher education sector has expanded and grown markedly in size, from a single public institution to a multiplicity of providers. Furthermore, the sector is increasingly becoming diversified. Currently, it comprises publicly-funded institutions, local private institutions, branch campuses of overseas institutions, one regional institution, affiliated institutions and overseas institutions through cross-border supply. Among the publicly-funded institutions, there is both diversity through mission and programme differentiation. The diverse institutions of the sector are offering a multiplicity of programmes ranging from Certificate to PhD and professional ones, and encompassing a wide variety of fields. The number of students enrolled at both the publicly-funded and non-publicly-funded institutions is increasing, indicating a growing demand for higher education and training. The growth of the private institutions has been achieved at no additional public cost and the diversified landscape is facilitating wider participation at the higher education level. As the private institutions award qualifications of overseas universities with which they have collaborative arrangements, they are providing cheaper alternatives to studying in the home campuses of these overseas institutions.

The Tertiary Education Commission

The Tertiary Education Commission (TEC) was set up in 1988 with the objective of fostering the development of higher education; promoting coordination amongst the higher education institutions; allocating funds to the higher education institutions; and making recommendations to the Minister of Education on the development of higher education; and advising on policy matters relating to scholarships. The Act of the Tertiary Education Commission was amended in 2005 and 2007 to make it responsible for regulating private provision of higher education, and to promote and enhance quality assurance in all higher education institutions, public and private.

The TEC has developed a Strategic Plan for the years 2007 to 2011. According to the plan the vision of the TEC is to 'Make Mauritius the intelligent island of the region in the global village' (TEC 2007: 5). Its mission is to 'Position Mauritius in the region as a world-class knowledge hub and the gateway for post-secondary education' (TEC 2007: 5). The goals of the Commission include:

- Creating an enabling environment for Mauritius to emerge as a regional knowledge hub and a centre for higher learning and excellence;
- Contributing significantly in the rapid transformation of Mauritius into the rank of developed countries;
- Developing Open and Distance Learning (ODL) as an instrument to increase access to post-secondary education and lifelong learning locally and regionally;

- Encouraging institutions to mount programmes that are relevant to the needs of learners, the country and the region;
- Promoting and enhancing teacher education and training in order to raise standards of feeder system to post-secondary education;
- Instilling the principles of good governance, transparency and accountability in the post-secondary education system;
- Ensuring optimum use of resources in the public higher education institutions;
- Sustaining research and consultancy;
- Fostering regional and international understanding and cooperation through a diversity of studentship and overseas institutions; and
- Reinforcing and empowering the TEC to fulfil its mission and objectives.

Access, Equity and Quality

Access

The high demand for higher education stems from the recognition of the close linkages between higher education and economic and social development. Higher Education means better jobs and a higher standard of living. With universal primary education being achieved in the 1970s and the pasing of legislation in 1977 making education both free and compulsory up to the age of 16, the challenges that policy-makers have had to face were related to broadening of access at the higher education level; improvement of quality and strengthening the management of the sector while ensuring equity.

Total enrolment in the higher education sector stood at 33 230 in December 2006. This represented a Gross Tertiary Enrolment Ratio (GTER) of 34.1%. The GTER is calculated as the percentage of the Mauritian population aged 20 to 24 years enrolled in higher education programmes locally and overseas.

Table 5.2 shows the enrolment of students by public and private institutions locally and overseas. From Table 5.2, it is evident that:

1. More than 74% of students were undertaking their studies locally of which 62% were in publicly-funded institutions.
2. Enrolment in public higher education institutions accounted for 46.5% of the total enrolment and 53.5% were in local private and overseas institutions.
3. The five higher education institutions taken together (UoM, MIE,

MGI, MCA and UTM), accounted for 42% of the higher education student population with 14 036 students and accounted for 91% of the enrolment in the public institutions.

4. The UoM is the largest supplier of tertiary education locally, accounting for 22.2% of total higher education enrolment, as opposed to 4.9% for the UTM, 12% for the MIE, 2% for the MGI and 1.2% for the MCA.

Table 5.2: Total Enrolment in Higher Education (2000/2001–2006/2007)

	TOTAL ENROLMENT						
	2000/2001	2001/2002	2002/2003	2003/2004	2004/2005	2005/2006	2006/2007
Publicly-funded institutions	9 057	11 021	9 880	12 710	11 713	13 397	15 464
Higher education institutions	8 255	10 204	8 832	11 387	10 385	12 020	14 036
University of Mauritius[1]	4 930	5 027	5 310	5 745	6 394	6 650	7 370
University of Technology, Mauritius	–	368	718	984	1 183	1 467	1 620
Mauritius Institute of Education	2 773	4 026	2 151	4 130	2 230	3 001	3 981
Mahatma Gandhi Institute	435	520	489	363	421	546	650
Mauritius College of the Air	117	263	164	165	157	356	415
Others	802	817	1 048	1 323	1 328	1 377	1 428
Swami Dayanand Institute of Management	503	508	569	689	701	632	626
Institut Superieure de Technologie	127	97	146	173	208	329	285
Industrial and Vocational Training Board	161	201	316	444	397	385	413
Mauritius Institute of Health	11	11	17	17	22	31	104
Distance education / private providers	5 255	6 100	7 242	7 507	7 515	8 110	9 293
Overseas	2 423	3 019	4 791	5 468	6 846	7 357	8 473
Total	**16 735**	**20 140**	**21 913**	**25 685**	**26 074**	**28 864**	**33 230**

Note:
1 - Excludes enrolment on joint MIE & MGI Programmes

Since 2000, total enrolment in higher education has grown from 16 375 to 33 230 in 2006. The GTER has more than doubled growing from 15.1% in 2000 to 34.1% in 2006.

A total of 481 tertiary-level programmes of study were offered locally in 2006/2007, of which 172 were full-time. The public higher education institutions accounted for 333 programmes and private/distance education providers, 148 programmes. About 17% of courses were at master's and 44% at degree level.

The number of new admissions in 2006 stood at 12 133 or some 36.5% of total enrolment. Of these, 7 086 students joined the public higher education institutions and 2 621 enrolled with private providers/distance education locally. Some 2 426 students, on the other hand, went overseas; the five most popular destinations were the UK (32.5%), followed by Australia (28%), France (13.1%), India (11.7%) and Ireland (5.8%).

The provision of opportunities in higher education to all those having survived the secondary cycle has resulted in the broadening of access over the years. As per the new strategic plan of the Tertiary Education Commission (2007–2011) and the White Paper on tertiary education projections the GTER is expected to reach 40% in the year 2010 and 45% in 2015.

To keep pace with rapid advances in knowledge and technology in Health Sciences and Medicine, education and training programmes in Medicine, Pharmacy, Nursing, Paramedical Sciences and Public Health have been undertaken with the establishment of a Medical College and a School of Dentistry.

The coming into operation of the Open University of Mauritius (approved by Parliament in 2005) is yet another step towards providing more opportunities for higher education.

Equity

Gender equity is not a major issue as evidenced by the fact that female participation in the higher education sector exceeds 50%. Table 5.3 shows the numbers and percentages of male and female students enrolled in the public higher education institutions from 2000 to 2006.

Table 5.3: Enrolment in Public Higher Education Institutions by Gender (2000/2001–2006/2007)

GENDER	2000/2001	2001/2002	2002/2003	2003/2004	2004/2005	2005/2006	2006/2007
Male	4 185	5 025	4 856	6 403	5 625	6 597	7 248
Female	4 872	5 996	5 024	6 307	6 088	6 800	8 216
Total	9 057	11 021	9 880	12 710	11 713	13 397	15 464
Male	46.2%	45.6%	49.1%	50.4%	48.0%	49.2%	46.9%
Female	53.8%	54.4%	50.9%	49.6%	52.0%	50.8%	53.1%

There is a perception that participation in higher education is predominantly by students from wealthier backgrounds. This is reinforced by the fact that enrolment in public higher education institutions is based on the best school-leaving results which are more likely to be achieved by students coming from the best and most elite secondary schools.

Enrolment in public higher education institutions by income group of households is shown in Table 5.4. This data reveals that more than 50% of enrolment in the public higher education institutions comes from the middle- and high-income groups (53.3% in 2002 and 58.4% in 2004).

Table 5.4: Enrolment in the Public Higher Education Institutions by Income Group

YEAR	LOW LESS THAN MUR 10 000 PER MONTH %	MIDDLE BETWEEN MUR 10 000 AND MUR 20 000 PER MONTH %	HIGH MORE THAN MUR 20 000 PER MONTH %
2002	46.7%	34.6%	18.7%
2004	41.5%	35.5%	22.9%

Quality

The concept of quality is not a new phenomenon in the Mauritian education sector. When the Master Plan on Education was being written in the early 1990s, views were expressed on the urgent need to improve standards and enhance quality across the whole spectrum of education. Since then the issue of quality has started assuming increasing significance in tertiary education as well – initially in the public higher education institutions under the purview of the TEC (as per its Act 1988) and recently in private higher education institutions (amended TEC Act 2005). Most quality initiatives in the sector, public and private, have been driven by the TEC as it explicitly has the statutory responsibility for ensuring quality of higher education in Mauritius by virtue of the TEC Act.

The mechanisms adopted by the TEC to assure quality in Hhigher education institutions are through institutional audits of the public institutions, and through registration of private institutions, accreditation of their programmes and quality assurance visits.

Prior to 2005, the private higher education sector was unregulated. The private higher education institutions were not only ill-equipped but were also offering courses that were not recognised. Their tutoring was geared towards passing examinations rather than providing a sound education. With the new regulatory framework and the centralising of the responsibility for quality solely in the TEC, the differences in terms of quality education provided by public and private higher education institutions are being eliminated.

Quality is assured in the private higher education institutions through their registration, through accreditation of their programmes and regular quality assurance visits by the TEC. As per the TEC Act no person can operate a higher education institution unless it has been approved by the TEC. The objective of accreditation is to ascertain whether the higher education institution is adequately equipped to fulfil its mission and that it has the necessary infrastructure and all the necessary wherewithal to offer and sustain its programmes.

Financing Higher Education

Sources of Funding

The financing of higher education is basically via the government and students/parents. Students enrolled in public higher education institutions are funded to a very large extent by the government. Students enrolled in local private higher education institutions and those in overseas institutions pay the full cost of their education.

The provision of higher education is said to be 'free'. It is important to clarify this concept of 'free' higher education. In fact this refers to the provision of higher education in public higher education institutions only. It is observed that all students enrolled in public higher education institutions pay general fees (application fees, registration fees and library fees). In terms of tuition fees, the position is as follows:

- At the UoM, full-time undergraduate students do not pay tuition fees, all other students (part-time and postgraduate) pay tuition fees although not the full cost.
- At the UTM, all students pay tuition fees although not the full cost. The funds generated annually by the UTM amount to approximately 70% of the requirement for the recurrent budget. The remaining 30% together with the capital budget are met through a government grant.
- At the MIE which runs mostly in-service programmes for teachers, no tuition fee is charged.
- The MCA, whose target group is the working population, provides life-long learning and continuous professional education, and charges tuition fees for all its programmes.
- Students in other higher education institutions do not pay tuition fees.

Hence there is no 'free' higher education in Mauritius but it is highly subsidised in public higher education institutions.

The unit costs of tertiary education vary depending on institution, type of award and field of study. At the UoM, currently the unit cost is MUR 41 700 annually for a degree in Law and Management as opposed to MUR 51 000 in Social Studies/Humanities, MUR 54 500 in Engineering, MUR 85 100 in Science and MUR 90 000 in Agriculture. The unit cost per programme at the UTM, on the other hand, averages MUR 47 300 per annum.

The costs in private institutions are much higher. The cost for an undergraduate-level programme per annum in the local private institution ranges from

MUR 60 000 to MUR 175 000. The cost borne by students who proceed overseas for their studies are higher than what they would have paid locally. These costs obviously depend on the country and the discipline being studied.

Taking into account an average annual cost of MUR 100 000 for local private programmes and MUR 300 000 for overseas students, the total expenditure for higher education (public and private) has been estimated in Table 5.5.

Table 5.5: Financing of Higher Education in Mauritius

Public higher education institutions	MUR
Government grants	1 000 000 000
Other sources	183 000 000
Total public higher education institutions (government funding + other sources)	1 183 000 000
Local private higher education institutions[1]	929 300 000
Overseas[2]	2 541 900 000
Total	4 654 200 000

Notes:
1 – Local Private: 9 293 students @ MUR 100 000
2 – Overseas: 8 473 students @ MUR 300 000

Total government expenditure on higher education is about MUR 1.0 billion. This includes grants to higher education institutions (including polytechnics) and scholarships. The higher education institutions raise some MUR 183 million by way of tuition fees, other fees and research and consultancy fees. Expenditure incurred by students studying in local private institutions and overseas amount to MUR 929.3 million and MUR 2.4 billion respectively. Total expenditure on higher education is therefore estimated at more than MUR 4.65 billion, out of which MUR 3 billion leaves the country in terms of foreign exchange.

The capacity of public higher education institutions to enrol students in Mauritius is limited. Out of the 33 230 students participating in higher education in Mauritius in 2006, 15 464 (about 46.5%) were following courses in public higher education institutions. The remaining 53.5% were following higher education programmes in private local or overseas institutions and these students pay the full cost of their higher education.

Although students enrolled in public higher education institutions are funded by the government to a very large extent, the proportion of state funding varies significantly amongst public higher education institutions. Education at the University of Mauritius became free in December 1976. The decision to abolish tuition fees was made in the wake of a political decision by the then government, taken on the eve of the December 1976 general elections. Tuition fees, however, were reintroduced in June 1980, only to be abolished again in 1988. At the University of Technology, Mauritius, all students, part-time and full-time, pay tuition fees, again not full cost, together with administrative charges. In the remaining non-university public higher education institutions, while some funds are generated, they depend mostly on public funding for both their recurrent and capital budgets.

The private institutions, local and overseas, receive no state funding and as such, are self-financing. They generate their income from various sources but mostly from tuition fees. The government recurrent grant to public higher education institutions are shown in Table 5.6.

Table 5.6: Government Expenditure on Higher Education

	2000	2001	2002	2003	2004	2005	2006
GDP	120 290	132 146	142 484	157 394	175 542	185 355	205 359
Total government expenditure	26 252	27 996	33 529	36 880	40 564	45 354	47 628
% of education expenditure on GDP	3.25%	3.23%	3.43%	3.33%	3.33%	3.29%	3.05%
% of education expenditure on total government expenditure	14.88%	15.27%	14.56%	14.20%	14.40%	13.45%	13.16%
Expenditure on higher education	504.5	656.2	674.7	622.0	796.7	684.7	700.0
% of expenditure on HE on GDP	0.42%	0.50%	0.47%	0.40%	0.45%	0.37%	0.34%
% of expenditure on HE sector on total government expenditure	1.92%	2.34%	2.01%	1.69%	1.96%	1.51%	1.47%
% of expenditure on HE on expenditure on education	12.91%	15.35%	13.82%	11.88%	13.64%	11.23%	11.17%

Expenditure on higher education increased from MUR 504.5 million in 2000 to MUR 700.0 million in 2006. However, in terms of the percentage of expenditure on tertiary education in relation to total expenditure on education this represented a decrease from 12.9% to 11.2%. In terms of GDP the share of government expenditure on higher education decreased from 0.42% in 2000 to 0.34% in 2006.

Financial Support for Students

The large majority of higher education students, including those enrolled in public higher education institutions, support themselves either from private sources or through loans contracted privately from financial institutions. A limited number of undergraduate and postgraduate scholarships and bursaries are available from both the public and private sectors and from donor countries and agencies. The University of Mauritius operates, on small scale, a grant system for students with special needs.

Student Loan Schemes

A national or state-supported student loan scheme proper does not exist in Mauritius. However, there are several student loans schemes that are operated by individual institutions, albeit on a small scale. In view of the profitable market, most of the financial institutions have introduced loan schemes to support students to study either locally or overseas. The conditions vary between institutions but the majority provides up-front money with pay-back during or after graduation and in some cases with a moratorium.

The different organisations providing loan schemes include the following: Ministry of Education and Human Resources; Employees Welfare Fund (EWF); SSR Foundation, MoE&HR; Trust Fund for Social Integration of Vulnerable Groups; Mutual Aid Association; and commercial banks.

The characteristics of the existing loan schemes in Mauritius can be described as follows:

- The loans provided by most of the institutions are close to commercial criteria.
- There is no targeting of the students. Students with financial difficulties may have difficulty in accessing loans.
- The objectives of the existing loan schemes are different. Most of the institutions assist students with a view to earning a profit as the rate of interest charged and the securities asked are almost the same as for any other type of commercial loan.
- The rates of interest vary by institution.
- The amount of loan differs by scheme.
- Repayment terms vary by scheme.
- Most of the schemes do not provide for any form of subsidy to the students.
- Some institutions grant loans only to their members and hence accessibility to loans may be restrictive.

Despite the above conditions/restrictions, there is significant demand for student loans. Even at a higher rate of interest, some students and parents take out loans to finance the higher education of their children.

Conclusion

Demand for Higher Education
A number of compelling arguments exist to support the fact that the demand for higher education will continue to increase in Mauritius. Mauritians believe that education is beneficial to themselves and their children. As a general rule, persons with more education obtain higher levels of income. There is already a high correlation between higher education and income at both the individual and the societal levels.

The growing demand will be due largely to the following factors:

- The continued growth in school-leaving numbers as the population bulge currently in the secondary sector moves through to the higher education sector;
- Demands from postgraduates, employers and mature aged learners and the need for employees to return to higher education periodically in order to update their skills;
- The internationalisation of higher education and the intention of the government to make Mauritius a knowledge hub in the region; and
- The increased importance of the knowledge industry for a globalised economy.

Based on an estimated annual average growth rate of 0.85%, the total population of Mauritius is expected to increase to 1 329 000 by the year 2010 and 1 371 000 in 2015. There were some 107 318 people aged between 20 and 24 years (higher education enrolment age group) in 2000. This represented 9.4% of the total population of the country. On the basis of population projection made by the Central Statistical Office, Mauritius, there will be 99 931 (7.5%) people aged between 20 to 24 years in Mauritius in the year 2010 and 96 000 (7%) in 2015.

The Tertiary Education White Paper provides for a 40% enrolment rate in the higher education sector by the year 2010 and 45% in 2015. With this targeted higher education enrolment rate (of 40%) there would be a student enrolment of 39 892 in higher education in the year in 2010 – an increase of 20% over the present student enrolment.

The Supply of Higher Education
A large proportion of demand for higher education remains unmet. In order to increase enrolment to attain the 40% GTER in 2010, either the capacity of existing institutions would have to be increased or new ones created. Both of

these courses of action require significant amount of funds to be invested in the higher education sector, be it from the government or from private sources.

With continued expansion in enrolment resulting from increasing and broadening of access to higher education coupled with national policies for promoting lifelong learning, there is a need to ensure that the sector is financially sustainable and remains competitive in a world of global accessibility and increased student choices.

The proportion of government expenditure allocated to the higher education sector as a percentage of the total expenditure on education is decreasing. Government expenditure on higher education as a percentage of GDP is also decreasing. Yet there is a need to significantly increase the GTER from its present level of 34% to 40% in 2010 and to 45% in 2015. It is less likely that the share allocated to the higher education sector would increase significantly in the next decade. It would be very difficult for the government to sustain such increases. Cost sharing in the higher education sector is therefore the only solution.

The present system of funding for higher education is inequitable. Even within the public higher education institutions the amount of government grant to students varies significantly. More than 50% of students enrolled in higher education have to pay the full cost of their education. The recent decrease in the share of total government expenditure on education allocated to higher education is a clear indication that the government is finding it more and more difficult to fund higher education.

Higher education is of critical importance to the socio-economic development and competitiveness of Mauritius, more so for the attainment of the objectives set by the government to develop the knowledge industry and to make Mauritius a knowledge hub in the region. Higher education undoubtedly will improve the country's competitive edge, economic growth, employment opportunities, productivity and social cohesion.

If Mauritius wants to position itself as a knowledge-based society, it will have to increase the participation rate in higher education. In view of its rising labour costs and competitive pressures from emerging economies like India, China, Malaysia and Indonesia, Mauritius will need to improve its skill-mix, not only to increase output per unit of labour, but also to produce high value-added goods and services. To this end, Mauritius will need more skilled technicians and professionals, and hence more and better quality higher education is necessary for the country's continued development.

Government, which has been playing a major role in the funding of higher education for decades, will find it more and more difficult to fund this sector. The availability of finance is one of the barriers to higher education expansion. It is therefore essential to look for alternative sources of funding for higher education, and private participation is probably one of the solutions.

There is consensus at the national level that there is a dire need to increase and widen access to higher education in order to achieve the enrolment targets set. It is also realised, however, that higher education is becoming more and more expensive and that more funds will be required. For quite some time now, discussions have been ongoing at governmental level on the financial sustainability of higher education in Mauritius without unduly straining the public budget. The issue of introducing tuition fees reflecting the actual cost across all the public institutions have been raised concurrently with the introduction of a national student loan system. Special support schemes for students from disadvantaged groups have also persistently surfaced. As cost sharing in an environment where the provision of higher education public higher education institutions is highly subsidised is inevitably controversial, the decision to shift more of the costs of higher education to parents and students will be highly political.

Chapter 6
MOZAMBIQUE

Arlindo Chilundo

Evolution and Structure of Higher Education

The first higher education institution in Mozambique was created in 1962 by the Portuguese as a branch of the Portuguese universities with the aim of serving mainly the children of Portuguese settlers. This institution was named Estudos Gerais Universitários and was upgraded to a university, the University of Lourenço Marques (ULM), in 1968. Initially, it offered nine programmes, namely Pedagogical Sciences, Medicine and Surgery, Civil Engineering, Mechanical Engineering, Electro-technical Engineering, Chemical Engineering, Agronomy, Silviculture and Veterinary Sciences. New programmes were added as the institution grew, reaching 17 degrees by 1974 (Chilundo 2002).

ULM maintained its discriminatory nature in relation to Mozambicans. In fact, until 1974, Mozambican students constituted less than 0.1% of the student population. With independence in 1975, Mozambique changed the nature and the goal of ULM. It was transformed and renamed Eduardo Mondlane University (UEM) in 1976. Its main mission was to train the critical mass and highly trained staff need by Mozambique to solidify the independence of the new Republic. Therefore, UEM became the first truly Mozambican university and it is still the major university in the country.

The higher education sub-system in Mozambique has grown rapidly in terms of student numbers, from about 3 750 students in 1989 to almost 40 000 students in 2006. Two-thirds of these students are enrolled in public institutions and one-third in private institutions. Over the same period, 24 new institutions have been approved/created, bringing the total number of institutions to 26 – 13 public and 13 private. This growth has been fed by substantial private sector involvement. The number of private institutions in Mozambique has been growing rapidly since their introduction in 1995. There are three types of institutions in Mozambique: universities, polytechnics and tertiary schools.

With rapid expansion, quality assurance, already a central governance objective in the strategic plan, has become an even more pressing issue. Also, the priority of the government is to safeguard and improve equity of access, aiming at a regional and gender balance across the country. At the same time, the government is committed to ensuring that quality standards are even across institutions and regions.

The geographic expansion of higher education has also been rapid, either through the establishment of satellite campuses or the opening of new universities in the provinces. Although most higher education institutions are concentrated in Maputo city, all provinces have some type of higher education institution, mainly in the form of a satellite campus.

At present there are about 40 000 students enrolled in higher education, covering the majority of the scientific areas. Female students account for about one-third of the enrolments, and two-thirds of all students enrolled are in the fields of Social Sciences, Humanities and Arts. The large enrolment in Social Sciences, Arts and Humanities is, on the one hand, a reflection of the availability of places in the higher education institutions and, on the other hand, the existence of employment opportunities in these areas.

The number of full-time academic staff is about 1 200, of which 15% are PhD holders, 25% are master's degree holders and 60% are holders of a first degree (bachelor's or licentiate). These numbers indicate that there is still a need for high investment in staff training at master's and PhD levels.

In spite of the growth in the number of university places, students in higher education institutions represent a very small segment in relation to the population as a whole. Only 0.16% or 40 in every 100 000 inhabitants of the age cohort 20–25 study at a higher education institution. In comparison, in Zimbabwe and Botswana, for example, there are 638 and 596 university students respectively for every 100 000 inhabitants (Chilundo 2004).

Higher Education Governance

Up to 2000, the higher education sub-system had been an integral part of the Ministry of Education. However, during the 2000–2004 period, the Mozambican Government recognised the importance of developing the high end of its human capital and with it the national capacity to generate and apply scientific and technological innovation in the different economic sectors as the key to pursuing a sustainable high-growth policy. Thus, the Ministry of Higher Education, Science and Technology (MHEST) was established in January 2000.

Through this legislation, two important councils were also established and have been crucial for MHEST in building support for the regulatory framework:

- **The Higher Education Council (CES)** bringing together MHEST and all higher education institutions at the highest level in a collaborative effort to shape the mechanisms in support of policy implementation in the sector.
- **The National Council on Higher Education, Science and Technology (CNESCT)** being the consultative organ for the Council of Ministers and a broader forum with the mandate to oversee the articulation and the integration of planning processes between the higher education, science and technology sectors. It was made up of representatives from various sections of government, the Council of Higher Education, representatives from research and higher education institutions, business associations and civil society. As a sounding board for evaluating progress of policy implementation CNESCT functioned as a crucial body in scrutinising new MHEST policies and proposals before they were presented to the Council of Ministers for approval and legislation. Crucially, the CNESCT also made recommendations to the Council of Ministers with respect to the creation of new institutions.

Following the election of a new president in 2005, the restructuring of a number of ministerial portfolios took place.

As a result, the approach of the bundling together of higher education, science and technology into a separate ministry was reversed. The MHEST portfolio has been split into higher education, on the one hand, and science and technology on the other. Higher education has been reintegrated with education in the new Ministry of Education and Culture (MEC). A new Ministry of Science and Technology (MCT) governs the science and technology sectors.

While the previous policy of bundling higher education, science and technology into one Ministerial portfolio put MHEST in a strategic key position to support overall development policies in Mozambique, the new policy seems to take a more functional approach to higher education, and therefore brings it back into the overall education portfolio.

Higher Education Planning

The strategic plan as a framework for policy implementation has driven change through a more system-wide approach in the higher education sector (Government of Mozambique 2000). The Ministry of Education (MINED) in the late 1990s, in response to the national conference on higher education, commissioned an analysis of the higher education sector in preparation for a strategic plan for a high-level political committee. The newly created MHEST developed the strategic plan itself together with an operational plan for 2000–2004. The strategic plan 2000–2010 became the main reference document for guiding and implementing policy in the higher education sector.

This plan offers a ten-year vision for the development of higher education in Mozambique, focusing on increasing access, reducing regional and gender disparities, and rationalising resources through the improvement of the internal efficiency of the whole sub-system. Implementing the plan requires a national effort based on collaboration between government at all levels, the higher education institutions and society at large.

The plan contains six major themes:

1. Improve access and equity by expanding the availability of higher education institutions physically and geographically, reforming access policies, and developing financial assistance policies and mechanisms for students in order to boost student numbers.
2. Increase flexibility and responsiveness of the system in order to meet market demand and the priorities of the national development agenda by creating training opportunities and opportunities for collaboration between the academic and private sectors, developing top-level public service curricula and increasing student access to labour market information. With these measures the intent is to make the system more relevant to its socio-economic environment.
3. Increase efficiency of higher education institutions by rationalising existing resources, improving management systems and diversifying sources of finance.
4. Increase diversity in higher education institutions' training programmes, and forms of delivery.
5. Improve quality assurance by improving teaching and learning conditions, establishing accreditation and quality evaluation mechanisms, and boosting innovation and research infrastructure within and between higher education institutions.

6. Governance: Redefine the role of government in higher education by developing a sector-wide higher education policy embedded within the national policy framework by developing and establishing the regulatory mechanisms for policy implementation, and by facilitating regional integration of the higher education sector and international cooperation with regard to the higher education sector.

This strategic plan is also the framework within which donor aid has so far been organised. The development of the strategic plan attracted strong interest from the World Bank, Swedish International Development Agency and the Dutch-funded Netherlands Organisation for International Cooperation in Higher Education (NUFFIC). Following the release of the strategic plan and the creation of MHEST, the trend in external funding has moved in favour of system-wide projects that now complement direct funding to the higher education institutions.

Higher Education Institutions

There are currently 26 higher education institutions in Mozambique, of which 14 are universities and 12 are professional and vocational institutions accredited by the Ministry of Education and Culture (MEC). (See Appendix for a full list.)

Most institutions are public (state-owned). Universities appear to be more attractive for the private sector, leaving professional and educational training as a responsibility of the state. There are four public universities and nine public professional and vocational institutions. In the private domain, there are nine universities and four professional and vocational institutions.

Among the higher education institutions, Universidade Eduardo Mondlane (UEM), the oldest and largest university, is by far the leading institution, dominating access of students to higher education. UEM offers courses in many areas (ranging from pure science, through engineering, technology, economics and business, to the arts) It is also located in different cities in the country. In 2006, UEM had 61% of student enrolments among the public higher education institutions in the country (41% of all student enrolments, public and private). With close to 12 000 enrolled students, UEM had more than double the students of the second largest higher education institution in the country, Universidade Pedagógica, which, in turn, was much larger than the rest.

Private institutions complement the effort of the state in terms of generating access to higher education, although with limited reach. All private higher education institutions together enrolled in 2005 a third of all higher education students. Of these institutions, ISCTEM, ISPU and UCM are the largest, all being university-type institutions. (See Appendix for full names of institutions.)

The focus of this study is UEM, since this institution dominates the sector and its data is most readily available. This decision was further supported by the fact that most of the smaller higher education institutions do not have adequate systems for data collection, storage and retrieval; therefore, they find it difficult to provide data and information at the level of detail and quality required for analysis.

Financing Higher Education

In 1999, government expenditure on education constituted about 3.2% of GNP and by 2001 this had increased to 6.5%. Of this figure, about 0.8% of the GNP goes to higher education with public expenditure of about US$ 1 700 per student. There is, however, some evidence that the government is paying special attention to the higher education sector. It is also expected that the public institutions will mobilise extra resources for research grants, provision of services and scholarships.

Students in the public system pay a low tuition fee (around US$ 100 per annum). However, studies on student unit costs have been carried out in the public higher education system and it is expected that after their conclusion a policy in higher education tuition and fees will be defined for the public system.

From an analysis of the state budget figures as approved by Parliament, public spending on education has been around 3% of the state budget, increasing from US$ 45 million in 2004 to US$ 59 million in 2006. In the education sector, the government normally funds:

- The Ministry of Education and Culture;
- Other intermediate-level education institutions; and
- Higher education institutions, usually through central budgets and, in one case (the Universidade Pedagógica), through provincial budgets for the campuses outside Maputo.

Over time, the Government of Mozambique (GoM) has implemented its commitment to funding education, one of the pillars in the *Action Plan for the Reduction of Absolute Poverty (PARPA)*. This action was also consistent with the GoM commitment under the Highly Indebted Poor Countries (HIPC) debt relief initiative, under which part of the debt service savings had to be converted into public expenditure in social sectors, including education.

State budget allocations to higher education increased by more than US$ 6 million per annum, having jumped from US$ 29 to US$ 40 million between 2004 and 2006. The respective amounts have systematically represented around 2% of the state budget.

Table 6.1: Public Funding of Higher Education as a Proportion of the Budget

	2004	2005	2006
State budget (US$, million)	1 492.6	2 047.9	2 021.1
Education (US$, million)	74.3	91.2	98.8
Higher education (US$, million)	29.2	35.6	39.7
Rest of education (US$, million)	45.1	55.6	59.1
Education funding as % of state budget	5.0	4.5	4.9
Higher education funding as % of total education budget	39.3	39.0	40.2

Within overall financing of the education sector, the funding for higher education has been significant, mostly due to the deliberate effort government has made in investing in higher education, especially in terms of:

- Building infrastructure, in order to improve the teaching and learning environment (i) at existing public institutions and (ii) at new public institutions in new geographical areas in order to reduce regional asymmetries in the country;
- Strengthening human capacity through a broad training programme for academic staff to pursue education and research at higher levels; and
- Information and technology infrastructure and equipment to accelerate access and transmission of knowledge to, from and among higher education institutions as part of the strategy of creating basic conditions for local research.

Consequently, in this period, public funding of higher education has been in the range of 39–40% of funding to education in general, as shown in Table 6.1.

The government finances higher education through basically two models:

1. Making funds available at the Ministry of Education and Culture for:
   - Reforming overall performance of the higher education sub-sector: e.g. quality assurance mechanisms, credit accumulation and transfer, information systems;
   - Both higher education institutions and their staff (scholars and

researchers), regardless whether they are public or private, through the Quality Enhancement and Innovative Facility (QIF). These funds can be accessed through applications on a competitive basis; and
- Students, through the Provincial Scholarships Fund (PSF), in which students from the rural provinces of Cabo Delgado, Gaza, Nampula, Tete, Niassa, Sofala and Zambézia can apply for funding to study at any of the accredited higher education institutions, either public or private.

2. Direct financing to the public higher education institutions:
   - Direct budgetary allocations to the institutions, through submission of specific proposals to the Parliament within the state budget proposals, which are eventually approved, being the funds disbursed directly to the beneficiary institutions, without further involvement of MEC;
   - Sourcing grant funds from development partners and directing them to the the higher education sector; and
   - Sourcing and allocating credit funds, under preferential conditions, to fill any possible gaps in public financing.

In summary, state funding for the higher education system is undertaken by the MEC through support to the higher education institutions, their staff and students especially those from disadvantaged provinces, with low income and higher education coverage. Since 2000 the government has made special efforts to provide funds for research, innovation and the strengthening of higher education institutions.

Quality Enhancement and Innovation Fund (QIF)
In 2002 the ministry launched the QIF, a programme which aims to provide financial and investment support to initiatives that enhance the quality of higher education. QIF is demand-driven and selects beneficiaries on a competitive basis, providing three types of financial support:

1. Institutional financial support – support for the higher education institutions to strengthen their capacity. When QIF finances public institutions, it is through a grant, whilst for private institutions it provides (reimbursable) loans;
2. Financial support to academic staff (individually), for programmes innovation, materials and teaching and learning methods; and
3. Financial support for academic innovation and scientific investigation.

In terms of institutional financial support, QIF has disbursed mostly grant funds to private higher education institutions (a total of eight institutions benefited from the funds in 12 projects), and it is clear that among these, the larger (and older) institutions were the ones with greater ability to access these funds. Only two public institutions have been financed in only three projects. In terms of the other two QIF components, by the end of 2005, the QIF Programme had:

- Received 117 applicants in five cycles of which only 36 projects were approved; and
- Disbursed an amount of US$ 810 000 to finance these projects.

Academic innovation and scientific investigation have received the majority of the funding.

Provincial Scholarship Fund (PSF)
In 1996 the government introduced private higher education institutions and at the same time started to examine the criteria for supporting poor students enrolled in both public or private higher education institutions. In 2006 a pilot provincial scholarship fund was introduced. In reality, this programme was designed to provide assistance (payment of tuition fees, learning materials, living expenses, travel and residence) to students who were not included in public higher education institutions' support programme. This model was introduced for families with low incomes. Scholarship recipients could use their funds to pursue their academic studies either in public or private higher education institutions.

Since 2002, the World Bank through IDA, has financed this programme. The first years of the implementation of the programmes were so successful that other partners, such as the Swedish Government, participated with a substantial financial contribution to the scholarship fund. The programme offers support to the more disadvantaged provinces in term of access to higher education institutions; consequently the central and northern provinces of Mozambique are the main beneficiaries of the programme. Thus far, the Provincial Scholarship Fund has benefited a total of 562 students (see Figure 6.1):

- IDA, from 2002 to 2006, financed 322 students from four provinces; and
- Sida, from 2005 to 2006, financed 240 students from three provinces.

To finance these students, the Provincial Scholarship Fund has spent almost US$ 4 million.

Figure 6.1: The Proposed Higher Education Funding Model

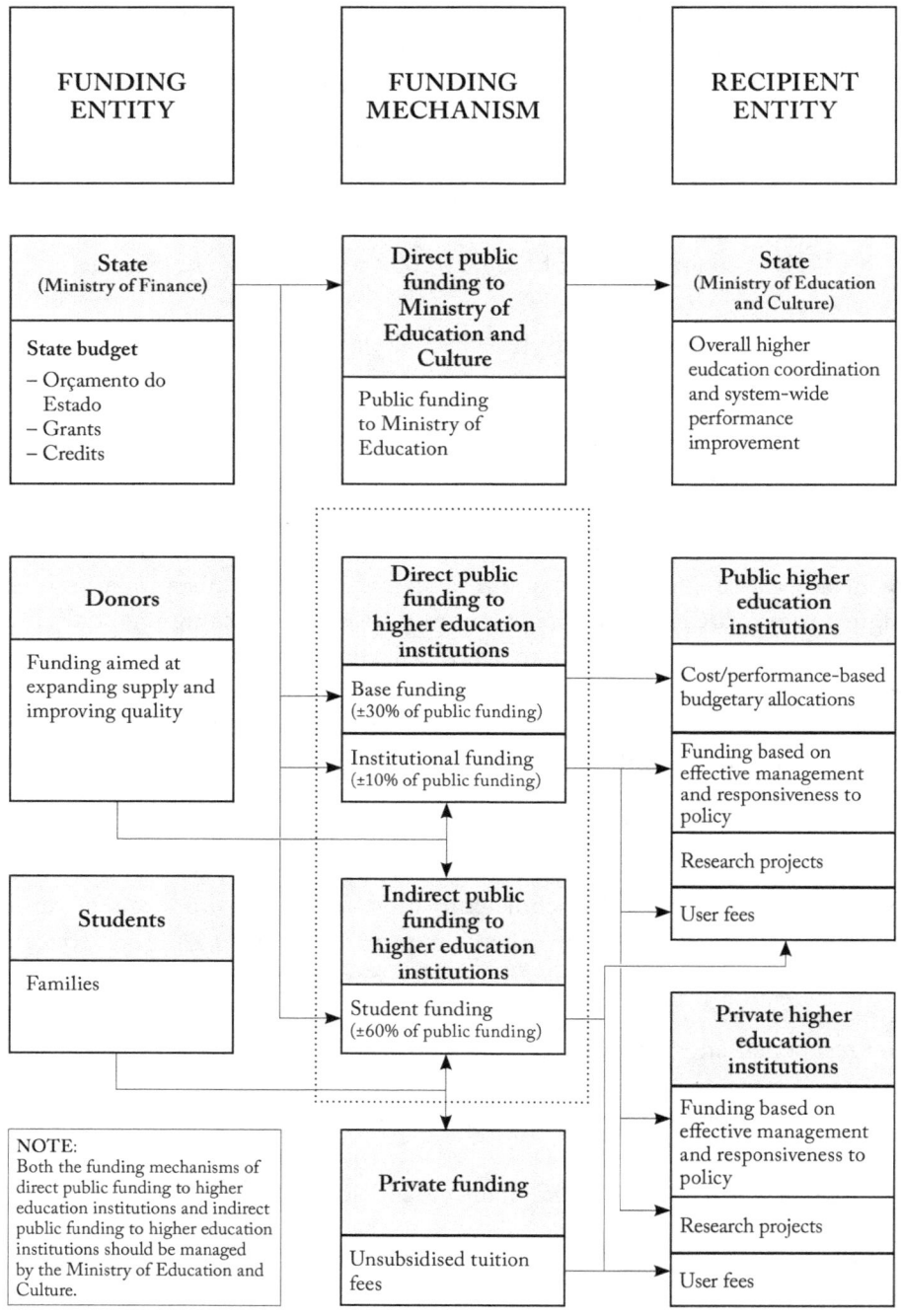

State Funding at the Institutional Level
The history and current status of higher education in Mozambique is such that one large public university (UEM) dominates student intake and enrolments. Consequently, public funding to higher education is dominated by UEM, as funding for public higher education institutions is incremental, based only on the number of students enrolled (inputs) and not on the number of graduates (success or output factors).

A system was designed in 2003 by the then-Ministry of Higher Education, Science and Technology (MESCT) and implemented at Mozambican higher education institutions to capture, classify and produce adequate information for educational cost centre analysis. The system, designed with technical support from international partners, was based on international best practice, adapted to the local reality and piloted at UEM.

Later, the system was further developed to cover the four major public Mozambican higher education institutions (UEM, UP, ISRI and ACIPOL) and also implemented in these institutions, establishing a system-wide coordinated educational cost accounting and reporting system.

This system, among other uses, allows for analysis of the pattern of state funding by type of higher education activity and expenditure. In its classification, and taking into account the Mozambican reality, the system accounts for the following classes of expenditure:

- Admission exams;
- Teaching and learning cost centres;
- Teaching support units;
- Administration and general service support units;
- Non-administrative/non-academic connected units;
- Common expenditures/scientific events; and
- Student support services.

Applying the system to UEM, with data from 2004, 2005 and 2006, it becomes clear that the bulk of the state funding is used at the teaching and learning cost centres. Administration and general support services cost centres are units where an important part of expenditure occurs. Because (i) some of the expenditures cannot be assigned and imputed onto one or more particular unit(s) in an unquestionable way, due to its nature, and (ii) UEM hosts some scientific events, going beyond a single unit, there is also a percentage of expenditure under 'common expenditures and scientific events'.

Public Funding for Private Higher Education Institutions
Private higher education institutions are not entitled to any direct funding or subsidies from the government. However, in 2002 the government introduced a provincial scholarship scheme which has benefited private providers. Since the principle is one of money following students, some of the private higher education providers, especially in programmes not offered by public higher education institutions, or those private higher education institutions in the remote provinces such as the Catholic University, managed to attract some scholarship holders to their institutions.

Direct Public Financing of Public Higher Education Institutions
Around 90% of the funds used in the public higher education institutions are obtained through direct public financing, through State Budget Funds. The determination and allocation of such funds is undertaken through bi-lateral budget negotiations between individual higher education institutions and the Ministry of Finance. Government allocates direct financing to the public higher education institutions, through a mix of:

- Direct budgetary allocations to the institutions, through submission of specific proposals to Parliament within the State Budget proposals, which are eventually approved, being the funds disbursed directly to the beneficiary institutions, without further involvement of the MEC;
- Sourcing grant funds from development partners and directing them to the higher education sector, as a complement to the annually approved State Budget allocations; and
- Sourcing and allocating credit funds, in preferential conditions, to fill up any possible gaps in public financing.

In using these funds, the public higher education institutions subsidise some students. In fact, studies on student unit costs carried out in the public higher education institutions, estimate the average cost to be around US$ 1 700 per annum, while the average annual tuition for the students paying full tuition is situated at around US$ 100. It is expected that after the conclusion of these studies, a policy on higher edcuation tuition fees will be defined for the public system.

Additionally, the government finances scholarships using two approaches:

1. Scholarships (either full or partial) granted directly by the public higher education institutions to its students based on specific eligibility criteria

and procedures. This scheme is part of the public direct financing to public higher education institutions; and
2. Scholarships through the Provincial Scholarships Fund (PSF), in which students from the provinces of Cabo Delgado, Gaza, Nampula, Tete, Niassa, Sofala and Zambézia can apply for funding to study at any of the accredited higher education institutions, either public or private.

In Mozambique, students and their families co-finance education at higher education institutions through the payment of tuition fees. Students who do not qualify for a scholarship, have to fully pay for their education.

Students in the public system pay a low tuition fee (around US$ 100 per annum), directly from their private resources, as part of their co-financing to their education costs.

This mechanism complements State Budget financing to the institutions. Owing to the precarious economic development stage of the country, this financing stream is still potentially exclusive for those students from poor families who fail to qualify for scholarships. In overall terms, students and/or their families currently co-finance only 3% of the financial resources collected by public higher education institutions.

In the current model, student mobility and choice are somehow limited by existing capacity, both institutional and within each existing study programme. However, higher education institutions (public and private) capacity is growing, and a future, improved higher education financing model should also be able to promote mobility. For that, reviewing the higher education institutions' financing mechanism through user fees can strongly contribute to overall system effectiveness improvement. It can create incentives for higher education institutions to increase capacity in the educational areas of highest demand, both by government and the private sector.

Meeting the Higher Financing Challenge

In the Mozambican context, it is important to improve the higher education financing model, taking into account the major objectives of social equity, which is of paramount importance in the government's strategy and policy guidelines. Such a model should be designed in an efficient way to accommodate the expected dynamics resulting from growing higher education activity in the country, as a consequence of the growth in demand for higher education.

This section presents some recommendations on courses of action that would improve overall higher education financing in the country.

An effective higher education financing model should depart from and improve on the current model, considering a mixture of direct and indirect funding mechanisms. Taking into account the current international thinking in higher education financing, the following modes for funding higher education are proposed:

- Direct funding, which should be the least important mode of financing higher education institutions:
  - Base funding to higher education institutions (between 20 and 40% of the funding to higher education institutions). This funding should be exclusively for public higher education institutions; and
  - Institutional funding to higher education institutions (between 10 and 20%). This funding should be mainly for public higher education institutions, but private higher education institutions could also access the funds, should there be sufficient justification; and
- Indirect funding: Student funding, which should be the majority of the funds (more than 50%). Students would access these funds on a competitive basis, taking into account policy priorities, in terms of areas of education. Therefore, both public and private higher education institutions would have access to payments from this funding mechanism.

Table 6.2 and Figure 6.1 show a version of the proposed higher education funding model. Table 6.2 summarises the three public funding mechanisms to higher education institutions.

Reviewing the system of public funding to the higher education system should also consider the role and responsibility of the MEC in providing system-wide strategic direction and coordination, providing a level playing field for all higher education institutions in the country. The role of MEC is crucial to enable the higher education institutions to make the best contribution possible to the development of the country, as well as overseeing the activity of the higher education institutions. Thus, the State, through the Ministry of Finance, should continue to allocate funds to the MEC, allowing the Ministry to have adequate resources to fulfil its mandate.

However, most of the funding arrangements intended for the higher education institutions currently active as part of the MEC structure (such as the current QIF and PSF), should evolve to being funding schemes managed under the direction of the MEC, but involving other stakeholders, to improve their linkages to the surrounding economy.

Table 6.2: Proposed Financing Model

PUBLIC FUNDING MECHANISM	INDICATIVE PROPOSED SHARE	PURPOSE	FORM AND DRIVERS
DIRECT FUNDING TO HIGHER EDUCATION INSTITUTIONS			
Base funding	30%	To provide stability for providers (20%)	*Form*: amounts per institution *Drivers*: key characteristics of the institution including the number of educational programmes
		To reward performance (10%)	*Form*: amounts per graduate *Drivers*: graduation output and educational programme cost band
Institutional funding	10%	To promote effective mgt. and institutional responsiveness to government policy (institutional improvement and innovation)	*Form*: approval of higher education institutions' proposals in competitive bids *Drivers*: policy response, institutional improvement and innovation: • policy support • infrastructure • research and • other competitive projects
INDIRECT FUNDING TO HIGHER EDUCATION INSTITUTIONS			
Student funding	60%	To fund tuition based on higher education institutions costs (46%)	*Form*: Scholarship fund *Drivers*: Number of students in each programme and average fee rates
		Contribution by students (14%)	

Direct Funding to Public Higher Education Institutions

A new system of direct public funding to higher education institutions would need to evolve from the current bi-lateral budget negotiations between individual higher education institutions and the Ministry of Finance, implying a major change.

Base Funding. Base funding should be intended exclusively for the public higher education institutions. It should be funded from allocations obtained from the Ministry of Finance, through the State Budget.

It should form between 20 and 40% of the overall financing to higher education – for indicative purposes, from this point onwards presented as 30%.

It should form the minimum financial allocations to the institutions to allow them to function, and should be determined by:

- Cost – base funding would take into account cost factors for different higher education institutions, providing minimum operational stability on the basis of specific cost structures; and
- Performance – base funding would increase for those institutions

showing better performance (in terms of throughput and graduation rates) when compared to others, in order to provide incentives for efficiency and effectiveness (performance).

Thus, it is advisable that the cost factor of the base funding should be based on the number of approved study programmes offered by individual higher education institutions There should also be some room for flexibility: negotiated funding should be provided for specific characteristics of the institution, consistent with policy options, and for which no funding is available from the other sources. That should be the case, for instance, when internship is mandatory and the institution is filling a human resource gap in state functions such as is the case of ACIPOL or the *Academia Militar*.

In terms of the performance factor, the guiding factor should be the number of graduates who complete a cycle (bachelor's, licenciatura, master's, doctorate) in any given year.

To allow for operationalisation of this funding mechanism, attention should be placed on the following measures during implementation:

- In computing both the cost factor and the performance factor, the study programmes should be divided in three cost bands, reflecting the levels of high-cost, medium-cost and low-cost programmes; and
- After definition of this base funding model, norms and procedures should be defined to regulate the relationships between the Ministry of Education and Culture, the Ministry of Finance, the Ministry of Planning and Development, and the higher education institutions.

Institutional Funding. Institutional funding should be the second direct funding mechanism. It should be intended mainly for the public higher education institutions, but also be granted to private institutions.

The source should also be allocations from the Ministry of Finance, through the State Budget, supplemented by donor funding aimed at expanding supply and improving quality. It should form between 10 and 20% of the overall financing to higher education – for indicative purposes, from this point onwards presented as 10%.

Institutional funding should be used to promote effective management and institutional responsiveness to government policy (specifically, institutional improvement and innovation) and appear in the form of competitive project-based funding, aimed at improving overall higher education system governance. Each institution should have a ceiling of institutional funds it can attract.

Thus, the competitive project-based institutional funding should be granted through the following windows:

1. Policy support projects – for projects to support implementation of higher education system-wide governance and policy aims, at the level of higher education institutions;
2. Infrastructure projects – for innovative infrastructure projects that cannot be financed out of other funding mechanisms. Inclusion of infrastructure projects in the funding model should allow the rates per student and graduate to include an allowance for maintenance of buildings and equipment, throughout the system;
3. Research projects – for projects that respond to national research priorities. These projects should focus on postgraduate-level research; and
4. Competitive projects – for any project not included in the windows mentioned above, but evaluated and judged to be of merit.

To put in practice this funding mechanism, it should be necessary to pay attention to the following:

- For infrastructure projects, emphasis should be placed on encouraging proactive investment in innovative infrastructure;
- For research projects in institutions with important research activities such as UEM, research costs should be separated from teaching costs, to allow for better quality of information; and
- After definition of the base funding model, norms and procedures should be defined to regulate the relationships between (i) the institutional fund and the higher education institutions; (ii) the institutional fund and the Ministry of Education and Culture, the Ministry of Science and Technology, the Ministry of Finance and the Ministry of Planning and Development; and (iii) the opening of the institutional fund to support from donors.

Indirect Public Funding to Higher Education Institutions: Student Funding
In Mozambique, students and their families co-finance higher education through tuition fees. In an improved financing model, student funding should be based on actual demand (demand driven), and aimed at:

- On the demand side, providing more mobility and choice of institutions and study programmes to the students; and

- On the supply side, enhancing responsiveness of the higher education institutions to student needs.

The student fund should be financed by (i) budget allocations from the Ministry of Finance, State Budget, (ii) student contributions, and (iii) donor funding aimed at expanding access and improving equity. The fund should be the main mechanism of financing higher education institutions – it should form more than 50% of the inflow of funds into the higher education institutions (for indicative purposes, it is presented as 60%).

Beneficiaries of the student should be chosen on the basis of merit, with selection criteria clearly spelt out. The fund should pay:

- Scholarships – paying the higher education institutions for each approved student, a percentage (for instance, of 25%, 50%, 75% or 100%) of educational costs (tuition fees). Students with less than 100% funding would have to pay the balance to the higher education institution. The percentage of the scholarship would be determined taking into account the need of the students resulting from means testing, and application of the results to an average tuition fee; and
- Social funding, for subsistence and lodging, for the students in need.

Before such student funding is embarked on, the following measures should be put in place to allow for proper implementation:

- Definition of socio-economic eligibility status for scholarships needs, to be coherent across the whole education sector and possibly within a wider social policy framework;
- Establishment of regulations and manuals, with norms and procedures defining and regulating the relationships between:
  (i)   the student and the student fund;
  (ii) the higher education institutions and the student fund;
  (iii) the student fund and the Ministry of Education and Culture, the Ministry of Finance, and the Ministry of Planning and Development; and
  (iv) the opening of the student fund to support from donors.

Private Households and Tuition Fees
It is proposed under the current model that those students with income enough to pay for their studies should pay the full tuition fees.

The current system should be implemented together with adjustments to the tuition fees at the public higher education institutions bringing them closer to the actual unit costs of education (the current fee level is set around US$ 100 per year, with average unit costs close to US$ 1 700 per student per year). Adverse selection, in the sense of social exclusion of students from low-income families would still be avoided through scholarship funding, provided that an effective screening (means testing) system is put in place, with appropriate procedures.

Closer tuition fees across public and private institutions would be beneficial for student mobility and create incentives to overall effectiveness improvements in higher education institutions, by increasing capacity in those educational areas of high need.

Appendix: List of Higher Education Institutions in Mozambique

Table A1: Accredited Public Higher Education Institutions

	INSTITUTION	TYPE OF TERTIARY INSTITUTION	LOCATION (PROVINCE)	DATE OF ESTABLISHMENT
1	Universidade Eduardo Mondlane (UEM)	University	Maputo	1962
2	Universidade Pedagógica (UP)	University	Maputo	1985
3	Instituto Superior de Relações Internacionais (ISRI)	University	Maputo	1986
4	Academia de Ciências Policiais (ACIPOL)	Academy	Maputo	1999
5	Instituto Superior de Ciências da Saúde (ISCISA)	Polytechnic	Maputo	2003
6	Academia Militar (AM)	Academy	Nampula	2003
7	Instituto Superior Administração Pública (ISAP)	Polytechnic	Maputo	2004
8	Instituto Superior de Contabilidade e Auditoria	Polytechnic	Maputo	2004
9	Escola Superior de Ciências Náuticas (ESCN)	Polytechnic	Maputo	2004
10	Instituto Superior Politécnico de Gaza (ISPG)	Polytechnic	Gaza	2005
11	Instituto Superior Politécnico de Manica (ISPM)	Polytechnic	Manica	2005
12	Instituto Superior Politécnico de Tete (ISPT)	Polytechnic	Tete	2005
13	Universidade de Lúrio (UniLúrio)	University	Nampula	2006

Table A2: Accredited Private Higher Education Institutions

	INSTITUTION	TYPE OF TERTIARY INSTITUTION	LOCATION (PROVINCE)	DATE OF ESTABLISHMENT
1	Instituto Superior de Ciências e Tecnologias de Moçambique (ISCTEM)	University	Maputo	1996
2	Instituto Superior de Transportes e Comunicações (ISUTC)	University	Maputo	1999
3	Instituto Superior Politécnico e Universitário (ISPU)	University	Maputo	1995
4	Universidade Mussa Bin Bique (UMBB)	University	Nampula	1998
5	Universidade Católica de Moçambique (UCM)	University	Sofala	1995
6	Universidade Técnica de Moçambique (UDM)	University	Maputo	2002
7	Universidade São Tomás de Moçambique	University	Maputo	2004
8	Universidade Jean Piaget (UJPM)	University	Sofala	2004
9	Escola Superior de Economia e Gestão (ESEG)	University	Maputo	2004
10	Instituto Superior Cristão (ISC)	Polytechnic	Tete	2004
11	Insituto Superior de Educação e Tecnologia (ISET)	Polytechnic	Maputo	2005
12	Instituto Superior de Investigação, Formação e Ciência (ISFIC)	University	Maputo	2005
13	Instituto Dom Bosco	Polytechnic	Maputo	2006

Chapter 7
NAMIBIA

Jonathan Adongo

Knowledge is a key engine for economic growth and social development. Namibia's national development framework seeks to transform the country into a knowledge economy (ETSIP 2005). One key pillar of a knowledge economy is education and, more broadly, human capital.

A shortage of skilled labour is one of the most significant barriers to Namibia's efforts to become a knowledge economy. One key source of capacity for knowledge creation and application that can alleviate the constraint caused by the shortage of skilled labour is higher education (Adams 2005).

Higher education, also referred to as tertiary education, is broadly defined as education beyond the secondary level, especially education at college or university level. This chapter defines higher education in Namibia based on its international definition, which includes both tertiary education – 'Type A' – provided by the universities and polytechnics; and adult education – 'Type B' – provided through vocational education.

Public financing of higher education is typically faced with a funding gap that arises for various reasons. The first is enrolment pressure where there are growing populations of primary and secondary school leavers with low current higher educational participation rates on the one hand, and inadequate higher educational capacity to meet the growing demand, on the other. Secondly, in both developing and developed countries there is an increasing scarcity of public revenue. This, in turn, arises because of three main reasons. The first is the ever-present competition from other public needs such as basic education, public infrastructure, health, the maintenance of public order, and environmental stabilisation and restoration. These competing needs are often more politically compelling than higher education. The second reason is the inability of many countries to rely on effective methods of raising public revenue. Taxation for public purposes appears to be exceedingly difficult in many African countries even if there is a tradition of tax compliance, and even if the legal and technical problems associated with tax collection could be resolved. The third reason is the degree and rapidity of change in higher education curricula and fields of studies in greatest need and/or demand. This has rendered many teachers, textbooks and educational infrastructure outdated and obsolete. Because of this, funding gap projections constantly need to be revised upward.

The growing dissatisfaction with the rigidities and inefficiencies of the public sector in addressing higher education financing problems is driving reforms in higher education financing structures. As these reforms are assessed, stakeholders grapple with various options available in designing new financing structures. In addition, there is an increasing awareness that that the operation of a market is influenced by who pays for the good – the consumer or a third party – and who produces it – private or government-operated providers (Gwartney *et al.* 2003).

Increasingly, the majority of reforms are drifting toward market solutions. This is in recognition that when consumers pay directly for goods and services, they are free to choose among suppliers and patronise those that provide them with the most value per unit of expenditure. In turn, their choices provide profit-seeking firms operating in open markets with a strong incentive to operate efficiently, keep prices down and cater to the preferences of consumers. Through this combination of forces – economising behaviour by consumers and competition among suppliers – a more efficient allocation of resources is meant to result (Gwartney *et al.* 2003).

Despite some differences, the nature of higher education financing reforms share many similarities in countries with widely differing politics, cultures, economies, ideologies and levels of development.

The objective of this chapter is to describe the financing of and the current levels of access to and equity in higher education in Namibia. The chapter also assesses higher education financing policies in Namibia in the context of three major themes that describe reform efforts in various countries, namely reform of public sector financing; restructuring of management and administration of the institutions with a focus on efficiency; and supplementation of public or governmental revenues with non-governmental revenues.

Higher Education Institutions

In Namibia institutions of higher education can be separated into two categories: tertiary education and vocational education.

Tertiary Education
Tertiary education in Namibia finds its legal basis in the White Paper on Higher Education of 1998. This White Paper emphasises the following:

- Expansion of access;
- Attainment and sustainability of high-quality programmes;
- Relevance to national development challenges; responsiveness to the needs of diverse constituencies;
- Facilitation of economic growth and competitiveness;
- Efficiency;
- Institutional coordination;
- Collaboration and integration; and
- Openness to innovation and diversity of types, modes and means of education (Marope 2005).

Two Acts of parliament have recently entered the statute book. The Acts are designed to take different aspects of the management of the higher education sector out of the political arena, but are yet to be operationalised.

The Higher Education Act, establishing the National Council for Higher Education, aims to provide mechanisms for making tertiary institutions more directly responsive to national needs. The Teacher's Education Colleges Act aims to bring to the colleges the level of professional and managerial autonomy enjoyed by other public tertiary institutions (ETSIP 2005).

The first tertiary institution in Namibia was established in 1992. Tertiary institutions in Namibia can be separated into three categories: public, private and branches.

Public Institutions. The public tertiary institutions in Namibia include the University of Namibia, Polytechnic of Namibia, four Colleges of Education, three Colleges of Agriculture and other tertiary institutions.

The University of Namibia is the only public university. It has nine campuses and centres in major towns around the country. It currently has seven faculties, namely Agriculture and Natural Science; Economics and Management Science; Education; Humanities and Social Sciences; Law; Medical and Health Sciences; and Science. These faculties offer certificate, diploma and degree courses with limited graduate- and postgraduate-level courses. Some courses are offered on-line through open and distance learning programmes. It also has five centres including the Centre for External Studies; the Multi-disciplinary Research and Consultancy Centre; the Language Centre; the Computer Centre; and the Information and Learning Resources Centre.

The Polytechnic of Namibia has four schools: Business Management; Communication, Legal and Secretarial Studies; Engineering and Information Technology; and Natural Resources Management and Tourism. It offers certificate, diploma and technology-orientated degrees. Some of these courses are also offered on-line through open and distance learning programmes. The Colleges of Agriculture fall under the University of Namibia and include Neudamm, Ogongo and Tsumis Park. Administratively they fall under the Ministry of Agriculture, Water and Forestry. Pre-service teacher training is offered through four Colleges of Education in Rundu, Caprivi and Ongwediva. In addition the National Institute of Education and Development offers a four- to five-year in-service education and training programme in collaboration with the University of Namibia and Centre for External Studies at the Ongwediva and Windhoek Colleges of Education. Other public tertiary institutions include the National Health Training Centre and the Israel Patrick Iyambo Police College.

Private Institutions. There are ten private institutions in Namibia including the International University of Management and the Institute of Management and Leadership Training.

Branches. Students in Namibia also have higher education opportunities offered by branches of South African and international universities operating in the country. These branches include the University of South Africa (Unisa), the Rand Afrikaans University (RAU – now University of Johannesburg [UJ]), Mancosa, East and Southern African Management Institute, the Cyprus Institute of Marketing, the University of London, the Association of Business Executives and the University of Maastricht.

In-service teacher education programmes are also provided by Unisa and UJ.

Vocational Education

The vocational education and training system in Namibia finds its legal basis in the National Vocational Training Act 18 of 1994 and its amended version of 1996. In 2004 a National Policy on Adult Learning was also adopted.

There are six vocational training centres in Zambezi, Rundu, Valombola, Okakarara, Arandis and Windhoek. Four are public and one is operated by its own board. In addition, the non-government Namibia Institute for Mining Technology (NIMT) also offers vocational training.

There are also Community Skills Development Centres in nine locations. The Centres are community-owned and offer training to promote self-employment. These provide non-formal, short-term training for youth and adults. There are also four Multi-Purpose Youth Resource Centres and two are under construction.

In addition, the College of the Arts serves students through its Windhoek campuses and the National Arts Extension Programme (ETSIP 2005)

Little consolidated information exists about the scope and characteristics of non-government skills training but it is thought to be considerable. Non-government vocational providers include non-governmental organisations (NGOs), parastatals and private profit-making institutions.

Financing

Namibia stands out as one of the biggest spenders on education and training in the region after Lesotho, with education expenditure comprising 7.2% of GDP compared to Lesotho's 10.4%. Education is funded directly through the government budget or through the Social Security Commission (SSC) development fund, which in 2003 was approximately N$ 39 million and focuses on providing training for the unemployed (Office of the Auditor General 2003).

Table 7.1 illustrates the share of education expenditure in the tertiary and vocational education segments. Both sub-sectors experienced growth in past years. However, the vocation education sub-sector is expected to experience reduced state funding. This decline is expected because of the planned introduction of the vocational training levy in 2007.

Within the education sector, the proportion allocated to tertiary education increased by three percentage points from 1996 to 2004 and then fell again to 2000 levels in 2005. The proportion of spending on administration and non-formal education has remained almost the same between 1997 and 2005. This is illustrated in Table 7.2. In 2005/2006, as Table 7.2 shows, 46% of education spending went to the primary sector, 22% to the secondary sector and 15% to tertiary education.

The programmes aimed at making the higher education sector more effective are illustrated in Table 7.3. The table which outlines the funding projections of the Education and Training Sector Improvement Programme (ETSIP), which is a national initiative aimed at making the education sector more effective.

Although Namibia has become less dependent on foreign aid since independence, donor financing of the education sector remains significant. Most of the donor funding contributes to the development budget, which mainly covers infrastructure, equipment and training. Table 7.4 shows contributions of different donors up to 2006.

Table 7.5 shows the distribution of funding within the higher education sub-sector between 2001 and 2003.

Table 7.1: Distribution of Public Spending on Higher Education (nominal N$, million)

INDICATOR	2000/2001 (ACTUAL)	2001/2002 (ACTUAL)	2002/2003 (ACTUAL)	2003/2004 (ACTUAL)	2004/2005 (EST.)	2005/2006 (ACTUAL)	2006/2007 (EST.)	2007/2008 (EST.)	2008/2009 (EST.)	2009/2010 (EST.)
TOTAL Tertiary education	221	254	263	337	335	327	368	379	394	404
Salaries & wages	31	35	35	39	40	44	54	44	47	49
Goods & services	8	7	9	9	7	8	17	15	8	9
Subsidies & other current transfer	146	185	191	266	268	267	268	287	311	320
Capital	36	26	29	23	20	8	29	33	27	26
TOTAL Vocational education	39	53	52	61	58	61	72	75	66	68
Salaries & wages	14	18	16	18	21	22	22	24	26	27
Goods & services	6	7	7	15	11	11	20	23	16	16
Subsidies & other current transfer	15	20	17	20	19	20	19	17	19	19
Capital	5	7	10	8	6	8	10	10	4	4

Source: State Revenue Fund 2002, 2003, 2004, 2005, 2007

Table 7.2: Breakdown of Education Spending by Economic Classification (%)

INDICATOR	1996/1997	1997/1998	1998/1999	1999/2000	2000/2001	2001/2002	2002/2003	2003/2004	2004/2005	2005/2006
Administration	11	10	10	10	10	10	11	11	11	14
Primary	45	49	48	48	48	47	49	50	47	46
Secondary	26	24	23	23	23	21	19	18	21	22
Tertiary	15	14	15	15	15	17	17	17	18	15
Non-formal	3	3	4	4	4	4	4	4	3	3

Source: State Revenue Fund 2004, 2005, 2007

Table 7.3: ETSIP Funding Component Projections (N$, million)

	2006/2007	2007/2008	2008/2009	2009/2010	2010/2011
TERTIARY EDUCATION	10.0	19.4	22.0	31.3	55.1
Develop the National Council for Higher Education	0.1	0.2	0.2	0.2	0.2
Implement the Teacher Education College's Act	0.3	0.2	0.2	0.2	1.2
Develop and rationalise the teacher education reform programme	0.2	7.9	7.8	6.9	4.2
Build capacity for graduate studies and research	0.0	1.1	7.0	5.1	4.2
Develop pre-entry, foundation programmes and student support	6.4	7.8	8.7	9.1	9.5
Enhance continuous professional staff development	2.9	3.2	2.8	2.9	3.0
Introduce quality assurance processes	0.0	0	0.8	0.6	0.7
Diversify financing resources	0.0	1.4	0.5	0.1	0.1
Use resources efficiently	0.0	0.0	0.6	0.2	0.2
Cost of absorbing increased throughput from expansion of secondary education	0.1	-2.5	-6.4	6.0	31.8
VOCATIONAL EDUCATION	8.1	60.4	103.2	81.8	57.8
Establish the Namibia Training Authority	0.5	1.9	4.3	1.3	1.4
Enhance management development at the vocational training centres	0.0	2.6	2.3	0.0	0.0
Establish competency-based training	0.0	2.8	2.7	0.0	0.0
Upgrade instructor qualification and expand outputs	0.4	0.6	0.1	0.0	0.0
Re-equip vocational training centres	5	0.2	0.1	0.1	0.2
Establish the levy system	0.1	1.0	1.3	0.6	0.6
Diversify and expand training provision	0.1	43.1	87.9	78.8	54.7
Developing the arts industry	2.0	8.3	4.5	0.9	1.0

Source: ETSIP 2005

Table 7.4: Donor Contribution to the Education and Training Sector (N$, 000s)

DONOR	2002/2003	2003/2004	2004/2005	2005/2006	2006/2007
Africa Group of Sweden		230			
Book Aid International	820	970	101	105	
EC/SIDA - ISCBF		14 753	15 915	16 880	9 731
Finnish Embassy		26	1 812		
GTZ	9 800	9 600	9 500	8 310	6 800
HIV/AIDS Global Fund		11 939	10 784	9 409	2 785
DANIDA (Ibis)			4 000		
KfW	24 352	39 116	5 037	4 000	
Lux Development		27 689	33 981	8 978	
Norway NAMAS			5 370		
UNESCO		820	1 220		
UNICEF	420	420	420	420	
USAID	24 880	24 880	32 400	32 400	32 400
French Embassy			800		
VSO Namibia	1 500	1 500	1 500	1 500	

Source: Ministry of Finance 2005

Table 7.5: Funding Distribution within Higher Education (%)

INDICATOR	2001/2002	2002/2003	2003/2004
Colleges of Education*	20	20	15
Vocational training centres*	15	15	15
University of Namibia	34	34	38
Polytechnic	19	19	20
Student Support	12	12	12

* Includes central administration costs
Source: Government revenue and expenditure 2002/2003 and 2003/2004

During the 2003/2004 financial year, more than N$ 48 million was allocated to student support through the Student Financial Assistance Scheme. A key concern is that only a few students benefit from the scheme. In 2002, only 40% (10% private sector bursaries and 30% government bursaries) of University of Namibia students received any kind of financial support (Marope 2005).

In the 2003/2004 financial year, the university and the polytechnic received almost 60% of the total allocation compared to teacher training and vocational education and training. This suggests that the allocation of government resources in higher education is not equitable (Marope 2005).

Tables 7.6 and 7.7 show respectively that the revenues and expenditures for the university and polytechnic have increased between 1996 and 2002. Since 1997, the university had a deficit, which was ultimately financed by the government. However, in 2002, the university recorded its first surplus since 1996. On the other hand, the polytechnic has had a consistent surplus between 1996 and 2002.

Table 7.6: Revenue and Expenditure for UNAM (N$, million)

INDICATOR	1996	1997	1998	1999	2000	2001	2002
REVENUE							
Government Subsidy	55	60.5	83.2	86.9	94.2	117.6	122.9
Tuition fees	10.1	9.3	11	12.6	15.6	22.9	39.9
Hostel fees	4.4	5	5.9	4.1	5.4	5.5	5.6
Other revenue	1.5	3.5	5.6	4.6	5.1	4.8	5.7
TOTAL	71	78.3	105.7	108.2	120.3	150.8	174.2
EXPENDITURE							
Personnel	47.8	57.9	86	96.8	91.1	110.1	112.8
Administration and other	19.7	27.6	36.5	38	37.3	37.1	42.4
TOTAL	67.5	85.5	122.5	134.8	128.4	110.1	112.8
Surplus/(deficit)	3.5	(7.2)	(16.8)	(26.6)	(8.1)	(3.4)	10.3

Source: Annual reports 1996–2002

Table 7.7: Revenue and Expenditure for Polytechnic (N$, million)

INDICATOR	1996	1997	1998	1999	2000	2001	2002
REVENUE							
Government Subsidy	27	35.2	41.7	47.3	51.2	65.2	68.1
Tuition fees	3.1	5.9	6.7	7.9	9.8	12.7	15.4
Hostel fees	2.3	2.2	2.6	2.9	3.8	4.1	4.3
Interest received	1.2	2.8	4.2	5.4	5.3	5.2	-
Rent received	0	0	0	0	1.7	1.9	-
Other revenue	1.8	1.5	2.4	4.1	2.5	4.4	19.5
TOTAL	35.4	47.6	57.6	67.6	74.3	93.5	107.3
EXPENDITURE							
Personnel	16.5	21.4	30.4	33.7	41.9	50.6	58.5
Administration and other	8.5	11	13.9	14.7	15.6	23	26.1
Depreciation	2.9	2.7	4.1	5.6	4.9	6.8	10.6
Delink subsidy	0	2.4	0	0	0	-	-
TOTAL	27.9	37.5	48.4	54	62.4	80.3	95.3
Surplus/(deficit)	7.5	10.1	9.2	13.6	11.9	12.1	11.1

Source: Annual reports 1996–2002

The government finances almost all the costs of the public vocational training centres. Less than 5% of the total cost is covered by tuition and other fees paid by trainees. Government financing includes staff salaries, equipment, materials and other operating expenses. A major share of expenses at the two non-government vocational training institutions, the Windhoek VTC and NIMT, is also covered by the government. In 2000, the government covered 82% of the Windhoek VTC costs and 53% of the total costs of NIMT (Grossman in Johanson & Kukler 2003: 63).

Unit costs indicate the extent to which resources are allocated optimally across levels of the education and training system. Table 7.8 shows that unit costs vary widely across levels and types of education and training in Namibia, indicating a skewed cost structure. The emerging picture is that of a very expensive post-secondary education and training system. Normalising the unit cost in primary education to 1, per pupil spending is estimated to be 12.6 for vocational education and training, 15.9 for Colleges of Education, 10.7 for the polytechnic and 12.6 for the university (Marope 2005).

For the colleges of education, head office costs were about 22% of the total cost in 2002. The unit cost estimates for vocational education are very high partly because the estimate includes administrative costs from the head office. These are difficult to disaggregate with any accuracy. Other prior analyses have roughly estimated the unit cost for vocational education and training, without administrative overheads, at about N$ 14 835. This is still about 6.56 times the unit cost of primary education. This figure is bound to be underestimated because it does not include tuition and other fees collected by vocational training centres and used to cover some of their expenditures (Marope 2005).

Table 7.8: Recurrent Unit Cost by Level or Type of Education and Training (2001)

LEVEL OF EDUCATION	PUBLIC SPENDING (N$ MILLIONS)	ENROLMENTS (PUBLIC)	PER PUPIL SPENDING	
			UNIT COST (N$)	UNIT COST (MULTIPLE OF GDP PER CAPITA)
Primary	896.6	396 252	2 263	0.14
Secondary	427	130 577	3 270	0.21
Vocational Education	52.7**	1 892	27 854	1.76
Colleges of Education	54.4	1 985	27 405	1.73
Polytechnic	74	3 170*	23 344	1.48
University of Namibia	136	4 849*	28 047	1.77

* Student FTE is used instead of raw enrolment; ** includes administrative costs   Source: Ministry of Finance, School of Census Data

Equity of Expenditure

One key indicator of equity in education systems is how different groups in society benefit from public spending on education. Evidence shows that overall public spending on education and training in Namibia is substantially skewed in favour of the rich. About 80% of the population shares only 40% of government subsidies (Marope 2005).

Besides the public sector, various private initiatives exist that finance higher education in the country. The four commercial banks in the country, i.e. Standard Bank, Nedbank, First National Bank and Bank Windhoek, provide collateral-based loans for higher education at commercial rates. Also, various local companies and multinationals operating in the country provide bursaries for higher education for students attending local and international (mainly South African) tertiary education institutions. (These bursaries are not the same as in-house staff development higher education financing programmes that are also available.) The bursaries are awarded to selected students to pursue degrees in fields in which the sponsoring institution is interested in developing a pool of future human resources.

Eduloan is a private finance company that was established in 1996. It provides educational finance in the form of loans at concessional rates for tuition and/or books to individuals or their dependants who do not qualify for the traditional financing through the formal banking sector or government aid schemes. It does this through a network of agreements with educational institutions in South Africa and bookshopss that allow its beneficiaries to use a smart card – Edu-Xtras – to make payments. The scheme also allows employers to operate a salary-deduction facility to recover their interest payments (Eduloan 2007). Eduloan is headquartered in South Africa, with a branch in Namibia. It is a majority donor-funded initiative (World Bank, International Finance Corporation, DEG [German] and AFD [French]) in partnership with Standard Bank and private shareholders (Eduloan 2007).

Besides the public and private sources of financing, households also pay fees. However, most households devote less than 1% of their total annual expenditure to their children's education.

Access

The nature and forms of education in Namibia have, to a significant extent, been shaped by the policies of both the German (1884–1915) and the South African colonial rulers (1915–1990). These two regimes forcefully regulated access to education in general and to schooling in particular by apartheid laws, policies and practices, with the clear purpose of enforcing and reinforcing the policies of separate development and bantustanisation based on race, ethnicity and tribe (Mutorwa 2004). Access to education prior to independence was further inhibited by the curriculum, i.e. a policy that prescribed the various courses or fields of study to be taught at schools, colleges and universities. Certain races were discouraged or barred from certain fields of study such as mathematics, sciences and law (Mutorwa 2004).

With this background, access in the country was defined to mean 'universal availability of basic education, as opposed to higher education, at both child and adult levels throughout the nation' at Namibia's independence in 1990 (Ministry of Education & Culture 1993b). This focus on access to basic education differs from a focus on higher education, which is the scope of this paper.

Access to tertiary education[1]

Table 7.9 shows that university enrolment increased by 137% between 1995 and 2002. Enrolment through distance education programmes offered by the Centre of External Studies grew by about 230%, accounting for about 40% of the total enrolment by 2002. Enrolment in non-distance education programmes increased by about 100% over the eight-year period. By 2002, enrolments were still very low in areas identified as having serious human resource shortages such as Science (7%), Agriculture and Natural Resources (2%), and Medical and Health Sciences (5%).

Table 7.9: University Enrolment Trends by Faculty

FACULTIES	1993	1995	1997	1999	2002
Agriculture and Natural Resources	–	–	67	141	211
Economics and Management Sciences	326	477	652	750	1 274
Education	397	597	782	676	1 187
Humanities and Social Sciences	377	436	389	415	897
Medical and Health Sciences	690	724	716	386	448
Law	–	45	89	106	225
Science	144	165	298	363	632
Centre for External Studies	1 705	1 092	544	1 239	3 572
Centre for Visual and Performing Arts	168	22	–	–	–
Total	3 807	3 558	3 537	4 076	8 446

– Not available; The first intake for the Faculty of Agriculture and Natural Resources was in 1996; The first intake for the Law faculty was in 1994; The Centre for Visual and Performing Arts was incorporated into the Faculty of Humanities and Social Sciences at the end of 1995.

Source: The University of Namibia Registrar's Office 2003

---

1   This draws from Marope 2005

Enrolments are also concentrated in undergraduate programmes. In 2001 postgraduate students accounted for 6% of enrolments. At this level, there were only three Science students and one Agriculture and Natural Resources student. This was relative to 140 students in the faculties of Education and Humanities.

Table 7.10 shows that growth in enrolment at the Polytechnic of Namibia has also been substantial, although much lower than at the university. Enrolment grew by close to 31% between 1996 and 2002. This fell far short of the demand for places. In 2003, for example, there were 5 000 applicants for fewer than 200 places.

Table 7.10: Polytechnic of Namibia Enrolment Trends by School

FACULTIES	1996	1997	1998	1999	2000	2001	2002
Business and Management Systems	1 803	2 417	2 388	2 507	2 763	2 597	2 297
Communication, Legal and Secretarial Studies	298	346	305	311	293	320	266
Vocational Training	196	64	–	–	–	–	–
Natural Resources Management and Tourism	124	133	154	243	313	388	381
Engineering and Information Technology	445	106	234	353	458	658	711
Distance Education Centre	315	142	–	–	–	–	–
Total	3 181	3 208	3 081	3 414	3 827	3 963	3 655

Note: Table does not include foreign students.

Source: Polytechnic of Namibia, Office of the Rector 2003; Ministry of Higher Education, Training and Employment Creation, annual statistics and Annual Reports of BETD INSET programme

Access to tertiary education, in terms of enrolment has rapidly increased since independence. By 2001, the gross enrolment ratio was 11% for tertiary education and training with about 80% of the population literate. Gross enrolment ratios for tertiary education in Namibia still lag behind that of other lower middle income countries, although it is comparable to other African countries. However, 12% of the population has never been to school.

A further challenge is the existing bottleneck of inadequate outputs at senior secondary level. The most significant cause of this shortage is that general education fails to provide the quantity and quality of output required to provide a base for higher-level human capital development, especially at the senior secondary level (ETSIP 2005). Unfortunately, the current education system is still ineffective to the extent that it renders most basic education graduates untrainable and unemployable (Marope 2005).

Access to Vocational Education
Enrolment in vocational training centres has increased more than 16 times, from about 174 trainees in 1992 to more than 2000 trainees in 2002.

Though access to these vocational training centres has increased, the demand for training still far outstrips supply. In 2002, about 30 000 youths completed grade 10; only about 1 000 (3%) of these could secure places in vocational training centres. This figure excludes students who may have dropped out of school before completing grade 10 (Marope 2005).

In 2002, the Valombola Vocational Training Centre had an applicant:admission ratio of 10:1 (2 000 applicants for every 200 places). At the Windhoek Vocational Training Centre, the demand for training places was also ten times greater than the available number of places (Grossman in Johanson & Kukler 2003: 63). The demand for places at NIMT was even higher – it received 3 000 applications for 150 places, a ratio of 20:1 (Grossman in Johanson & Kukler 2003: 91).

Trainee enrolment is concentrated in a narrow band of fairly traditional trades with just eight trades from the 19 offered accounting for over 70% of the enrolments. The most popular trades are automechanics, bricklaying, carpentry and joinery, electrical general, plumbing, welding and fabrication, and secretarial work.

It is striking that second-year enrolment is 55% of the first year enrolment. This may suggest a substantial expansion of year 1 enrolment in 2002 and/or a high drop-out rate between year 1 and year 2. It is assumed that the difference between year 2 and year 3 enrolments is due to repetition. However, reliability and consistency of data obtained are low (Marope 2005).

Access by women to vocational training centres reflects existing gender stereotyping. Subjects that are 'traditionally female professions' have the most number of women; including clothing and knitting craft, hospitality, secretary and administration, and business practice.

Multipurpose Youth Resource Centers are also experiencing an increase in enrolment with occupancy increasing from 1 800 in 2001 to 5 480 in 2002 (Marope 2005)

Access to Branches
Up to 50% of tertiary education students in Namibia study through distance education (ETSIP 2005). In 2002 about 5 389 Namibians were enrolled in South African institutions for this purpose.

Equity

In Namibia, disadvantaged groups have inadequate access both to inputs and outputs. Inequalities are most evident in the distribution of resource inputs and learning outcomes. These inequalities render the education system a weak instrument for facilitating poverty eradication and for reducing social inequalities. They represent a failure to realise the productive potential of a large proportion of the population (ETSIP 2005).

This section presents data on inequalities in access to tertiary education, focusing on location and gender inequalities. Further exploration of inequity according to other socio-economic dimensions was limited by a lack of data.

Location

Learning outcomes are inequitably distributed to the disfavour of learners in the previously disadvantaged rural, northern regions. For example, the urban population has greater tertiary educational opportunities (69%) when compared with the rural population (31%) in Namibia.

Inequalities in learning outcomes mirror major disparities in the distribution of resource inputs. Overall, schools in the northern regions (Caprivi, Kavango, Kunene, Oshana, Ohangwena, Omusati and Otjikoto) have lower physical, human and financial resources. This results in only 40% of the grade 10 graduates from the northern regions qualifying for entry into senior secondary schools on national examinations compared with over 60% in the rest of the country. This low achievement translates into under-representation of these regions at the tertiary level (ETSIP 2005).

Gender

Women have consistently accounted for about 60% of the university enrolment. This is mainly due to their predominance in Health Sciences (excluding Medicine), Education, as well as in Humanities and Social Sciences. It is encouraging to note that women constituted 40% or more of the enrolment in fields that are ordinarily dominated by men.

While the number of females enrolled at the Polytechnic of Namibia has been increasing over time, the enrolment of females in Engineering and Information Technology fell over time.

Equity in Vocational Education

Opportunities for vocational education are inequitably distributed to the disfavour of women. In 2002, women accounted for 19% of the total enrolment. The situation seems to be getting worse. Between 2000 and 2002, the enrolment of males rose form 1 390 to 1 650 while female enrolments dropped by 26% from 510 to about 380. This reduced the proportion of females from 27% to 19%. There are no other data indicating other forms of inequities in access to skills development and vocational education and training opportunities (Marope 2005).

There is, however, gender equity in pre-service basic education teacher diploma programmes offered by the colleges of education.

Financing Reforms

The high levels of current government expenditure on education makes efforts to increase the share of education in the total government budget by mobilising more government funds in the future, seem both inefficient and counterproductive. However, other reforms can still be pursued to ensure that higher education gets the funding it needs. Financing reforms can be pursued at the budgetary level or by raising additional funds from new sources.

Budgetary Reform
Since 2001/2002, at the budgetary level, the education ministries have been refocusing their budgeting processes from input-based to output-based allocations. The Medium Term Expenditure Framework (MTEF) developed by the Ministry of Finance provides expenditure ceilings across line ministries. Line ministries then allocate these ceilings across priority programmes in their Medium Term Plans (MTPs).

Despite the increase in financial resources allocated to higher education institutions, there are no clear criteria for how funds are allocated and no agreed performance indicators to account for the funds received. In the absence of clear criteria, the Ministry of Education seems to have adopted a policy of incremental budgeting. Efforts to pursue performance and other new forms of public budgeting should be cautious of experiences where they have been accompanied, in many instances, with unintended and sometimes unwanted consequences.

The gap between what institutions request and what they are allocated is huge and growing. This partly arises due to differences in the institutions' and the government's financial year. The financial year for the institutions commences in January, while the government's financial year begins in April. The national budget is presented to parliament in mid-April. Thereafter, it takes the Ministry of Education a couple of months before it can allocate funds to institutions. Therefore, the institutions only know their exact allocations in the middle of their financial year. This creates not only uncertainty, but also a risk of overspending. The synchronisation of financial years could be one step towards facilitating better planning (Marope 2005).

To address this problem, the university and polytechnic advocate for a formula-based budget allocation (per learner formula). Formula-based funding that reflects national development priorities should only be adopted with proper staff training on its use. If the funding formula is easy to understand and include adequate but as few indicators as possible, it will be viewed as rational, fair and transparent, and allow for planning. This could address most of the concerns relating to lack of transparency, inadequate funding and uncertainty of funding (Marope 2005).

Another reform at the budgetary level is the introduction of per capita funding. This should encourage equity. In addition, there can be a restructuring in the allocation of public spending on education. This could take the form of a re-adjustment on spending on a particular level of education – pre-primary, primary, secondary, tertiary or vocational.

Another way of mobilising resources is shifting between budgets. In most countries a proportion of educational expenditure particularly that associated with training is spent by ministries other than the ministry of education, e.g. ministries of labour, agriculture, industry, housing, and information and broadcasting.

Diversifying Sources of Financing
Diversification of funding sources could be towards public and non-public sectors. The rest of this section deals with diversification of sources of financing towards public sources. This can be further categorised into internal and external sources.

Internal. One approach to diversifying sources of financing could be to earmark specific government revenues to be allocated exclusively to the education sector. For example, the allocation of a percentage of revenues from certain economic sectors or an earmarked tax for education on some goods or services such as alcohol, cigarettes, gambling, horseracing, cinema and theatre tickets. Earmarked taxes have been used in Nepal, China, Botswana and Turkey in order to finance expansion of education programmes. Pakistan introduced a surcharge on some imports, designating the proceeds to the education system. South Korea introduced a five-year education tax on the sale of tobacco and on income from interest and dividends.

Another approach would be to promote efforts aimed at involving other government agencies in financing the costs of higher education. This can include inviting regional authorities to finance some of the costs by setting up regional education funds.

External. External funding for the higher education sector can occur by borrowing through the issue of public debt instruments, e.g. government bonds.

This would be relatively easy for Namibia because its sovereign debt is rated as investment grade by Fitch (a global credit rating agency). However, stakeholders in the education sector view this as a last option to be adopted citing its macro-economic implications, without specifying whether these will be negative or positive (ETSIP 2005).

Another source of external funding for higher education are external donor agencies. These donors can provide grants, soft loans and/or technical assistance either bi-laterally or multi-laterally. Although this source of financing is already being used to finance education in Namibia, it could be relied on to a greated degree.

The benefits of donor financing of higher education can be maximised if it is allocated within a framework that coordinates among different needs and is linked to projects that are well integrated in the national plan for education. To address this donors have been providing direct support for the education sector to the Namibian Government through its budget from 2003/2004 to 2006/2007 based on a memorandum of understanding. The funds were routed to the education sector through the Ministry of Finance. Continuation of donor support depended on whether certain conditions were met including the assessment of the education sector at a Joint Annual Review.

Unfortunately, a greater proportion of development budget funds are being used to subsidise the recurrent budget with general budget support than without it. Therefore, a significant proportion of donor funds assigned for development (investment) purposes are being used to absorb the excess costs of, for example, remuneration and utilities (ETSIP 2005).

Efficiency Reforms

The high level of expenditure in education in Namibia is mainly driven by increases in learner numbers, non-implementation of staffing norms for teachers, salary increases projected as an average of actual increases awarded in the past three years and an increase equal to inflation on other inputs into the sector.

High costs of tertiary education per student arise in part because of lower weekly teaching hours by staff compared with the lower levels of the education system, smaller average class sizes, higher average salaries and more extensive requirements for facilities, including student boarding (ETSIP 2005). Evidence of inefficient use of resources at present include high repetition and drop-out rates from tertiary institutions, in some cases small department and class sizes, and underutilisation of some facilities. As an example, the ratio of teaching staff to students is 1:12 in Colleges of Education compared with international norms which are closer to 1:20. This inefficiency has resulted in cuts in other discretionary areas such as textbooks.

In the absence of any constraints imposed on these cost drivers, the education sector will face both a decline in quality of education provided (through a decline in the provision of key inputs) and an over-expenditure on its allocated budgetary ceiling. However, constraints should not focus on cutting the amount of expenditure but can shift to focusing on reforming the patterns and mechanisms of allocation of available resources and their efficient spending with the aim of reducing unit costs. Increasing efficiency and reducing unit costs through better spending enable better use of available resources, improved management of the system and achievement of more with the same means. The resulting funds that are mobilised by efficiency gains can then be channelled toward efforts to improve the future performance of the sector.

An efficiency reform measure that has been identified by the Namibian Cabinet as one that could be pursued is greater productivity in tertiary education. For the same amount of expenditure more students could be enrolled resulting in an increase in the average number of students per faculty, per lecturer and increased utilisation rates of physical facilities. This would result in more students graduated from tertiary institutions for the same unit cost as at present or alternatively reduce costs per graduate.

Another efficiency reform measure that has been recognised by the Namibian Government is instituting normative financing as a basis for allocation of public funds among institutions. Such reforms include establishing baseline costs per programme and institution. These measures will provide incentives to institutions to economise in the use of resources.

Another way to reduce costs is the incorporation of information and communication technology (ICT) in Ministries of Education and higher education institutions. This has the added benefit of giving instant access to libraries and other information. Unfortunately, the current experience is that technology continues to be incorporated by management mainly as 'add-ons' to conventional teaching and curricula, without the accompanying changes in the instructional production function that are required to realise useful productivity gains.

Although the financing of higher education is increasingly taking into account measurable output indicators, the quest for productivity and efficiency is still dominated by cost-side considerations at the expense of outputs or learning. This is evidenced by findings that there is a low level of effort to measure the learning added by a higher education institution, or to maximise learning in ways that have been proven to be effective.

Efficiency reforms that focus on reduction of staff face problems. This is because public education sectors in most countries continue to have great difficulties shedding redundant and unnecessary staff and closing inefficient and outdated institutions. An alternative option would be to optimise allocations per category of expenditure, e.g. salaries and benefits, and non-salary and investment.

Private Higher Education

Private financing of education is limited, both in terms of private provision and in terms of expenditure by the private sector and households. On average, households devote less than 1% of their total annual consumption to their children's schooling. Therefore, the beneficiaries (graduates in terms of higher earnings and enterprises in terms of qualified workers) pay little if any of the costs (Marope 2005).

The Namibian Government recognises that partnerships with the private sector need to be strengthened if higher education aims to finance a larger share of its operating costs from non-government sources (ETSIP 2005).

Increased partnership with the private sector entails a shift in the burden of increasing educational costs from the general taxpayer or general citizen (who may be 'paying' for the government's deficit financing through the erosion, or confiscation, of purchasing power) to parents and students especially, but also to philanthropists and to purchasers of educational services. This can occur through greater cost sharing with beneficiaries, raising income from the private enterprises, generation of own income by tertiary institutions and sourcing income from philanthropies.

Individual Financing

Individual financing of higher education should shift towards cost-sharing mechanisms. There are three primary vehicles through which this can occur, tuition and fees, student loans and a graduate tax.

Tuition and user fees. More countries are shifting the cost burden of higher education from the taxpayers to parents and students in the form of tuition and user fees. The former is a partial source of revenue for the support of instructional costs. The latter is a partial or complete source revenue for the support of non-instructional costs such as examinations, library, laboratory and learning materials or institutionally provided room and board for what are usually governmentally supported maintenance, or cost of living, grants. User fees try to alleviate the cost of various forms of hidden or open, direct or indirect contributions in cash, kind or labour.

In Africa, the introduction of tuition and the movement toward more nearly full cost recovery on accommodation and catering seems to be widely recognised as both necessary and sound. Implementation has generally been slow, sporadic and unevenly applied, with some reported progress in, for example, Uganda, Kenya and Zambia. While many countries maintain free primary and lower secondary education, fees or other charges and contributions often exist or are being introduced throughout Africa for upper secondary and tertiary studies.

Like other African countries, free primary education is entrenched in the Namibian Constitution. However, this does not apply to the post-primary level. Thus Namibia can be part of the trend where more and more developing nations are shifting the cost burden of higher education from the taxpayers to parents and students in the form of tuition (official fees) and user fees. The former is a partial source of revenue for the support of instructional costs.

The introduction of tuition and user fees has to be cautious and carefully programmed. The introduction of, or substantial increases in, tuition for non-compulsory education sectors not supported by constitutions or framework laws and hitherto supported primarily or wholly by public revenues, will face the sheer political power of the student class.

Where they already exist in some higher education institutions, efforts to increase tuition and fees may face less resistance. Where they do not exist, efforts to shift costs through tuition and fees should, at least for the immediate future, focus on foreign students, or students admitted with entrance examination scores just below a threshold cut-off through a differentiated tuition scheme.

Another issue to be aware of is that increases in tuition fees, for example, may simply lead to commensurate withdrawal of public revenue, effecting a shift in the cost from taxpayers to families, but seeming to give the students and his/her parents little or nothing extra for their additional money.

In terms of wider social goals, the introduction of tuition and fees needs to be cautious because it can affect access to education and its equity. As more children from poor households enrol in tertiary education and training, the ability of households to contribute to financing education will become increasingly limited (Marope 2005).

To maintain equity of access to these levels of education, mechanisms for pro-poor education should be developed and implemented. One example of such a mechanism is a system of means tested grants to subsidise selectively those students in greatest financial need so that students from poorer families are exempted, or pay only a proportion of the total cost of their education. The proposed National Education Fund to support cases of hardship is one such mechanism (ETSIP 2005).

Some countries also impose an 'effective tax' on income and/or assets in the form of an expected parental contribution toward the higher education expenses of their children. In Namibia, many schools have a school development fund. A school development study conducted in 2002 estimated that approximately N$ 100 million was being raised annually by way of the School Development Fund (ranging from N$ 55 to N$ 1 400 per learner per year). The study also noted that only 2% of the learners were exempted from the School Development Fund (Marope 2005).

Student loans. With cost sharing in higher education resulting in increasing costs borne by students and families, student loans are also being increasingly used as a means of overcoming problems related to access and equity. These loans are usually provided through state-supported schemes and have been developed in more than 60 countries worldwide. In Namibia, the Student Financial Assistance scheme has shifted from a bursary scheme to a student loan scheme (Marope 2005).

Student loans ease the pressure on national budgetary funds by shifting some of the costs of higher education away from the government (and/or taxpayers) to the main beneficiaries of higher education – the students. Student loans also enable students to study now and pay later through the receipt of income that additional education makes possible when they are employed. If they are targeted at disadvantaged groups, they can lead to greater access by the poor to higher education, thus contributing to improved social equity. If they are targeted at priority fields, they can lead to the loosening of human resource bottlenecks that inhibit national and social development. Since students pay for their studies they are more likely to seek value for money. This helps in improving quality, efficiency and effectiveness, through the promotion of market forces in the higher education financing structure.

For effective loan recovery to occur some studies advocate the provision and administration of loans (including recovery) by private financial institutions or by an autonomous body that is able to create a sustainable, revolving fund. These entities should be sufficiently capitalised with efficient loan administration. Efficiency in debt collection mechanisms can be enhanced through the use of private debt collectors who can be more effective as they are less susceptible to political pressure in pursuing defaulters (Marope 2005). Without effective recovery, student loan systems are largely ineffective in shifting a significant higher educational cost burden from governments or taxpayers to students. While this is recognised, some studies advocate that subsidised interest rates can be provided through guarantees or the government topping up of the rate of interest (Marope 2005; ETSIP 2005).

Graduate tax. An alternative to student loans would be a graduate tax. Instead of receiving a loan that has to be repaid, students would receive a grant. This would be repaid later through an additional charge to the students' annual tax bill (surtax) that is incurred on his/her income without regard to any amount individually owed, after they are employed and their earnings reach a minimum threshold. In Brazil, a tax amounting to 2.5% of the wages of employees in the private sector is levied by the government, and earmarked specifically for primary schooling.

With a graduate tax, there is no immediate relief to the government's current cash obligation for the support of the universities or the students, although the government secures a stream of future income surtax payments, which are of somewhat uncertain present value, but are collectively (potentially) substantial. The students continue to receive their usual subsidies in the form of low or no tuition and perhaps living grants. However, they incur obligations for greater income tax payments than would have been the case in the absence of their higher educational experience. The effect is a shift in ultimate cost burden, without an immediate change in the immediate cash burden on the government.

Thus far, no country has successfully adopted a pure graduate tax. The applicability to developing countries depends largely on the degree to which there is likely to be confidence in the income tax system.

Efforts to make individuals in Namibia pay for their higher education expenses through these mechanisms will be hindered by the perception that the ability of households to contribute is limited due to income disparities and poverty (ETSIP 2005). In addition, efforts to implement these mechanisms will be politically undesirable partly because of the widespread popular belief that the government alone is responsible for provision of quality education at all levels in Namibia. This belief is blamed on the initial impression that the government created of being able to cope with ever-increasing needs of the education sector (ETSIP 2005).

Firm Financing
Employers form part of the indirect beneficiaries of education. They have a vested interest in the supply of knowledgeable and skilled graduates and in lifelong learning to upgrade and update their workforce. Since they benefit from the 'outputs' of the education system, it seems fair that they contribute to the financing of higher education.

Firm financing can be obtained either through an industry-wide training levy, which can be used to reimburse the higher education institutions that provide the training, and also to finance industrial training centres.

The theoretical case for a levy rests on two pillars. Firstly, public funds are limited by overall deficits in public spending and other urgent national priorities. Given widespread poverty, training fees are relatively inelastic as a way of increasing income to higher education institutions. Second, firms currently under-train, in part because they may lose trained staff to competitors. A levy should be designed to give all enterprises a financial incentive to train their employees (ETSIP 2005).

On a more practical level, various stakeholders have recognised the need to strengthen management capacity of the vocational education system to be more responsive and to involve employers in policy decisions, i.e. to make it more demand led; to decentralise public skills provision to respond better to local requirements; to stimulate an increase in the number and variety of vocational education providers; and to stimulate initiatives that reduce reliance on the government for financing the much-needed expansion of vocational outputs and provisioning of skills development (ETSIP 2005). With this in mind, the 1994 National Vocational Education and Training Act allowed for a levy on payrolls to be used to finance vocational training. Although it has never been implemented, the establishment of the Namibia Training Authority with majority employer control creates an opportunity to introduce a levy to suit the needs of employers.

What has been proposed is that private employers with more than 20 employees should pay a training levy of 1% of their wage bill with the possibility of the rate to be reconsidered and, if necessary, readjusted periodically (Marope 2005). However, decisions still need to be made on the levy method – whether raising revenue, levy exception, levy rebate or levy grant should be used. In addition, the rate of collection, size of firms levied and mechanisms for collecting the levy also need to be agreed upon.

Despite all its advantages, one potential disadvantage of a levy scheme is to increase the cost of labour, which can encourage more capital-intensive production in industry. In addition, levies elsewhere, depending on the type, have proved difficult to administer (Marope 2005).

Own Financing by Institution

Higher education institutions can also contribute by generating their own financing. This can occur through engaging in business enterprise, research and consultancy, or by leveraging their alumni network.

Conclusion

A shortage of skilled labour has been identified as one of the most significant barriers to Namibia's efforts to become a knowledge economy. One key source of capacity for knowledge creation and application that can alleviate the constraint caused by the shortage of skilled labour is higher education.

In Namibia institutions of higher education can be separated into the tertiary education and vocational education sub-sectors. This chapter described the financing of, and the current levels of access to and equity in, higher education in Namibia.

The chapter showed that the university and the polytechnic receive the majority of the total budgetary allocation to higher education by the government compared to vocational education and training, and teacher training. Thus it can be argued that the allocation of government resources in higher education is not equitable. In addition, unit costs, which indicate how optimally resources are allocated across levels of the education and training system, were found to vary widely across levels and types of education and training in Namibia reflecting a skewed cost structure.

Higher education and training was found to be very expensive. Even in this environment, evidence showed that the overall public spending on education and training in Namibia is substantially skewed in favour of the rich.

The nature of financing, which depends on a country's financing policies, determines the levels of access to and equity of higher education in a country. These policies were determined to a large extent by the country's history that resulted in the general education system failing to provide the quantity and quality of output required to provide a base for higher-level human capital development, especially at the senior secondary level. To address this, 'access' in Namibia was defined to mean 'universal availability of basic education, as opposed to higher education, at both child and adult levels'.

Using participation as its definition of access and measuring it using enrolment, it is evident that tertiary and vocational enrolment has rapidly increased since independence. However, gross enrolment ratios for tertiary education in Namibia still lag behind that of other lower middle-income countries, although it compares favourably relative to its neighbours. In addition, enrolments were found to be low in areas identified as having serious human resource shortages. Furthermore, university enrolments were concentrated in undergraduate programmes.

Even though enrolment in higher education was found to have increased rapidly, it fell far short of the demand for places. If the basic education system is improved to cater to the 12% of the population that have never been to school and new entrants, the need for more higher education institutions should increase substantially.

Enrolment in vocational educational institutions was found to be concentrated in a narrow band of fairly traditional trades. In addition, access in this category of higher education reflected existing gender stereotyping with subjects that are 'traditionally female professions' having the greatest number of women.

With the university offering limited graduate- and postgraduate-level courses, more Namibians acquired senior degrees abroad, particularly in South Africa.

In terms of equity, this chapter analysed inter-group inequalities in higher education by focusing on location and gender inequalities. In this regard, the urban population has greater tertiary educational opportunities than the rural population. In addition, women account for the majority of university enrolments, mainly due to their predominance in Health Sciences (excluding Medicine), Education, the Humanities and Social Sciences. They also make up a significant number of university enrolments in fields that are ordinarily dominated by men. Also, gender equity in pre-service basic education teacher diploma programmes offered by colleges of education was found.

Polytechnic enrolment of females in Engineering and Information Technology has fallen over time. In addition, opportunities for vocational education are inequitably distributed to the disfavour of women and seem to be worsening.

Moreover, disadvantaged groups have inadequate access both to inputs and outputs. This resulted in inequalities in learning outcomes and schools in the northern regions (where the majority of previously disadvantaged groups reside) having lower physical, human and financial resources. This translates into a relatively lower level of qualification for entry into senior secondary schools on national examinations compared with the rest of the country and under-representation of these regions at the tertiary level.

The costs of higher education in Namibia are borne at present almost completely by the public budget. The high level of government expenditure on education makes efforts to increase the share of education in the total government budget by mobilising more government funds in the future seem inefficient and counterproductive. Given its role in promoting development, all stakeholders (foreign donors, households, private enterprises, non-governmental organisations and private donations) must support the government in all aspects of higher education including financing.

In recognition of this, the objective of this chapter was to present a synthesis that assessed higher education financing policies and practice in Namibia in the context of three major themes, namely reform of public sector financing; restructuring of management and administration of higher education institutions;

and supplementation of public or governmental revenues with non-governmental revenues.

In terms of budgetary reform, the MTEF ceilings in MTPs inform ETSIP of the government funds available to implement its objectives. This results in the actual implementation of ETSIP being grounded in the MTPs. In addition, the integration of ETSIP into the MTEF and the MTP of the Ministry of Education has been achieved.

Other reforms at the budgetary level include per capita funding, which encourages equity and formula-based funding, which reflects national development priorities. In addition, a re-structuring in the allocation of public spending on education can be pursued. Finally, shifting between budgets so that a proportion of educational expenditure is spent by ministries other than the ministry of education is also an option.

In terms of diversifying sources of financing, earmarking specific government revenues collected by a tax and allocating this to the higher education sector is an option. Another option is to involve other government agencies in financing the costs of higher education, e.g. regional authorities. Although donors have been providing direct support for the education sector to the Namibian Government through its budget from 2003/2004 to 2006/2007 this option can be pursued further. The benefits of donor financing can be maximised if it is allocated within a framework that coordinates among different higher education needs and is linked to projects that are well integrated in the national plan of higher education.

Efficiency reforms focus on reforming the patterns and mechanisms of allocation of available resources and their efficient spending with the aim of reducing unit costs. One such reform measure is greater productivity in tertiary education. Another is to institute normative financing as a basis for allocation of public funds among institution. Also, institutional autonomy and school-based management, or the devolution of authority from public authorities, at whatever level, to institutions, is also an option. In addition, the incorporation of technology in Ministries of Education and higher education institutions is another option.

Rather than pursuing efficiency, reforms that focus on reduction of staff face problems. An alternative option would be to optimise allocations per category of expenditure, e.g. salaries and benefits, non-salary and investment.

Beyond setting up their own higher education institutions, public–private partnerships can be created in formerly, purely public institutions. The involvement of the private sector in the operation and management of public institutions brings their know-how and management capabilities into this arena.

For the sustainability of these partnerships, appropriate incentive frameworks, laws and regulations should be put in place for the operation of these establishments. This should help address the alleged lack of quality and questionable long-run sustainability. The perception that increased privatisation of currently public institutions will threaten efforts to preserve access to education can be addressed through the provision of cash grants to higher education institutions.

With limited financing of education by the private sector and households, the Namibian Cabinet recognises that partnerships with the private sector need to be strengthened. A key justification for a partnership in higher education financing that involves the private sector is the expected returns to individuals and to society. Empirical evidence shows that private and social returns to education beyond the junior secondary level are high in Namibia. In addition, many higher education students come from households that are not as poor. Therefore, more private financing of higher education is justifiable.

Although free primary education is entrenched in the Namibian Constitution, this does not apply to the post-primary level. Thus Namibia can be part of the trend where more and more developing nations are shifting the cost burden of higher education from the taxpayers to parents and students in the form of tuition (official fees) and user fees. However, introduction of tuition and user fees has to be carefully programmed because such efforts tend to face the sheer political power of the student class.

To maintain equality of access to higher education, as the ability of households to contribute to financing education becomes increasingly limited when more children from poor households enrol, pro-poor mechanisms should be developed and implemented. One mechanism is a means tested grant to selectively subsidise those students in greatest financial need. The proposed National Education Fund to support cases of hardship is one such mechanism.

Student loans are also being increasingly used as a means of overcoming problems related to access and equity. These loans enable students to study now and pay later through the receipt of income that the additional education makes possible when they are employed. Since students pay for their studies they are more likely to seek value for money. This helps in improving quality, efficiency and effectiveness, through the promotion of market forces in the higher education financing structure.

Without effective recovery, student loan systems are largely ineffective in shifting significant higher educational cost burden from governments, or taxpayers, to students. While this is recognised, some studies advocate that subsidised interest rates can be provided through guarantees or the government topping up of the rate of interest.

A graduate tax can also be instituted. Instead of receiving a loan that has to be repaid, students would receive a grant. This would be repaid later through an additional charge to the students' annual tax bill (surtax) that is incurred on his/her income without regard to any amount individually owed, after they are employed and their earnings reach a minimum threshold.

Efforts to make individuals in Namibia pay for their higher education expenses through tuition and fees, loans and/or graduate taxes are hindered by the perception that the ability of households to contribute is limited due to income disparities and poverty. In addition, efforts to implement these mechanisms will be politically undesirable partly because of the widespread popular belief that the government alone is responsible for provision of quality education at all levels in Namibia.

Employers form part of the indirect beneficiaries of education. They have a vested interest in the supply of knowledgeable and skilled graduates and in lifelong learning to upgrade and update their workforce. Since they benefit from the 'outputs' of the education system, it seems fair that they contribute to the financing of higher education.

Financing from private firms can be obtained either through an industry-wide training levy, which can be used to reimburse the higher educational institutions that provide the training and also to finance industrial training centres.

Higher education institutions can also contribute by generating their own financing. This can occur through engaging in business enterprise, research and consultancy, or by leveraging their alumni network. Own financing by higher education institutions can also occur through the emerging concept of educational self-help service and as an experiment for teaching and applied skills.

Financing for higher education can also occur through philanthropy, which is defined as private, voluntary giving as opposed to financing from the public, non-governmental sector. This category of financiers includes non-profit organisations, private enterprises, religious bodies, charitable foundations, high net-worth individuals, etc.

In addition to certain pre-conditions an appropriate legal framework with proper incentives is as important for philanthropy financing to succeed. Such a framework includes fiscal incentives such as favourable tax treatment of charitable contributions. Also, due to the volume of philanthropic financing there is a need to have appropriate laws on donations and endowments, which would regulate the issue of donations and endowments, their record and distribution at all levels.

As these reform efforts are instituted the role of the government funding will change. It will become more of a regulator for the whole education system but will remain a key player for the provision of education at the basic level. In this capacity it will be responsible for, amongst other things, the elaboration of national educational legislation, and monitoring and evaluating its implementation.

Chapter 8
SOUTH AFRICA

Pundy Pillay

Introduction: Structure and Financing of Higher Education

In the new democracy, South Africa's racially-based higher education institutions were rationalised through a merger process into 23 non-racial universities. There are currently three categories of universities in the country: universities (those institutions that were defined as such during the apartheid period and remain so); universities of technology (the former technikons or technical universities); and comprehensive universities (which are merged universities and technikons).

The 23 universities serve about 800 000 students of whom more than 200 000 study through distance education offered by the University of South Africa (Unisa). The end of apartheid also witnessed a tremendous growth in both local and international private higher education. Currently, there are more than 90 private institutions serving about 35 000–40 000 students. The most prominent international provider of higher education is Monash University from Australia.

The public universities are state-funded institutions, with a varying base of private income and all increasingly dependent on student tuition income. The private higher education instiutions receive no state funding and are largely dependent on tuition income and private sector investment.

All higher education institutions, public and private, are regulated through an accreditation system led by a statutory body, the Council on Higher Education (CHE), and its implementation arm, the Higher Education Quality Committee (HEQC). The HEQC has been responsible for closing down programmes and even whole institutions that have failed to meet specific quality assurance standards.

There are several features of the South African higher education financing framework that are somewhat unique in the African context. First, given intersectoral competition for financial resources, there appears to be a fairly serious public commitment to spending on higher education as manifested, for example, in the recent substantial increase in the higher education budget in nominal terms between 1996 and 2008 (Table 8.1). As a percentage of the education budget, higher education spending increased from 4% to 14.5%. However, spending on higher education as a proportion of both GDP and overall government expenditure, declined during this period (Tables 8.2 and 8.3). Moreover, there has been a significant decline in student per capita expenditure across the system.

Table 8.1: Higher Education Spending in South Africa (ZAR billion)

BUDGET ITEM	1996	2000	2005	2008
Total education	42.1	51.1	83.3	110.2
Higher education excluding NSFAS*	4.1	7.1	10.8	14.5
NSFAS*	0.30	0.44	0.86	1.18

Spending as % of GDP

ITEM	1996	2000	2005	2008
Total education	6.62	5.36	5.27	5.14
Higher education	0.82	0.74	0.68	0.68

Spending as % of government budget

ITEM	1996	2000	2005	2008
Total education	23.97	21.82	26.38	27.74
Higher education	3.0	3.0	2.6	2.4

* NSFAS – National Student Financial Aid Scheme   Source: Department of Education, South Africa 2007a

Second, the system has always had a fee-paying component. In fact, tuition fees comprise a significant component of institutional revenue, on average about 32% (Duncan 2009).

Third, higher education institutions are free to generate 'third stream' income through, inter alia, research and entrepreneurial activities. Such third stream income constituted 23% and 27% of total revenue in 2004 and 2007 respectively (Duncan 2009). In 2007, the government subsidy as a proportion of total revenue ranged from 60% in the Central University of Technology and Walter Sisulu University to 31% at the University of Stellenbosch. Fees as a proportion of revenue ranged from 43% at Unisa to 19% at North West University. The total of first and second stream income for historically white universities (HWUs) was

64% in 2004 and 60% in 2007; for historically black universities the respective figures were 83% and 76%. The average for all higher education institutions was respectively 77% and 72% (Duncan 2009).

Fourth, South Africa has developed one of the most effective student loan schemes for higher education. Called the National Student Financial Aid Scheme (NSFAS), it is an income-contingent scheme designed for needy students. The scheme is funded by the government (to the tune of ZAR 1.18 billion [about US$ 170 million] in 2008, up from ZAR 300 million [US$ 43 million] in 1996) and loans are paid back through the tax administration system when the graduate is employed and has reached a particular income threshold. Under this scheme, the number of grants awarded increased from almost 100 000 in 2002 to nearly 141 000 in 2007. The number of students assisted increased from more than 86 000 to 113 500 in the same period. Moreover, unlike most student loan schemes, this scheme has one of the most acceptable recovery rates internationally. In South African rand terms, the amount recovered increased consistently from ZAR 155 million in 2002 to ZAR 479 million in 2007.

Fifth, there is a close link between planning (at both the institutional and system levels) and funding. Higher education institutions are required to submit three-year 'rolling plans' to the government as part of the state's planning and Medium Term Expenditure Framework (MTEF) budgeting process.

Sixth, a key component of the higher education financing framework is that it is underpinned by a funding formula.

Historical Background

Before the advent of democracy in 1994, the South African government's tertiary education funding policies mirrored apartheid's divisions and the different governance models which it imposed on the higher education system (Bunting 2002). The original funding framework was introduced in 1982/1983 when the main focus of government was to address the needs of the historically white institutions, specifically the historically white universities.

Between 1994 and 1997, there were no substantive changes to the funding framework. In 1997 the government announced its intention to introduce a new funding framework which was intended as a mechanism for steering the higher education system towards the goals and targets established in the National Plan for the transformation of the higher education system.

The original funding model developed during the apartheid era had two key features. First, it treated students as agents who were able to respond rationally to the demands of the labour market. It was assumed that their choices of institutions, qualifications and major fields of study followed labour market signals and their reading of these signals. As a consequence, the only role which the model gave to government in the national higher education system was that of funding student demand, and of correcting any market failures which might occur.

The main concerns with the original funding framework related to equity (access, particularly of the disadvantaged black majority of the population) and efficiency (of outputs and outcomes, particularly, but not only, at the historically black higher education institutions).

The 1997 Education White Paper rejected this student-as-rational-agent model. It stated that the model had not worked in South Africa, and added that this rationale had to be dropped if higher education were to emerge from its apartheid past. The White Paper replaced the student-as-rational-agent model with a planning-steering model of higher education funding that aimed to bring equity and efficiency into the system. In this new model government takes account of labour market signals, but does not adopt either a narrow 'human resources' planning stance or the 'hands-off' stance which is embedded in the student-as-rational-agent model.

In a dual economy such as South Africa's, the student-as-rational model was only partially successful. It worked for a relatively small proportion of students (largely from the minority population groups, and who were mainly city-based), for whom adequate labour market information and career guidance was available. For the majority of the black population, such labour market information was extremely limited. Poor labour information coupled with an almost total absence of vocational counselling at black schools had resulted in a failure of the student-as-a rational model for many. Furthermore, the new government felt that the higher education system needed some 'guided intervention' as the 'market' did not always ensure optimal outcomes in terms of developing countries' human resource needs.

The new model represented a major change in focus. It emphasised that the primary purpose of higher education is to teach, research and play a pivotal role in the improvement of the social and economic conditions of the country. Hence government would fund institutions for training students, conducting research and assisting with the development needs of society and the economy. The 'production process' would be left in the hands of the institutions.

The second feature of the apartheid model was that it contained an implicit assumption that government is the funder of last resort of the higher education system. As such, government subsidies for universities and technikons are supposed to be based on (a) determinations of the actual costs of reasonably efficient institutions; and (b) decisions on which of these costs should be covered by government subsidies. The costs not covered by government subsidies would have to be met by institutions from their private income sources, primarily their student tuition fees.

The new model's view on prices is radically different from that of the old model. In the new model, government first decides on how much it can afford to spend on higher education and then allocates the funds according to its needs and priorities. It would be possible to determine the underlying unit costs for the activities but, within this new framework, the government's basis for allocation is not computed unit costs.

The capacity of the institutions to understand and work with the formula varies substantially, particularly between the historically white and black institutions. With the old formula, the government provided bulky and incoherent supporting documents, a substantial disincentive to enhancing the understanding of the workings of the system. With the new formula, the Ministry of Education (MoE) has produced succinct explanatory documents to foster a greater understanding of the formula.

The Planning Framework for Higher Education

In the Education White Paper 3: A Programme for the Transformation of Higher Education (1997), it was stated that a new funding framework was required to facilitate the transformation of the higher education system.

The White Paper argued that the new funding framework must be goal-orientated and performance-related in order to enable it to contribute to fulfilling the vision and goals for the transformation of the higher education system, which include:

- More equitable student access;
- Improved quality of teaching and research;
- Increased student progression and graduation rates; and
- Greater responsiveness to social and economic needs.

The implementation framework for achieving the vision and goals of the White Paper was outlined in the National Plan for Higher Education (NPHE 2001). The NPHE established indicative targets for the 'size and shape of the higher education system, including overall growth and participation rates, institutional and programme mixes and equity and efficiency goals', including benchmarks for graduation rates (NPHE 2001: 12).

The NPHE furthermore indicated that the 'planning process in conjunction with funding and an appropriate regulatory framework will be the main levers' (NPHE 2001: 10) for achieving goals and targets set. The NPHE goes on to state that the 'effective' use of funding as a steering lever requires the development of a new funding formula based on the funding principles and framework outlined in the White Paper.

The White Paper argued that the development of the higher education system cannot be left to the vagaries of the market as it was singularly ill-suited to addressing the legacy of the past and the reconstruction and development challenges of the future.

The White Paper proposed the replacement of this market model with a planning model in which the development of the higher education system would be 'steered' and national policy goals and objectives achieved through a combination of instruments, namely national and institutional three-year rolling plans, that is, 'indicative plans which facilitate the setting of objectives and implementation targets that can be adjusted, updated and revised annually' (MoE 1997: 13), a responsive funding framework and an appropriate regulatory framework.

The planning model of higher education funding therefore involves three steps:

1. The Ministry determines national policy goals and objectives;
2. Higher education institutions develop three-year rolling plans indicating how they intend to address the national goals and objectives; and
3. Interaction between the Ministry and institutions results in the approval of institutional plans, which would lead to the release of funds based on the quantum of funds available.

As stated earlier, the new funding framework is radically different from the previous framework. It replaces the market-cum-cost model with a planned model in which the starting point for the allocation of funds to higher education institutions is not institutional costs, but affordability linked to the achievement of national policy goals and objectives. The new framework accepts the principle that institutional costs tend to be functions of income, that is, of what is available to be spent. In this regard, funds allocated by the government to institutions are not designed to meet specific kinds or levels of institutional costs, but are intended to pay for the delivery of teaching and research-related services linked to approved institutional three-year 'rolling' plans.

In short, the new framework is a goal-orientated and performance-related distributive mechanism, which explicitly links the allocation of funds to academic activity and output, and in particular to the delivery of teaching-related and research-related services which contribute to the social and economic development of the country.

The new funding framework and the associated planning processes are in line with the government's Medium Term Expenditure Framework (MTEF), which underpins the national budget process. The MTEF involves the development of three-year rolling budgets, which are adjusted, updated and revised annually based on a review of factors such as the growth of departmental budgets in the context of revenue generation and affordability, the relationship between departmental policy priorities and the government's strategic objectives, expenditure patterns, inflation adjustments and sector specific issues. In the case of higher education, examples of such sector specific issues are enrolment and output patterns and trends, cost pressures and efficiency measures, in particular, in relation to personnel and infrastructure and special policy initiatives such as the current institutional restructuring process.

The Minister of Education releases an Annual Statement on Higher Education Funding for each MTEF period. This contains the review of key trends and indicates what changes, if any, are to be made in determining the allocation of funds to the different categories and sub-categories of the funding framework.

The New Funding Framework

The various mechanisms in the new funding framework come into operation only after government has determined (a) the total of public funds that should be spent in a given year on higher education; and (b) what services should be delivered by the higher education system. Higher education institutions play no role in the determination of the overall amount of funds for higher education. This is primarily an outcome of the government's budgeting process. However, institutions are required to submit to the Ministry three-year rolling plans indicating their planned inputs and outputs.

Main Elements
In terms of the new funding framework, higher education institutions receive (i) block funds, which are undesignated amounts made available to each institution; and (ii) earmarked funds, which are designated for specific purposes.

Block funds consist of:

- Research funds generated by approved outputs;
- Teaching funds generated by (a) planned full-time equivalent (FTE) student enrolments and (b) by approved teaching outputs; and
- Institutional factor funds.

Institutions know in advance the total amount of block funds that have been allocated to them. However, because of National Treasury regulations these funds are disbursed over the first eight months of the fiscal year as follows: a three-month allocation paid in April (the first month of the fiscal year); another three-month allocation in May; from June to October, monthly allocations; and the remainder of the allocation paid during November. The process is further complicated by the fact that the fiscal (April–March) and academic (January–December) years do not coincide. This forces some institutions to obtain bridging finance from commercial banks (and hence at some cost) for the first three months of the academic year.

The details of the various elements of the new funding framework are outlined below.

Separation of Teaching and Research Funds
The new block-funding formula includes requirements that (a) teaching and research funds are separated; and (b) teaching funds must be standard across institutions. The two central features of the new funding framework are therefore as follows:

- **Teaching funds**: Teaching funds are based on teaching inputs and teaching outputs. In allocating teaching funds to institutions, the model treats all institutions equally.
- **Research funds**: Research funds are based on research outputs and on earmarked funds for specific developmental purposes. The new framework makes no separate provision for a 'blind' research element or so-called research input funds, that is, a subsidy amount which institutions will receive regardless of whether or not they engage in research activities. Research training is regarded as a sub-component of teaching and provision for research training has therefore been made within teaching funds.

Block Grant Funding
Block grant funding has three components: research output funds; teaching funds;

and institutional factor funds. Furthermore, teaching funds are further broken down into teaching funds based on outputs, and teaching funds based on inputs.

Research Output Funds
With the new funding arrangements the total funding available for research is divided into earmarked and block grant funds. The earmarked component is used for such activities as capacity development, collaborative research projects and research student scholarships. Between 10 and 15% of the total for research is allocated each year to the earmarked component.

The block grant component is based on the research outputs of institutions. The total allocated in the form of block grants for research outputs is based on publication units, on research master's graduates and on doctoral graduates. Because of delays in obtaining data from institutions, research output funds for year n will be based on the publication units and research master's and doctoral graduates of year n-2. The weightings employed are: publication units 1, research master's graduates 1, and doctoral graduates 3. These weightings are intended to emphasise the need for the doctoral graduate total to increase, and to give added incentives to institutions to achieve these goals.

Teaching Funds: Outputs
The National Plan for Higher Education emphasised that student graduation rates must improve from historically low levels. Incentives designed to encourage institutions to increase their graduation rates have thus been included in the new funding framework. These incentives take the form of a teaching output subsidy built into the framework.

Teaching output funds for year n are based on the total of non-research graduates produced in year n-2. Research master's and doctoral graduates are not included in the teaching output subsidy because they are major components of the research output subsidies discussed earlier. Teaching outputs are weighted according to the ratios shown in Table 8.2.

Table 8.2: Weighting Factors for Teaching Outputs

1st certificates and diplomas of 2 years or less	0.5
1st diplomas and bachelors' degrees: 3 years	1.0
Professional 1st bachelor's degree: 4 years and more	1.5
Postgraduate and postdiploma diplomas	0.5
Postgraduate bachelors' degrees	1.0
Honours degrees/higher diplomas	0.5
Non-research masters' degrees	0.5

Teaching Funds: Inputs

Inputs for teaching funds for year n are based on two main elements:

- A funding grid based on aggregations of educational subject matter categories and course levels.
- Full-time equivalent (FTE) student places and/or planned FTE student enrolments.

Funding Grid

This funding grid for teaching inputs is set out in Table 8.3.

On the basis of cost studies, a fixed set of ratios should hold between the average costs per FTE students in the various funding groups. These are shown in Table 8.4.

Table 8.3: Funding Grid for Teaching Inputs

FUNDING GROUP	DISCIPLINES
1	education, law, librarianship, psychology, social services/public administration
2	business/commerce, communication, computer science, languages, philosophy/religion, social sciences
3	architecture/planning, engineering, home economics, industrial arts, mathematical sciences, physical education
4	agriculture, fine and performing arts, health sciences, life and physical sciences

Table 8.4: Ratios between Funding Groups in Funding Grid

Funding group 1	1.0
Funding group 2	1.5
Funding group 3	2.5
Funding group 4	3.5

FTE enrolments in the funding grid are weighted according to course level as well. These are shown in Table 8.5 and they take account of (a) the high priority the National Plan gave to the need to increase postgraduate student enrolments, especially at master's and doctoral levels; and (b) an argument that, given the ways in which FTE enrolments are calculated, weighted totals of FTE enrolled postgraduate students constitute better strategic incentives to institutions than the unweighted ones.

Table 8.5: Weightings of FTE Enrolments within the Funding Grid

Undergraduate	1.0
Honours and equivalent	2.0
Master's and equivalent	3.0
Doctors and equivalent	4.0

Table 8.6 sets out the full funding grid which is to be used to generate teaching input subsidies for universities and technikons.

Table 8.6: Weightings within the Funding Grid

FUNDING GROUP	UNDERGRADUATE & EQUIVALENT	HONOURS (4TH YEAR) & EQUIVALENT	MASTER'S & EQUIVALENT	DOCTORAL & EQUIVALENT
1	1.0	2.0	3.0	4.0
2	1.5	3.0	4.5	6.0
3	2.5	5.0	7.5	10.0
4	3.5	7.0	10.5	14.0

FTE Student Places and Planned FTE Student Enrolments

The funding formula had to make provision for both FTE student places and planned FTE student enrolments as the primary input values for the new block formula. It refers in particular to planned FTE student places because of the necessary link between funding and planning in the new funding framework. This link implies that teaching funds cannot be paid to institutions solely on the basis of historical student enrolments. These inputs have to be moderated by approved institutional three-year rolling plans.

A key issue for the new block formula is that of finding a proxy for FTE student places. Given that most institutions lack the capacity to provide acceptable forward projections of their student enrolments, it was decided that enrolled data for year n-2 would have to be used as proxies for student places in determining the input teaching subsidies of institutions. Provisions are made for later adjustments to these figures on the basis of actual enrolments and other necessary modifications.

The new framework does not include regular inflation-based adjustments of the rand values of cost unit. Since the proposed model contains no cost units, inflation is dealt with in terms of government's annual budgetary allocation for higher education, the assignment of planned FTE-enrolled students to institutions and the calculation of prices per cell in the funding grid.

Institutional Factors

The original formulas for higher education institutions made provision for institutional set-up subsidies. These are amounts which higher education institutions received to compensate them for basic running costs, irrespective of the size of their student body. These set-up subsidies had an important effect on the block funds of higher education institutions. They increased the unit subsidies of smaller institutions (their subsidy payments per enrolled student) and dampened those of larger institutions.

In the new funding framework, the set-up subsidies are replaced by institutional adjustment factors, which take account of three sets of institutional circumstances: (a) the proportion of contact (or on-campus) FTE student enrolments from previously disadvantaged groups; (b) the approved size of each institution in terms of FTE student enrolments; and (c) the approved shape of the institution in terms of FTE student enrolments in the teaching input funding grid. In each case the FTE student enrolment total is an unweighted one; that is, one which does not take account of the weightings by level built into the new funding grid. A further important point to note is that these institutional adjustment factors are applied only to the teaching input funds of each institution. They are not applied to teaching and research output funds.

Students from disadvantaged or poor backgrounds are, for this purpose, deemed to be African and Coloured students who are South African citizens and who are enrolled in contact education programmes. It was recognised that these population group categories are too broad to serve as long-term indicators of disadvantage and some new factor would have to be developed as a proxy for 'disadvantage'.

Earmarked Funding

Earmarked funds budgets are used primarily for the following purposes:

- The national student financial aid scheme;
- Research development;
- Foundation programmes and teaching development;
- Interest and redemption payments on approved loans;
- Approved capital projects, as and when funds for these purposes are made available as part of the national higher education budget; and
- Any other purpose either identified in the current national higher education plan; or
- Determined by the Minister from time to time.

Foundation Programmes

The new funding framework also provides funds for 'foundation' programmes to enable students from educationally disadvantaged backgrounds to adjust to the demands of higher education. Foundation students are funded as additional FTE student places awarded to an institution. This means that such students generate more funds for the institution than it would otherwise receive.

It was decided that foundation programmes would be funded in this way for at least the first five years of the operation of the new funding framework.

A total equivalent to about 15% of the expected FTE enrolment of first-time entering undergraduate students in contact education programmes were to be assigned each year to foundation programmes. This proportion would be increased in the future if assessments of institutional foundation programmes suggested that appropriate provision should be made for larger totals of first-time entering undergraduate students. These FTE foundation students would be funded at the price applicable to funding Group 1 in the teaching input grid. The foundation funds generated will be earmarked, in the sense that they will have to be used for foundation purposes only. These funds would be allocated to institutions by the Ministry when assessments are being made of their three-year rolling plans.

Assessing the Funding Framework

The new funding framework developed for higher education in South Africa has a number of important implications for equity and efficiency (Pillay 2006).

Predictability

Implementing a formula-driven approach ensures a level of predictability, particularly with regard to 'certainty of revenue'. Institutions are aware of the factors driving the formula and will know within certain parameters, the magnitude of resources that will flow to them over a certain period. Such certainty undoubtedly enhances institutional planning.

Recognition of a Hard Budget Constraint

The new funding framework is driven by the availability of public resources for higher education rather than by the costs of provision. The various mechanisms in the framework come into operation only after government has determined (a) the total of public funds that should be spent in a given year on higher education and (b) what services should be delivered by the higher education system.

Promoting Institutional Autonomy and Equity
By using a mixture of block and earmarked grants the formula achieves both these goals to a certain degree. Block grants confer a degree of freedom of use of funds by institutions while earmarked grants by definition are directed towards the attainment of specific goals such as equity – for example, in research development, and through foundation programmes for the historically disadvantaged.

Efficiency Incentives
The formula-driven framework provides for this in a number of ways:

- The block grant component rewards efficiency of outcomes in research. Grants are based on the output of publications and of master's and doctoral graduates. Research grants are moreover not based on a predetermined monetary amount but against benchmarks based on academic capacity.
- Inadequate research performance by the system as a whole will result in surpluses of funds allocated for research. These funds provide a further incentive to stimulate output in that they are distributed on a pro-rata (output) determined basis.
- The formula is designed in such a way that it rewards the output of certain categories of graduates more than it does others (for example, professional bachelors' degrees as against other bachelors' degrees). Such a funding mechanism can enable the government to stimulate the development of skills that are in short supply. As with research, teaching output funds are determined not by pre-set amounts of funding but developed through a set of benchmark graduation rates, based on the National Plan for Higher Education. In line with this, the formula promotes differential funding in line with the country's human development needs (for example, Agriculture and Health Sciences as against Librarianship and Psychology).
- Through institutional funding, the framework promotes economies of scale and thus lower institutional unit costs.

Equity
Equity is enhanced in a number of ways:

- Earmarked funding, inter alia for capacity building, research development and foundation programmes for the historically disadvantaged;

- Institutional factoring for students from historically advantaged backgrounds (African and Coloured students); and
- Institutional factoring for small institutions, especially those in rural areas.

However, Le Roux and Breier (2007) argue that the funding formula is likely to have significantly different outcomes from those intended by the government. They argue that the funding formula needs to be adjusted, in order to allocate more funds to institutions which accommodate students from socio-economically disadvantaged backgrounds.

The main argument developed by Le Roux and Breier is that the new funding framework has the unintended consequence of discouraging higher education insitutions from accommodating students who might have the ability to succeed but are badly prepared for university and/or cannot afford full-time study. The new funding framework places a strong emphasis on improving success rates for diplomas and degrees. Institutions are effectively penalised if they admit students who cannot complete the degree or diploma in the required time, either because of an inability to pass all the courses or because they may wish to study part time in order to also earn an income. Moreover, the new funding framework further cuts back significantly on the rewards for a course-work master's degree compared to a master's degree based on a full thesis, which again discourages institutions from accepting students from disadvantaged backgrounds for a master's programme. In this view, the new funding framework also penalises universities if students take longer than the standard period to complete their degrees or diplomas, which means that it strongly discourages universities from accommodating part-time students.

In Le Roux and Breier's view, a situation has arisen in which universities are

> rewarded for selecting students who are well prepared for universities and punished if they are not. This builds in a strong bias against accommodating students from disadvantaged backgrounds and puts higher education institutions that traditionally focused on these students at a tremendous disadvantage, particularly at a time when most historically white institutions have managed to attract many of the better qualified black students from the traditionally black institutions. Ironically, the very low African and Coloured participation rates are far more likely to improve if the present race-based elements of the formula are scrapped and replaced by a number of measures aimed at increasing the throughput of students from socio-economically disadvantaged backgrounds. (Le Roux & Breier 2007)

Le Roux and Breier suggest that the reasons for not effectively applying the new formula are obvious. All of the traditionally black higher education institutions that have remained separate institutions will do significantly worse than the historically white institutions. As far as teaching output is concerned, the black universities have, since apartheid legislation disappeared, lost many of their stronger students to the historically white institutions, and they are taking in students primarily from the old 'Bantu education' system, who are far less prepared for university, than students from the former white schools as well as private schools. For these reasons as well as the poor quality of staff at many historically black institutions, these institutions are unlikely to ever come close to meeting the output demands of the formula.

Le Roux and Breier note that the new funding framework brought in a scale factor, rewarding universities which had a large number of black students or increased their contingent of black students, changed the funding given to different disciplines, restricted the expansion of distance students to a low rate, and gave a much higher reward to research publication, full theses master and PhDs, simultaneously reducing the subsidy for course-work masters significantly. However, in their view, some of these changes have been to the detriment of students from poor and educationally disadvantaged backgrounds and also part-time students. They also suggest that the most fundamental weakness of the new funding framework is that like the NSFAS it uses race as a proxy for disadvantage, rather than developing a direct measure of socio-economic need.

Trends in Higher Education Financing

As pointed out by Wangenge-Ouma and Cloete (2008), the funding of higher education is critical for the attainment of the key policy goals identified by the National Plan on Higher Education. These policy goals are:

1. Producing the graduates needed for social and economic development;
2. Achieving equity in the higher education system;
3. Achieving diversity in the higher education system;
4. Sustaining and promoting research; and
5. Restructuring the institutional landscape of the higher education system (NPHE 2001).

The most important source of funding for South Africa's public universities is the state. However, the degree of dependence varies. Some universities receive slightly more than 30% of their total income from government while others receive 65% of their total revenues from this source (Wangenge-Ouma & Cloete 2008).

A recent study at Rhodes University (Duncan 2009) has shown that the proportion of institutional revenue received from the state (the so-called first stream of income) has declined, on average, from 62% in 1986 to 41% in 2007. 'Second stream' income (tuition fees) increased from 15% to 32% and 'third stream' income (research, consultancies, investment income, etc), increased from 23% to 27% during the same period.

However, in both real and student per capita terms, funding has declined. A recent analysis shows that between 2000 and 2004, government funding of higher education declined by 3.1% in real terms (DoE 2007b). From 1995 to 1999, total state spending per FTE student in higher education increased annually by ZAR 352 in real terms (in 2000 rand) but declined annually by ZAR 515 between 2000 and 2004. This decreasing pattern continued in the period to 2009 and is unlikely to be reversed in the light of the MTEF projections to 2012 (Table 8.7).

As a percentage of GDP, state funding of higher education has also declined from a high of 0.82% in 1996 to a low of 0.68% in 2008. As a percentage of the government budget, after peaking at 3.0% in 2000, it has consistently declined reaching 2.4% in 2008.

Table 8.7: Average Annual Increase in State Funding of Higher Education per FTE Student (2000 ZAR)

	1995–1999	2000–2004	2005–2009
Higher education (formula funding)	173	-655	-142
Higher education (total)	352	-515	-5

Importantly, discretionary funds per FTE student (i.e. as per the funding formula) have declined more rapidly than earmarked funding, that is, subsidies not directly contributing to operational costs such as NSFAS (Wangenge-Ouma & Cloete 2008). For instance, whereas, the state's total funding for higher education per FTE student increased by an annual average of ZAR 352 (in 2000) between 1995 and 1999, discretionary funding in the same period increased by an annual average of ZAR 173. In the 2000–2004 period, discretionary funding per FTE equivalent declined by an annual average of ZAR 655 in real terms compared to an decrease of ZAR 515 for total state expenditure on higher education per FTE student.

Expenditure on higher education comprises only about 2.5% of total government expenditure. Table 8.8 shows that for 2008/2009 and 2009/2010 this proportion stood at 2.4% and is projected to rise only marginally to 2.5% for the next two years of the current Medium Term Expenditure Framework.

Table 8.8: Higher Education Expenditure as a Proportion of Total Government Expenditure

BUDGET ITEM	2008/2009	2009/2010	2010/2011	2011/2012
Higher education (ZAR, billion)	15.5	17.1	19.5	21.6
Total (ZAR, billion)	633	739	792	849
Higher education total %	2.4	2.4	2.5	2.5

Source: National Treasury 2009

In the higher education budget, the two main items are transfer payments to the higher education institutions and the NSFAS. Table 8.9 shows that the transfer payments to NSFAS ranged between 8% and 10% for the fiscal period 2005/2006–2007/2008, but is expected to stabilise around 12.0–12.5% for the next four fiscal years.

The transfer payments to the higher education institutions increased at an average annual rate of 12.3% between 2005/2006 and 2008/2009 (this was significantly above the average inflation for this period, and thus represents a 'real' increase of around between 3-5%). This expenditure is projected to continue to increase at an average rate of 11.2% over the medium term, again significantly above the projected inflation rate for the period (6–7%) (computed from National Treasury 2009 figures).

Table 8.9: Higher Education Budget: 2005/2006–2011/2012 (ZAR, billion)

	2005/2006	2006/2007	2007/2008	2008/2009	2009/2010	2010/2011	2011/2012
NSFAS	0.864	0.926	1.333	1.702	2.145	2.333	2.710
HEIs	9.616	10.895	11.864	13.737	15.229	17.449	18.935
Total HE	10.633	11.940	13.304	15.537	17.374	19.782	21.645
NSFAS/HE (%)	8.1	7.8	10.0	12.4	12.3	11.8	12.5

Note: Higher education institution (HEI) allocation here excludes capital allocations.   Source: National Treasury 2009

Transfers to NSFAS are expected to rise at an average annual rate of 16.6% over the medium term 'mainly due to additional allocations for specific bursaries such as the initial supply of teachers bursary and for students at FET colleges' (National Treasury 2009).

The National Student Financial Aid Scheme (NSFAS)

As stated earlier, by developing country standards, South Africa has developed an effective loan scheme for higher education students.

The parameters of NSFAS assistance in 2007/2008 are summarised as follows:

- Financial assistance is only made available to those who are both financially needy and academically competent;
- The maximum award is ZAR 35 000 and the minimum award is ZAR 2 000;
- Up to 40% of the award may be converted into a bursary where the extent of this conversion is determined by the student's academic results;
- Interest on loans accrues as at 01 April 2007 at 7.0%;
- Interest on the component of the award which is converted into a bursary will be written off;
- A credit balance on a student's fee account will be returned to NSFAS by 31 March 2007 and will be regarded as the student's first loan repayment;
- The loans are income-contingent, with loan repayments beginning at 3% of salary at ZAR 30 000;
- Funds are recovered from debtors at the remuneration source; and
- NSFAS awards can be packaged with other awards as long as the total amount granted does not exceed the student's full cost of study for the year; and
- an own contribution of some kind must form part of the total package.

Table 8.10 shows the trends in awards and recovered funds between 2002 and 2007.

Table 8.10: NSFAS – Trends in Awards and Recovered Funds

	2002	2003	2004	2005	2006	2007
Number of awards	99 949	112 264	113 693	122 696	124 730	140 901
Number of students assisted	86 147	96 552	98 813	106 852	107 586	113 616
Recovered funds (ZAR, million)	155	208	245	329	392	479

Source: NSFAS 2008

Notwithstanding the impressive data presented above, NSFAS does continue to present a number of challenges to policy-makers and implementers, the most important of which are the following:

- Providing adequate funding to all financially needy students who qualify to enter the higher education system, so that they are able to meet the 'full costs of study';

- Financial allocation to higher education institutions is based on race (as a proxy for need) rather than on direct measures of socio-economic need; and
- Further improvement is needed in the loan recovery rates.

Conclusion

South Africa has reached a relatively high level of sophistication in the development of its higher education funding mechanisms particularly with the close link between its planning and budgeting processes, and its implementation of a relatively simple funding formula. The system has also benefited from always having had a fee-paying system so no new cost-sharing mechanisms had to be developed. Finally, there is also a strong systemic thrust towards greater equity exemplified in both the funding formula and the student loan scheme.

However, the South African system does face enormous challenges with respect to quality and efficiency. The apartheid legacy of differentiated systemic quality and efficiency continues except that the main determinant is no longer race but socio-economic status and region.

With respect to the new funding framework, more recently, serious questions are being raised about the adequacy of the instruments within the formula to promote inter-institutional equity. In fact, it is being argued that the funding mechanism currently in place may be serving to entrench and even accentuate inequalities between previously advantaged and previously disadvantaged institutions. In practice, this is occurring for at least three reasons at the current time:

1. The formula rewards research outputs but most disadvantaged institutions do not have research capacity and in the light of their heavy teaching burdens are not likely to develop this capacity in the short to medium terms.
2. Capital expenditure, while increasing substantially in the past few years, falls far short of requirements in the light of increased access.
3. Earmarked grants provided for in the funding formula, may be inadequate to 'level the playing field' and thus address the equity challenge more effectively.

Chapter 9
TANZANIA

Johnson M Ishengoma

Introduction

For the first seven years after independence in 1961, Tanzania retained the free market economy it inherited from colonial rule. However, a fundamental and radical shift in Tanzania's development, economic and educational policies, including higher education financing policies, was made in 1967 through the Arusha Declaration, a political blueprint that intended to make Tanzania a socialist and an economically self-reliant state. According to one of the principles of the Arusha Declaration, access to scarce resources such as education was to be regulated and controlled by the government to ensure equal participation by all socio-economic groups (TANU 1967).

The implementation of the Arusha Declaration led to the nationalisation and control of the major means of production by the state, including the abolition of school fees in primary and secondary education and tuition fees in higher education. Until 1967, students in higher education institutions paid tuition fees but poorer students were assisted through government bursaries. Local government authorities, which were considered to be in the best position to make judgements on a person's ability to pay, largely determined a student's eligibility for a bursary (Ishengoma 2004: 15). These bursaries – which were actually disguised income-contingent loans – were recovered through deductions from monthly salaries upon graduation and subsequent guaranteed employment in the civil service and other public sectors. Galabawa (1991: 54) also points out that a student revolving loan scheme used to operate in Tanzania in the 1960s and 1970s, but collapsed due to the lack of supervision and commitment by stakeholders. This interest-free loan scheme recovered loans through monthly deductions from salaries of graduates for a period of 18 months after obtaining government-guaranteed employment.

When Tanzania adopted socialism in 1967, bursaries were granted to all students admitted at the then University College of Dar es Salaam on signing of a bond to work for the government for the period of at least five years. Failure to honour this bond, would compel the recipient to refund the government all the costs incurred at university (Ishengoma op. cit.: 16). In 1974, the government abolished the bursary system and took over the responsibility of paying all the costs for higher education. The rationale for this change was to make higher education accessible to all socio-economic groups in order to achieve one of the major goals of the Arusha Declaration of building an egalitarian society. The government continued to finance all the costs of public higher education until 1992/1993 when it reinstituted cost-sharing in higher education policy.

Structure of Higher Education

According to the National Higher Education Policy (1999), higher education encompasses all courses of study leading to the award of a first degree, advanced diploma, postgraduate or any higher level degree. In the context of this definition, the system of higher education in Tanzania is dual, composed of: (i) universities and university colleges; and (ii) non-university higher education institutions (institutes and colleges) offering mainly three-year advanced diplomas in professional fields, such as Accountancy, Engineering, Social Welfare, Materials Management, Community Development, Business Administration and related fields of study. Very few institutes offer first degrees. The duration for the first degree is between three and five years depending on the field of study, and 18 months for a master's degree in the social sciences and humanities, while the minimum duration for a doctorate is three years.

Higher Education Agencies and Regulatory Bodies
Public universities and university colleges fall under the jurisdiction of the Ministry of Higher Education, Science and Technology (MHEST), while public non-university institutions are regulated by respective government ministries. The Directorate of Higher Education in the Ministry coordinates all the activities of public universities.

There are two quality control and assurance organs in the higher education sector. The Tanzania Commission for Universities (TCU) established by the

Universities Act No. 7 of 2005 to replace the Higher Education Accreditation Council (HEAC), sets, monitors and ensures the standards, appropriateness, relevance and adequacy of all inputs, processes and outputs of university education in Tanzania. The National Council for Technical Education (NACTE) established by the Act of Parliament No. 9 of 1997 registers, accredits both public and private non-university higher education institutions. The Higher Education Students' Loans Board (HESLB) established by Parliamentary Act No. 2005 disburses loans to qualified students admitted in both public and private higher education institutions. Table 9.1 shows a list of public and private universities and universities colleges and their locations, while Table 9.2 provides a list of non-university higher education institutions.

Both tables demonstrate the predominance of Dar es Salaam city as the major location of 19 or 42% of the public and private higher educations in Tanzania raising some critical questions about the equitable distribution of these institutions and their accessibility to the majority of Tanzanians especially those in rural areas.

Table 9.1: Tanzania Public and Private University Colleges Registered by the Tanzania Commission for Universities, July 2007

PUBLIC UNIVERSITIES/UNIVERSITY COLLEGES/INSTITUTES		
INSTITUTION	LOCATION	TOTAL ENROLMENT (2006/2007)
University of Dar es Salaam (Main campus)	Dar es Salaam City	14 363
Muhimbili University College of Health Sciences	Dar es Salaam City	1 459
University College of Lands & Architectural Studies	Dar es Salaam City	1 129
Dar es Salaam University College of Education	Dar es Salaam City	2 032
Institute of Journalism & Mass Communication	Dar es Salaam City	n/a
Open University of Tanzania	Dar es Salaam City	12 613
Mkwawa University College of Education	Iringa Town	870
Sokoine University of Agriculture	Morogoro Town	2 439
Moshi University of Cooperative and Business Studies	Moshi Town	850
Mzumbe University	Morogoro Town	3 116
University of Dodoma (New)	Dodoma	n/a
State University of Zanzibar	Zanzibar	376
Total enrolment in public universities		39 242

PRIVATE UNIVERSITIES AND UNIVERSITY COLLEGES		
INSTITITUTION	LOCATION	TOTAL ENROLMENT (2006/2007)
St. Augustine University of Tanzania	Mwanzay	3 099
Bugando University College of Health Sciences	Mwanza	151
Ruaha University College	Iringa	499
Mwenge University College of Education	Moshi	n/a
Tumaini University-Dar es Salaam University College	Dar es Salaam	2 157
Tumaini University-Makumira University College	Arusha	633
Tumaini University-Iringa University College	Iringa	2 123
Tumaini University-Kilimanjaro Christian Medical College	Moshi	374
Hubert Kairuki Memorial University	Dar es Salaam	478
International Medical & Technological University	Dar es Salaam	531
Zanzibar University	Zanzibar	n/a
Aga Khan University	Dar es Salaam	109
Mount Meru University	Arusha	452
University of Arusha	Arusha	658
Muslim University of Morogoro	Morogoro	367
Teofilo Kisanji University	Mbeya	313
College of Education Zanzibar-International University of Khartoum	Zanzibar	466
Tumaini University-Bishop Stephano Moshi Memorial University College	Moshi	n/a
Tumaini University-Sebastian Kolowa University College (New)	Lushoto	n/a
St. John's University	Dodoma	n/a
Total Enrolment in Private Universities		12 410
Grand Total		51 652

Source: Adapted from: United Republic of Tanzania (URT) 2006a

Table 9. 2: Tanzania Non-University Higher Education Institutions Recognised by the National Council for Technical Education (NACTE), 2006/2007

PUBLIC NON-UNIVERSITY INSTITUTIONS		
INSTITUTION	LOCATION	TOTAL ENROLMENT
Dar es Salaam Institute of Technology	Dar es Salaam	674
Mbeya Institute of Technology	Mbeya	149
Arusha Technical College	Arusha	405
Mwalimu Nyerere Academy of Social Sciences	Dar es Salaam	120
Mweka Institute of Wildlife Management	Moshi	65
Institute of Social Work	Dar es Salaam	989
Community Development Training Institute	Arusha	715
Institute of Accountancy Arusha	Arusha	2 636
Institute of Finance Management	Dar es Salaam	4 101
National Institute of Transport	Dar es Salaam	394
Tanzania Institute of Accountancy	Dar es Salaam	2 134
College of Business Education	Dar es Salaam & Dodoma	2 152
Institute of Rural Development Planning	Dodoma	1 149
Dar es Salaam Maritime Institute	Dar es Salaam)	167
Total Enrolment (2006/2007)		15 445
PRIVATE NON-UNIVERSITY INSTITUTIONS		
INSTITUTION	LOCATION	TOTAL ENROLMENT
St. Joseph College of Engineering	Dar es Salaam	645
Masoka Institute of Management & Administration	Moshi	282
Total Enrollment		927
Grand Total		**16 372**

Source: Adapted from: United Republic of Tanzania (URT) 2006a pp 57

Participation Rates in Higher Education

The most recent available data cited in the URT (2005: 6) revealed that the university-age participation rate is 0.27% compared to 1.47% for Kenya and 1.33% for Uganda. The low participation rate in higher education in Tanzania can be attributed to the low participation rate in secondary education, which in turn is attributed to low budgetary allocation to secondary education compared to primary education.

Available research evidence shows that Tanzania has an abysmally low participation rate of 6% of the age cohort in secondary education, compared to Kenya and Uganda which have participation rates of 16% and 31% respectively (Ishengoma 2004: 89).

Table 9.3 presents data on the rates of application and admission for the University of Dar es Salaam from 2001/2002–2005/2006 as a proxy measure for trends in participation rates in Tanzania public higher education. Data in Table 9.3 show that the admission rate at the University of Dar es Salaam declined from 37.8% in 2000/2001 to 30.5% in the 2005/2006 academic year, apparently due to high admission criteria/cut-off points set by the University, particularly for government-sponsored students through the Higher Education Students' Loans Board (HESLB). A second explanation for declining admission rates is that new enrolments had to be kept in balance with the University's inadequate accommodation and teaching-learning facilities, in order to maintain academic quality. Despite the capacity expansion which has been undertaken by the University in recent years through internally generated funds and external investors, teaching-learning facilities at the University of Dar es Salaam – as in other public universities – are still inadequate to enable the institution to admit all qualified students.

Table 9.3: Application vs. Admission Rates at the University of Dar es Salaam, 2000/2001–2005/2006

YEAR	APPLIED	ADMITTED	ADMISSION RATE (%)
2000/2001	5 325	2 015	37.8
2001/2002	5 276	2 776	52.6
2002/2003	6 171	3 423	55.4
2003/2004	6 036	3 582	59.3
2004/2005	8 616	4 785	55.5
2005/2006	15 589	4 757	30.5

Source: University of Dar es Salaam (UDSM) 2004 & 2006 pp 7 & 8

Education Financing

Financing of the education sector in general is to a large extent the responsibility of the government with some limited shared responsibility between the government, parents, institutions, communities and donors at all levels of education. However, the financing of higher education in Tanzania, according to policy on cost sharing in higher education introduced in the 1992/1993 academic year, is currently *supposed* to be a shared responsibility between the government and beneficiaries, i.e. parents, students and other stakeholders.

Table 9.4 shows the education sector budget allocation as percentage of total government budget, and as a percentage of GDP.

Table 9.4: Education Sector Budget Allocation as Percentage of Total Government Budget and GDP, 1999/2000–2006/2007 (TZS, million)

YEAR	TOTAL BUDGET	EDUCATION SECTOR BUDGET	GDP (CURRENT PRICES)	EDUCATION SECTOR AS % TOTAL BUDGET	EDUCATION SECTOR AS % GDP
1999/2000	1 168 778	138 583	6 706 381	11.9	2.1
2000/2001	1 307 214	218 051	7 624 616	16.7	2.9
2001/2002	1 462 767	323 864	8 699 887	22.1	3.7
2002/2003	2 106 291	396 780	9 816 319	18.8	4.0
2003/2004	2 607 205	487 729	11 331 638	18.7	4.3
2004/2005	3 347 538	504 745	13 063 317	15.1	3.9
2005/2006	4 176 050	669 537	n/a	16.0	n/a
2006/2007*	4 850 588	958 819	n/a	19.8	n/a

*=Estimates
Source: Adapted from URT 2006b pp 89

The data in Table 9.4 reflect an increasing trend in the education sector budget as a proportion of the total budget from almost 12% in 1999/2000 to 20% in 2006/2007. In comparative international terms, education expenditure at around 4% of GDP is close to the average for African countries. However, the picture is less promising with respect to capital expenditure. The government allocation for capital/development expenditure increased consistently from TZS 20 billion in 2000/2001 to TZS 92 billion in 2004/2005 before falling dramatically to TZS 35 billion in 2005/2006.

Table 9.5 shows the trend in the budgetary allocation to education by sub-sectors. The table shows:

- That the allocation to primary education declined from around 73% in 1998/1999 to 65% in 2006/2007;
- During the same period the allocation to secondary education increased from 7% to 12.5%;
- The allocation to teacher education fell from 2.4% to 1.1%; and
- The share going to higher education increased from 18% to 22%.

The budgetary allocation to higher education is therefore high as a proportion of the education budget. However, this allocation still appears to be inadequate given the critical role of higher education in the economic and technological development of the country. This explains why all public higher education institutions are currently involved in various revenue diversification activities to generate the much needed extra income to finance some of the operations of these institutions. However, some of these activities have been counterproductive to quality improvement in higher education.

Table 9.5: *Government Budgetary Allocation by Education Sub Sector, 1998/1999–2006/2007 (TZS, million)*

YEAR	TOTAL EDUCATION SECTOR	EDUCATION SUB-SECTOR							
		PRIMARY		SECONDARY		TEACHER EDUCATION		TERTIARY & HIGHER	
		TOTAL	% SHARE	TOTAL	% SHARE	TOTAL	% SHARE	TOTAL	% SHARE
1998/1999	107 457	78 000	72.6	7 857	7.3	2 600	2.4	19 000	17.7
1999/2000	138 583	92 845	67.0	10 492	7.6	2 752	2.0	32 494	23.4
2000/2001	218 051	144 658	66.3	21 453	9.8	5 261	2.4	46 679	21.4
2001/2002	323 864	236 618	73.1	24 359	7.5	5 872	1.8	57 015	17.6
2002/2003	396 780	289 718	73.0	29 876	7.5	6 646	1.7	70 540	17.8
2003/2004	487 729	361 425	74.1	32 464	6.7	7 700	1.6	86 140	17.7
2004/2005	504 745	322 196	63.8	92 045	18.2	6 189	1.2	84 315	16.7
2005/2006	669 537	418 455	62.5	104 483	15.6	8 540	1.3	138 059	20.6
2006/2007	958 819	618 534	64.5	119 987	12.5	10 439	1.1	209 859	21.9

Source: URT 2006c pp 90–91

Analysis of the higher education budget shows that recurrent expenditure increased from TZS 111 billion in 2005/2006 to TZS 167 billion in 2006/2007. Furthermore, there was a declining trend in the percentage share of student direct costs (SDC) and students' loans from 1999/2000–2002/2003 from 12% to 9% and from 17% to 14% respectively, compared to an increasing trend in personal emoluments (PE) which increased from 29% to 41% in the same period.

The declining trend in allocations to the students' loan item might explain why the HESLB is currently facing a financial crisis in meeting student demand for loans.

Current Higher Education Funding Model

Financing of public higher education in Tanzania is a shared responsibility between the government, students and their parents, communities and external donors.

In 1998, the government Task Force on Financial Sustainability of Higher Education identified major sources for financing public higher education and consequently developed a financing formula which, to some extent, is currently being applied. The distribution of contribution to higher education financing according to source was suggested as follows:

- Central government, local governments and communities   82%
- Students, parents and households   12%
- Higher education institutions plus donors   4%
- Other sources plus higher education institution staff   2%
  (URT 1998: xvii)

The Task Force also proposed that government should be responsible for most of capital development expenses, recurrent and other administrative expenses, and personnel emoluments; parents and students. Institutional staff should generate income through consultancy and commissioned research. In addition, the Task Force made specific recommendations on the three *main* sources of funding public higher education, including strategies to attain a financially sustainable public higher system within the context of cost sharing. The details of these recommendations are summarised in Table 9.6.

While to some extent the suggested formula for financing of public higher education is currently being applied in public higher education institutions, in practice, the government – despite its systematic declining subventions to public higher education institutions – remains the major source of financing, specifically financing for capital development and recurrent expenditure.

The government's recurrent funding to the universities is currently based on capitation grants to universities developed from unit costs of different courses and student numbers targeted to be enrolled in a given academic year (URT 2007: 113).

Table 9.6: Recommended Main Sources of Funding Public Higher Education in Tanzania

MAIN SOURCE	FINANCING STRATEGIES
A. Central and local government	
	1. Government direct subventions to higher education institutions
	2. Educational levies
	3. Government grants administered by designated bodies
	4. Bi-lateral and multi-lateral agreements
	5. Tax relief on imported educational materials
	6. Tax relief to third party investors on infrastructure
	7. Borrowing funds from international agencies and banks
	8. Mobilisation of public moral and material support to the sector
	9. Guaranteed core funding
	10. Performance-based investments on campuses
B. Students through cost sharing	
	1. Payment of fees from their earnings
	2. Payment of fees from parents' earnings
	3. Private loan scheme for qualifying students
	4. Public (government) loan scheme
	5. Employers' scholarships for their employees
	6. Extended family contributions
	7. Trust funds and other scholarships
	8. Work study schemes
C. Institutional-generated income through revenue diversification	
	1. Privately sponsored student tuition fees
	2. Faculty contracted research and consultancy and service delivery
	3. Running short courses
	4. Lease operations of buildings, facilities and land
	5. Rationalisation of the mode of offering of various services on campuses
	6. Institution of cost-cutting measures
	7. Donor and alumni donor funds, endowments and gifts
	8. Accruals from fixed deposits
	9. Sale of patents
	10. Sale of prototypes
	11. Sale of books and other academic items

Source: Adapted from URT 1998 pp 102–110

The government is also the major source of financing for tuition-dependent private higher education institutions by providing loans to students enrolled in private universities and university colleges through the HESLB established by the Parliamentary Act No. 8 of 2004, as well as loans to institutions through the Tanzania Education Authority (TEA) established by an Act of Parliament in 2002.

While the share of external donors in financing Tanzania public higher education has been declining over the years, their financial contribution to public higher education is still significant.

The TEA is a public-funded facility which receives annual allocations from the Treasury, and can raise additional financial resources from individuals and foundations. The TEA provides grants and soft loans to both public and private education institutions at all levels from primary to university. By July 2005 it had disbursed grants totaling TZS 10.9 billion and TZS 5.1 billion in soft loans to 34 private education institutions (including private universities and university colleges) and 62 public education institutions (Omari & Mjema 2007: 23).

In summary, it is evident that the government is the major source of funding of public higher education, followed by external donors. Institutional contributions, despite the fact that all public universities are undertaking various income generation activities as a part of a revenue diversification strategy, are still small, specifically for the University of Dar es Salaam, Sokoine University of Agriculture and University College of Lands and Architectural Studies.

Private universities rely heavily on external donors for their core funding and on tuition fees. Private universities also rely on limited government support mainly through the HESLB which provides loans to students enrolled in specific programmes and the Tanzania Education Authority (TEA) which provides grants and soft loans for capital development in private education institutions.

Student Financing Scheme in Tanzania: The Higher Education Students' Loans Board

In implementing cost sharing in higher education policy, the government introduced a student loan scheme in the 1992/1993 academic year initially to cover student accommodation and meal costs. A revolving student loan scheme had existed in Tanzania in the 1960s and 1970s, but collapsed due to lack of supervision (Galabawa 1991: 54).

The student loan scheme which was introduced in 1992/1993 operated as a unit in the Ministry of Science, Technology and Higher Education until July

2004 when the HESLB was established. By July 2003 a total of TZS 26 billion in loans were due for recovery (URT 2005: 16) but until recently, no loan recovery had taken place so far, mainly because the HESLB has no viable loan recovery mechanism and because of the politics surrounding the student loans scheme.

However, serious attempts at loan recovery have been made since 2007, and the HELB has so far recovered more than TZS 900 million (approximately US$ 1 million).

The HESLB was established by Parliamentary Act No. 9 of 2004 and began its operations as an independent government organ in July 2005. The Act which established the HESLB stipulates that eligible and needy Tanzanian students who secure admission in higher learning institutions may seek loans from the Board to meet some of the costs of higher education in line with paragraph 6.2. of the 1999 National Higher Education Policy which requires students to contribute to higher education costs (URT 1999: 16).

The major objectives of the HESLB are: (a) to strengthen the implementation of cost-sharing policy in higher and technical education by providing financial assistance on a loan basis to academically able but needy students unable to meet higher education expenses; and (b) to recover monies lent to students who have graduated and are serving the nation in different sectors within and outside the country (HEAC 2005: 16).

The HESLB is mandated to give loans to needy Tanzanian students pursuing higher education in either public or private universities within Tanzania; students studying abroad under development partnership scholarships; and a limited number of needy Tanzanian students pursuing master's or doctoral degrees in local public or private universities. Students enrolled in both public and private universities may apply for loans to cover tuition fees as charged by institution study not exceeding TZS 1.5 million for humanities and social sciences courses; TZS 4.0 million for Medicine; and TZS 2.0 million for science, engineering and technological courses.

In addition to the above expenses, the HESLB also pays for meals and accommodation (TZS 3 500 per day for 26 weeks); books and stationery (TZS 120 000 per academic year); field research (TZS 100 000 per academic year); special faculty requirements which vary from faculty to faculty; and practical training (TZS 6 000 per day for 42 days per academic year).

Due to serious operational problems, mainly resulting from the Act which established it, the HESLB issued new guidelines and criteria for granting loans with effect from the 2006/2007 academic year on 31 May 2006. Under these revised guidelines, the Board, 'subject to the provisions of the Act, may provide, on loan basis, financial assistance to any eligible student who is *really* [author's emphasis] in need of and has applied for such assistance as required to meet all or any number of the students' welfare costs of higher education.' The critical question is how to determine an eligible student who is *really* in need. As Omari and Mjema (2007: 27) correctly observe, 'the scheme pays for students in both private and public higher education institutions without means testing to target the poor. Thus both the rich and the poor have access to highly subsidised "loans".' The fact that the Board currently grants loans to all students in both public and private higher education institutions grossly contradicts its own over-emphasised principle of giving loans to *needy* students (Ishengoma 2006a: 59).

According to the revised guidelines and criteria, loans are granted to students pursuing *first degrees* or advanced diplomas in national priority courses such as Medical and Physical Sciences; Engineering and Technology; Accountancy; Economics; Commerce; Finance; Law; and Education. Furthermore, under these new guidelines, the Board provides loans of up to 60% of the required tuition fee, 60% of the recommended special faculty requirements and practical field expenses and up to 100% of the recommended research expenses in the following fields of studies only: Medicine (including Human, Veterinary and Dental Surgery), Pharmacy, Engineering, Architecture and Agricultural Sciences.

In addition to the above guidelines, the HESLB imposes a cap on the maximum number of new students to be financed for each respective higher education institution, both private and public. Apart from a general statement contained in the Loans Conditions section in the application form that the loan shall be mandatory due for repayment after *one year* of the completion of studies or within such a period as the HESLB may decide to recall the loan, whichever is earlier, conditions for loan repayments are not stipulated.

As a response to the public universities students' strike in April 2007 opposing 40% contribution to higher education costs, the HESLB in May 2007 issued new guidelines for loans but retained the same loan items for 2007/2008 academic year. According to these new guidelines, the percentage of loan for various approved loan items including tuition fees will differ from one student to another depending on the socio-economic status of student, parents or guardian and the maximum loan amount allowable for each loan item. Loans will now be approved according to means testing results. Depending on the means testing results loans will be approved in the following categories: A (100% full loan), B (80% loan), C (60% loan), D (40%), E (20%), and F (0% or no loan) (HESLB 2007). While these new guidelines appear to promote equity in access to loans and consequently access to higher education, given the Board's current operational problems, the implementation of the above guidelines is likely to be problematic. Already the Board is facing serious operational problems such as issuing loans to non-Tanzanians and ineligible Tanzanian students.

Available data shows that in 1999/2000 a total of 10 292 students received loans. Moreover, the HESLB disbursed a total of TZS 38 billion (US$ 71 million) as student loans from 1999/2000–2004/2005, most of which has not been recovered.

Unit Costs in Higher Education Institutions

In 2003 the Ministry of Science, Technology and Higher Education commissioned a team of experts to conduct a study on unit costs in higher education institutions. Using three methods (full, variable and incremental costing) they derived a series of unit costs for public universities, non-university higher education institutions, and private universities. Table 9.7 provides a summary of these institutional costs. Compared to private universities, student unit costs in public universities are lower. On the full costing method, while the public universities exhibit a wide range, it is difficult to say whether actual costs are higher given the absence of average costs by discipline/course. Variable costs appear to be much lower at both private universities and non-universitiy public institutions.

Table 9.7: Unit Costs by Type of Higher Education Institution (HEI) (TZS)

TYPE OF HEI	FULL COSTING	VARIABLE COSTING	INCREMENTAL COSTING
Public universities	976 000–3.4 m	423 000–1.2 m	274 000–3.5 m
Non-university HEIs (public)	808 000–1.3 m	240 000–248 000	713 000–1.07 m
Private universities	774 000–1.4 m	396 000–723 000	768 000–1.4 m

Note: Incremental or incremental marginal costing involves adding both the variable and fixed incremental or marginal costs.

Financing Higher Education, Access and Equity

This chapter adopts Johnstone's (2003a cited in Ishengoma 2005: 5) two definitions of the concept of equity in higher education. The first construction of equity in higher education is that higher education is accessible to all with interest and academic ability (academic preparedness) to benefit from it. This, according to Johnstone, is a narrow view of higher education equity because in the context of cost sharing in higher education, higher education can be made more or less equitable to the degree that need-based student loans or grants are provided to students from low-income families.

Another conception of equity in higher education is that of fairness, based on the principle that those who benefit most from higher education and have the economic ability to pay for higher education should at least bear some, if not all, the costs of higher education.

Current financing of higher education in Tanzania, specifically the current student loans scheme, exacerbates the already existing inequities in higher education. Empirical studies on equity in higher education in Tanzania reveal that higher education is inequitable because of disproportional representation of children from upper- and middle-class families in both public and private higher education. For example, a study by Voipio and Hoebink (1998 cited in URT 2003b: 48) revealed that the benefits of public expenditure on higher education in Tanzania accrued to the richest 20% of the population. These findings are also supported by Omari (1994: 54) who observed that the top 20% of the Tanzania population in terms of wealth consumes 40% of all government spending in education because they are unequally represented in secondary and higher education.

A World Bank study in 1995 revealed that very poor students have a remote chance of entering higher education institutions. This situation has arisen with the introduction of cost sharing and liberalisation of private secondary schooling, the transition to advanced levels of education is confined largely to the children from advantaged homes because of the high private costs involved (URT 2002: 49). Ironically, despite this acknowledgement, the government continues to grant loans to students enrolled in both public (under government sponsorship) and private universities without rigorous means testing. Furthermore, studies by Ishengoma (2004 & 2006b) also revealed that access to higher education in Tanzania is greatly influenced by unacceptable correlates such as socio-economic class, religion, ethnicity and gender.

To implement a student loans scheme without proper means testing – as Tanzania is currently doing – is essentially to consolidate inequities in higher education because there is abundant empirical research evidence to show that 'the children of the wealthy in all countries disproportionately benefit from higher education' (Johnstone 2003b). As Castro-Leal *et al.* (1999 cited in Omari & Mjema 2007: 22) correctly observe, public social spending in education programmes in African countries favour not the poor, but those who are better off.

To a large extent, financing of higher education through the Tanzania Education Authority also exacerbates inequities in higher education financing. As pointed out earlier, TEA grants soft loans and grants to private higher education institutions, most of which are affiliated to religious organisations in Tanzania and abroad, and charge higher tuition fees when compared to public higher education institutions. These institutions are also characterised by low enrolments.

Internationally, as Omari and Mjema (2007: 23) correctly argue, there are strong objections to giving public taxpayers' money to private and religious education institutions because of:

- The lack of accountability to tax payers;
- The lack of public scrutiny through public auditing as is the case with public institutions;
- The fact that private higher education institutions charge higher tuition fees and pay higher salaries than public institutions;
- Exclusivity – some of religious institutions admit only members of a particular faith;
- Unequal competition with public institutions in raising additional funds from philanthropic organisations; and
- Elitism – some private higher education institutions are only for the rich; for example, one private university in Tanzania charges its tuition fee in US dollars for both Tanzanians and non-Tanzanians.

While there is no broad objection to some form of public financial support to private higher education when the need arises, the fact that government financing of its own universities and university colleges has been on the decline makes the above practice to some extent misguided as is the case with granting loans to all students in public and private universities.

Summary and Conclusions

Whereas some reforms have been introduced in the financing of public higher education, the current formula or mode of financing public higher education in Tanzania leaves much to be desired as it generally promotes inequity.

Most public universities depend heavily on decreasing government subventions and they are unable to raise the much needed internally generated funds through enrolling more privately sponsored students as is the case in Kenya and Uganda. For example, research shows that Makerere University is generating large amounts of revenue from the private entry scheme increasing its revenue from UGS 4 billion (US$ 3.3m) (equivalent to 17% of the total funding) in 1995/1996 to UGS 29 billion (US$ 16.5m) (equivalent to 53%) of the total funding in 2003/2004 (Carol 2004 cited in Johnstone 2006: 11)

The apparent confusion in the implementation of the student loans scheme and the fact that currently only a few loans have been recovered from TZS 50 billion [US$ 92 559 794] given out by 2004/2005, raises questions about the sustainability of financing of higher education in this way. While the government introduced cost sharing in higher education as a major means of financing higher education in 1992/1993, in practice the government remains the major source of funding for public higher education and to some extent private higher education with the conspicuous absence of the private sector and other stakeholders.

The fact that the government remains a major source of financing for higher education in Tanzania is a contradiction to its own stated objective of introducing cost sharing in higher education policy, i.e. moderating government expenditure in higher education. This scenario raises some critical questions about the financial sustainability of higher education in Tanzania because, as is the case with all governments in all developing countries, the government also has to finance other compelling public needs, apart from higher education. This explains why the government almost always approves slightly above half or at times less than half of the funds requested by public higher education institutions for recurrent expenditure.

Moreover, the percentage of external donor contributions for research and capital development in public higher education institutions has declined over the years, although external donors remain a relatively significant source for funding research and capital development projects in public higher education institutions. Although donor dependency is not entirely strange in a country where almost 42% of the national budget depends on external donors, despite the declaration to be economically self-reliant for the past 40 years, it is clearly not appropriate for public universities which are supposed to be independent in knowledge production and dissemination.

On the basis of the above observations and conclusions, it is recommended that for higher education in Tanzania to be financially sustainable, there is a need for a new higher education financing formula which will ensure that all stakeholders and beneficiaries of higher education contribute to its costs. This will entail serious implementation of cost sharing in higher education policy. More importantly, the current modus operandi of the HESLB needs to be overhauled to make it effective.

Designing an Appropriate Model for Financing Higher Education in Tanzania
Despite the existence of a plethora of beneficiaries of higher education and various stakeholders in higher education the major source of financing of both public and private higher education is the government. This is so despite the introduction of cost sharing in higher education policy 14 years ago and despite the obvious fact that the government's ability to finance higher education is limited because of other competing needs. The contribution of the major beneficiaries of higher education (students, parents, the private sector and the community) and other key stakeholders to higher education costs remain very low.

At the same time, evidence confirms that public universities have not been able to generate adequate extra income from revenue diversification activities to lessen their dependence on government subventions because of their inability or reluctance to raise revenue from privately sponsored student programmes. Compared to Kenya and Uganda, Tanzania public universities enrol a negligible number of students in privately sponsored student programmes. Yet, available evidence shows that tuition fees from privately sponsored students, if properly harnessed, could generate substantial extra income, compared to other revenue diversification activities undertaken in public universities.

The HESLB established in 2004 primarily to give loans to the *needy* Tanzanian students currently *indiscriminately* disburses loans to all students enrolled in both public and private higher education institutions including those studying abroad. However, it is clear that higher education in Tanzania is inequitable because of the disproportional representation of students from the upper and middle classes in both public and private higher education institutions. In practice, the current student loans scheme perpetuates the already existing inequities in higher education in Tanzania. Furthermore, the HESLB has so far not been able to recover, to any significant extent, loans disbursed since 1993/1994 when the loans scheme officially came into effect, making the establishment of a revolving loan scheme impossible.

There is thus evidence of a lackadaisical attitude in the implementation of cost sharing in higher education policy, including unnecessary politicisation and strong opposition to policy by stakeholders although the policy is clearly justified and clearly spelt out in the Education and Training Policy, namely that:

> the funding of tertiary education and training in public institutions is mainly undertaken by the state with insignificant contribution from parents, students and institutions themselves. This has resulted in inadequate resources, low enrollments, high unit costs, institutional inefficiency, students' unrests, non accountability and laxity. (URT 1995: 78)

In the context of the above observations, the current state of financing higher education in Tanzania calls for a new formula/model for financing higher education – an example of which is proposed in the following sections.

Key Financing Principles for the Proposed Financing of Higher Education Model
The new framework for financing higher education in Tanzania should be guided by the following principles: shared costs or cost sharing, equity and human resource development. The principle of cost sharing is based on the fact

that because of the high private returns from higher education the beneficiaries of higher education, i.e. students, parents and potential employers of the graduates, should share the costs. The principle of cost sharing also encompasses the equity principle, while the principle of human resource development links higher education financing to the production of critical human resources for the economic and social development of a nation. Other principles to be considered in designing a model for financing higher education in Tanzania are efficiency, financial sustainability and quality. The strengths and weaknesses of some possible higher financing education strategies for Tanzania are summarised in Table 9.8.

Table 9.8: Strengths and Weaknesses of the Possible Financing of Higher Education Strategies in the Tanzanian Context

STRATEGY	STRENGTHS	WEAKNESSES
Student Loans	• Equitable if rigorous means testing and targeting are conducted • Expanded access to higher education	• Higher default rates • High administrative costs • Attribution of value
Income Generation/Revenue Diversification	• Can generate supplementary income for the institution • Development of entrepreneurial sprit	• Low collection if management and internal control systems are weak • Diversion of attention from core university functions • Susceptible to corrupt practices
Education Levy	• Equitable to users of higher education products	• Double taxation
External Donor Funds	• Large sums can be received	• Unpredictable • Dependence syndrome • Threat to academic freedom
Contracted Research and Consultancy	• Improved quality and quantity of research • Identification of the higher education institutions with industry sector • Market positioning of the institution	• May divert interest from teaching • Susceptible to corrupt practices
Government Funding	• Main source of funds for higher education institutions • Large sums of funds can be received • Most reliable source	• Declining economic ability and competing needs may lead to reduced budgetary allocations • Ad hoc allocation

Source: Adapted and modified from: URT 1998 p 86

Proposed Model for Financing Higher Education

In the Tanzanian context it is almost impossible to propose a viable model for financing higher education because of the heavy politicisation of financing higher education and the current 'socialist' mindset of 'free higher education' among the majority of Tanzanians (including the elite). This chapter proposes the general *market model* of financing higher education, which appears to have been successful in Kenya and Uganda. This model is also proposed within the context of the strengths and weaknesses of the possible financing higher education strategies depicted in Table 9.8. The 'market model' is also proposed in the context of two major trends that have characterised changes in the higher education sector in Tanzania since late 1990s when the government decided to liberalise the higher education sector, i.e. some limited privatisation of public higher education, and the emergence of the private sector.

The market model proposed here is also advocated by Oketch (2003) in reference to higher education in Kenya and by Lamptey (1994) who stresses the injection of some market principles and market-driven approaches into the financing of higher education to make it completely self-financing. Oketch (2003) views the market model of financing higher education in terms of *financial diversification* and *partial privatisation of public universities*, while Lamptey advocates the adoption of the contemporary marketing concepts of product, price, place and promotion (the 4 Ps) in higher education.

Lamptey further argues that the higher education sector is composed of the following market segments: students who are direct beneficiaries of higher education and therefore they constitute a major market segment of higher education; society, an ultimate beneficiary of higher education products – an indirect market; and intermediaries, composed of government, employers, donors and alumni.

While the market model of financing public higher education has been criticised and branded as *academic capitalism* driving universities into entrepreneurial competition for extra income and external funds with adverse effects on educational quality and external efficiency, the model, if cautiously adopted, can turn around the finances of government-dependent public higher education institutions in Tanzania. This model has worked at Makerere and Nairobi Universities, and there is no reason why it should not work in Tanzania where the injection of market principles in the economy has led to improved economic growth.

Bloom *et al.* (2005: 3) also argue that since higher education is a product and service, and can produce both public and private benefits and may create greater tax revenue, higher education can be marketed using an effective marketing mix through opening up dialogue with markets.

The market model in the Tanzanian context is justified in the larger context of the market economy Tanzania has adopted since the late 1980s and in the wider context of improving higher education efficiency (internal and external), accountability and quality improvement. The market model can also address the ever-increasing demand for higher education and at the same time maintain higher education quality. Table 9.9 summarises some basic components of the market model in terms of proposed major sources of funding public higher education institutions and viable financing modes.

Table 9.9: Proposed Model for Financing Public Higher Education in Tanzania

RESPONSIBLE INSTITUTION & RANK ORDER	FINANCING MODE	COST/BUDGET ITEM	LEVEL OF FINANCING IN % (ANNUALLY)
1. Higher education institutions	Revenue diversification and privatisation of services; contracted research and consultancy; enrolment of privately sponsored students	1, 2 & 4	1 = 5% 2 = 5% 4 = 100%
2. Students and their parents	Cost sharing	3	100%
3. Government	Direct subventions to higher education institutions; introduction of an education levy	1, 2 & 4	1 = 95% 2 = 95% 4 = 0%
4. Private sector/Potential graduate employers	Direct donations to responsible institutions; student and professorial chairs sponsorships; sponsorship of contracted research and consultancy	1	Variable
5. External donors	Direct grants to higher education institutions, faculty, departments, bureaus, etc.	1	Variable
6. Financial institutions	Creation of a Higher Education Bank from which students can and their parents can borrow money to pay for tuition and related costs at a market/ commercial interest rate	Variable	Variable
7. Alumni	Direct donations to institutions to establish Endowment and Trust Funds	1 & 3	Variable

KEY: 1 = Capital Development; 2 = Direct Training Costs; 3 = Students' Direct Costs; 4 = Other Administrative and Personal Emoluments Costs

The model shown in Table 9.9 proposes that higher education institutions should take the lead in self-financing through revenue diversification to cover 5% of the capital expenditure and direct training costs and 100% of other administrative and personal emolument costs, which consumes the largest share of public higher education budgets. The government, on the other hand, through direct subventions and capitation grants should cover 95% of both capital development and direct training costs, and 0% for other administrative and personal emoluments budget.

The model also proposes the establishment of a Higher Education Bank to replace the current ineffective Higher Education Students' Loans Board which offers interest free loans and has so far failed to recover loans. Such a bank can provide loans to students/parents to cover tuition fees and other related costs at a commercial interest rate. The proposed bank can also provide loans to higher education institutions. Currently, there is only one private commercial bank (Azania Bank) which provides education loans to parents and individuals.

Chapter 10
UGANDA

Nakanyike Musise and Florence Mayega

History of Ugandan Higher Education

Uganda's higher education system has its origins in the early 1920s with the founding of Makerere as a technical college to serve students from the British East African territories of Kenya, Tanganyika and Uganda. From its inception, but more so after the Currie Report of 1933, the architects of higher education envisioned a system that would almost wholly be financed by the state. In justifying this position, the Currie Report reasoned that there was a link between social demand and the possibility of increased social, cultural, economic and political returns from investing in higher education (Ashby 1966: 478 quoting Currie Report paragraph iv)

The combination of high expectations of social returns from higher education and principles which to a large extent have shaped Uganda's higher education system were underscored and grounded by the Channon Memorandum and Channon Report almost ten years later (1940 and 1943 respectively). The Channon Report recommended that fees for higher education in the colonies should be abolished. In the Memorandum, Channon provided a cost-benefit analysis to justify the proportion of public funding which would be necessary for the provision of higher education. It was assumed that financial responsibility for higher education in the colonies would lie with the British Government for the foreseeable future.

But perhaps the most important report for the development of higher education system in Uganda was the Asquith Commission on Higher Education in the Colonies Report (1945). The Report established a pattern of higher education in all former British colonies whose remnants persisted for over forty years after independence. For instance, access was to be dependent upon academic merit alone – open to all social classes without distinction of wealth, race, sex or creed. No mention was made of fees for students. The Report proposed high admission requirements and on this basis proposed that scholarships should be awarded on the basis of merit for 'a selected few'. In addition, adequate funds were to be made available from universities for prospective students seeking entry. The Report specifically rejected as undesirable any form of bonding arrangements which might require recipients of scholarships or grants to enter government or other services. Its emphasis upon quality rather than cost was fully accepted and embraced by the colonial government. Most important for the financing of higher education in Uganda, the report entailed an in-built assumption that a large proportion of university expenditure, both capital and recurrent, would be met by Britain (Girdwood 1992). The origins of a financial dependency relationship of African universities have been attributed to this report. In fact, Girdwood (1992) has accused Asquith of presenting a model which established the expectations towards which education planners continued to aspire, even when the economic base necessary to make such aspirations viable was no longer present (Girdwood 1992: 13). Girdwood states that the 'the model created was one which was designed, from the outset, to rely upon foreign financial assistance, and was therefore to remain very vulnerable to external agendas' (Girdwood 1992: 2).

The 1950s represented an even more significant period for the funding of Uganda's higher education system and saw the introduction of a bigger role taken on by the international aid agencies and the erosion of British monopoly over its present and former colonies. During this period the USA started to supply a substantial proportion of the funding necessary for the expansion of higher education on the continent. The Rockefeller and Ford Foundations and the Carnegie Co-operation of New York emerged as new major players. Equally important, the multilateral agencies also begun to take an active interest in the financing of higher education in Africa.

Whereas the attainment of independence ushered in a new way of looking at higher education in Uganda, it never challenged the colonially initiated financing arrangement. However, higher education was also expected to play a role in nation building (Coleman 1983) and hence state funding was further justified. Not diverging from the Asquith recommendations, the entire cost of university buildings, equipment and other facilities continued to be borne by the three East African states with students paying no tuition fees and being given subsistence allowances. This level of funding reflected the weight of social expectations from higher education.

In 1970, owing to the nationalist pressures in the region, the University of East Africa for which Makerere College had been a Constituent College since 1963 dissolved into three fully fledged independent universities (Makerere University in Uganda, University of Nairobi in Kenya and University of Dar es Salaam in Tanzania). Makerere University, like other national development initiatives, was to remain a public undertaking financed and supported from public sources.

The World Bank's *Education Sector Working Paper: Education and Basic Needs* published in 1974 was the first major treatise to present a new development approach which would have more serious repercussions for higher education in Uganda. The document emphasised that lending to higher education would have to decline. This had two implications for borrowing countries. First, that national spending on higher education would be expected to reduce and second, as a corollary, higher education should find alternative and 'relevant' roles for itself. The document posed some fundamental questions about education structures, questions such as 'Who should be educated, how, for what and at whose expense?' (1974: 11). With the agenda (to neglect higher education) having been set by this document, the World Bank published its *Education Sector Policy Paper* (1980) with an underlining philosophy of putting key emphasis on primary and secondary education, and the bank paid little attention to higher education. In the last 20 years or so, financing Uganda's higher education system has been influenced by the World Bank policy framework on education of the 1980s and 1990s.

Overview of Ugandan Higher Education

Public Expenditure on Education
Public expenditure on education as a percentage of GDP has increased from 1.5% in 1991 to 5.2% in 2002–2004. As a percentage of government expenditure, it has grown from 11.5% (1991) to 18.3% in 2002–2004, compared to Kenya's 29.2% (2002–2004) (UNDP 2006). The highest proportion of this goes to the primary education sub-sector.

Public financing of education constitutes an average of 25% of the national budget. A survey of the expenditure trends over the period 1997/1998–2005/2006 indicates a range from 27% in 1998/1999 to 22% in 2003/2004. With the adoption of the Sector Wide Approach to budgeting and the medium-term expenditure framework in 1997/1998, all education-related activities were clustered in the education sector budget. This coupled with the introduction of universal primary education and a priority shift to basic education was the genesis of the decline in public support to higher education.

Table 10.1: Education Sector Expenditure in relation to National Government Expenditure 1997/1998–2005/2006 (UGS, billion)

	1997/1998	1998/1999	1999/2000	2000/2001	2001/2002	2002/2003	2003/2004	2004/2005	2005/2006
Total education sector spending	208	267	322	373	456	505	518	567	626
Total national expenditure	810	984	1 226	1 496	1 895	2 037	2 343	2 433	2 686
% education sector at national level	26%	27%	26%	25%	24%	25%	22%	23%	23%

Source: National Budget estimates 1997/1998 to 2005/2006

Demand for Higher Education

The Gross Enrolment Ratio (GER) in higher education is about 3.5% which is comparable to the sub-Sahara African average of around 4% but much lower than the world average of 27%. Enrolments increased by more than 260%, moving from 30 000 in 1995 to 109 208 by 2005, a more than three-fold increase in a decade. With the country's high population growth and the introduction of universal primary education and, more recently, universal secondary education, the demand for higher education is likely to continue growing. In addition, the demand for higher education in Uganda is likely to increase as a result of such factors as (i) the increases in household incomes; (ii) growing recognition of the role of higher education in national development; and (iii) the expected high private returns to higher education.

The response to the unprecedented growth in demand for higher education has been an expansion in service providers, particularly the number of private institutions.

Structure of Higher Education

The higher education sub-sector in Uganda is stratified as follows: (i) degree awarding universities; and (ii) other tertiary institutions (commonly referred to as the technical sub-sector) offering diplomas and certificates. Universities are further categorised into public and private institutions. Public- or state-funded institutions are established by Acts of Parliament while the private universities are chartered, licensed or unlicensed. The 'other tertiary institutions' are similarly categorised into public and private.

By 2005, the higher educaiton sub-sector had 152 institutions – 51 of these were public and 101 private. The university tier had 28 institutions, of which 5 were public, 13 chartered and licensed private, and 10 were unlicensed universities. There were 124 other tertiary institutions of which 46 (37%) were public. Public, 'other tertiary institutions' are predominated by National Teachers Colleges (NTC), Health Training Institutions (HTI) and Theological Institutions.

Private 'other tertiary institutions, mainly comprise Colleges of Commerce and Management Institutions (NCHE 2005).

Table 10.2: Composition of Higher Education Institutions (2005)

INSTITUTIONS	PUBLIC	PRIVATE	UNLICENSED
Universities	5	13	10
NTC	10		1
Technical Institutes	6		
Colleges of Commerce	5	42	
Forestry College	1		
Cooperative Colleges	2		
Hotel and Tourism	2		
Management Institutions	3	19	
Health Training Institutions	10	4	
Agricultural Institutions	3		
Fisheries Institutions	1		
Aeronautical Institutions	1		
Development Centres	1		
Communication Institutions		3	
Theological Institutions		9	
Meteorological Institutions	1		
Total	51	90	11

Source: National Council for Higher Education 2004

Three public 'other tertiary institutions' do not fall in either category. These are the Uganda Management Institute (UMI) which is a degree-awarding institution mainly at the postgraduate level; the Law Development Centre (LDC) which is a diploma awarding-institution mainly for postgraduate law students from the various universities and the Makerere University Business School (MUBS) which offers degree programmes from Makerere University and also has independent diploma and certificate programmes.

Equity and Access

There are three main avenues for entering the university system. The first avenue is where secondary school graduates with two principal passes in the University

Advanced Certificate of Education Examination (A levels) can be directly admitted into the university, while the second allows diploma holders to be considered for entry. The third avenue is the mature entry scheme for lifelong learners and adults who missed the opportunity for direct entry through the formal school system.

The state has reserved 4 000 positions per annum for government sponsorship to students admitted into the five public universities. The system is merit based and students with the highest grade points are awarded scholarships based on the individual requirements of the institutions and the faculties where the students are to be based. The 4 000 students represent only 17% of the students who qualify for university entry and a mere 10% of the students who sit for entry examinations.

In 2005/2006 a new system was introduced primarily to redress the enrolment imbalance between the sciences and the humanities. In the new system 75% of the 4 000 government-sponsored students are admitted on the basis of merit but are limited to subjects deemed crucial to national development specifically in Science and Technology, Law, Performing Arts and Economics. A quarter of the 4 000 posts is left to address equity gaps. A quota system was introduced for the best students in each district, persons with disabilities and sportsmen and -women who meet the minimum requirements of specific institutions and programmes. Students who do not qualify for government sponsorship are admitted through the private sponsorship scheme or to the other tertiary institutions. State-funded scholarship therefore is highly competitive and mainly favours those from the higher social strata who can afford the best secondary schools.

Although higher education has traditionally been regarded as a public good in Uganda, it has remained elitist. Mayanja (1998) showed that 60% of students admitted to Makerere University were from the middle- and higher-income groups. Unfortunately this situation has not changed; the 4 000 students who access state scholarships in the four public universities are mainly those from the higher-income brackets as evidenced by the secondary schools they attended. For example, 47% of the students admitted at Makerere University in 2004/2005–2006/2007 for government sponsorship came from the 25 most prestigious and highly selective schools.

Students selected for state sponsorship receive 'free' university education including tuition, accommodation, meals and other welfare costs. Additionally, because of the merit-based entry mechanisms, these students are admitted to professional courses such as Law and Medicine. This further increases the divide between the urban rich and the rural poor.

Currently, only 18% of the more than 70 000 students in public universities are government-supported for all costs including tuition, accommodation and welfare costs.

Apart from this quota system, other initiatives undertaken to address issues of equity and access particularly from the gender perspective in Makerere University are (i) an additional 1.5 points to the entry grades scored by females (this initiative increased female enrolment from 36% in 1998/1999 to 46% by 2005/2006); and (ii) The Carnegie Female Scholarship Initiative which is a three-year renewable US$ 1 million grant to Makerere University to cater for female students from disadvantaged socio-economic backgrounds admitted specifically to science-based programmes.

Enrolment in Public Universities

According to the National Council for Higher Education (NCHE), enrolment in public universities in 2005 stood at 54 435 students. This represented 76% of total university enrolment. Makerere University as the largest public university had 75% of the total enrolment in public universities in 2004 but this was reduced to 61% in 2005 (see Table 10.3).

Table 10.3: Student Enrolment Share of Public Universities in Uganda 2004/2005

INSTITUTION	ENROLMENT		% SHARE OF ENROLMENT	
YEAR	2004	2005	2004	2005
Makerere University	34 955	33 108	75.0	60.8
Mbarara University	1 086	1 139	2.3	2.0
Makerere University Business School	6 562	10 111	14.2	18.6
Kyambogo University	3 323	7 588	7.1	14.0
Gulu University	640	2 489	1.4	4.6
Sub-total	46 566	54 435	100.0	100.0
Aggregate university enrolment in Uganda	68 079	71 279		
% Share of public university enrolment to total university enrolment in Uganda			68.4	76.0

Source: National Council for Higher Education 2005 and 2006

Of the 33 108 students enrolled at Makerere in 2005/2006 only 7 000 (21%) were government-supported students. Data from Kyambogo University revealed that only 2 485 (18%) of the 13 000 students enrolled in the 2005/2006 academic year were government sponsored. At Mbarara University of Science and Technology, 389 (16%) of the 2 464 enrolled were government sponsored. In total, public university government-sponsored enrolment has been kept almost constant while the number of private fee-paying students has increased dramatically.

The Regulatory Environment

Legal Framework
The Universities and Other Tertiary Institutions Act of 2001 sets the legal framework for the provision of higher education in Uganda. This Act replaced the various statutes that established and governed individual public institutions. The Act was promulgated to attain four basic goals: (i) to provide for the widening of access to higher quality institutions; (ii) to provide an environment for equating professional or other qualifications of the same or similar courses offered by different institutions; (iii) to ensure quality at all tertiary institutions; and (iv) to oversee and guide the establishment and management of those institutions while respecting the autonomy and academic freedom of these institutions.

The National Council for Higher Education (NCHE)
The regulatory role of higher education is vested in the NCHE as established by the Act. Among other responsibilities the NCHE is charged with:

- Receipt and processing of applications for the establishment and accreditation of public and private institutions of higher education;
- Monitoring, evaluation and regulation institutions of higher education;
- Ensuring minimum standards for courses of study and the equating of degrees, diplomas and certificates awarded by the different public and private institutions of higher education;
- Setting and coordination of national standards for admission of students to the different institutions of higher education;
- Certifying that an institution of higher education has adequate and accessible physical structures and staff for the courses to be offered by it; and
- Advising the government on policy and other matters relating to institutions of higher education.

Jurisdiction over Tertiary Education
The Act stipulates that the Higher Education Department within the Ministry of Education and Sports (MoES), has jurisdiction over tertiary education. However, in practice, this is only true in the case of universities, as the Teacher Education Department is responsible for all the National Teacher Colleges while the Department of Business, Technical, and Vocational Education and Training (BTVET) is still responsible for some of the technical tertiary institutions particularly Health Training Institutions, Colleges of Commerce and Technical

Colleges. At the same time, other government ministries have jurisdiction over some of the other tertiary institutions. For example, the Aeronautical College falls under the Ministry of Defence, and the Law Development Centre falls under the Ministry of Justice and Constitutional Affairs.

Financing Higher Education

Post-1986 Reforms in Education Sector Financing
Education sector reform is based on Unesco's Education for All (EFA) campaign. The 1991 Government White Paper, among others, prioritises primary education over other sectors and encourages the promotion and fostering of private resources in the provision of higher education – new private providers as well as permitting public higher education institutions to raise funds from private sources.

Government thus adopted new modalities for the funding and coordination of the whole education sector as part of this reform. The government, in a pact with the international donor agencies, instituted the Education Sector Investment Programme (ESIP) in 1998 with, among others, the primary goal of confronting and addressing the financial challenges emerging out of the implementation of univeral primary education. From its inception, ESIP I and its successor programme ESIP II, became the blue print for allocating funds between different education sub-sectors.

A notable outcome of the ESIP has been the decline in public expenditure on higher education (Table 10.4) and a deliberate move by the government to encourage public universities to generate resources from private sources, as well as encouraging the private sector to play an increasingly significant role in the provision of higher education.

The government's reluctance to finance higher education has led to an increase in private expenditure on higher education and public institutions bidding to develop various mechanisms for generating funds from private households. The wave of privatisation of higher education has become so strong in Uganda that there was a time when almost every six months there was a new university being created. Moreover, in public institutions, most students now pay fees as a result of the dual track entry scheme. This dual track scheme was instituted in 1992 and legalised by the Universities and Other Tertiary Institutions Act (2001).

Appleton (2001) observed that despite the increase in enrolment from 2.4 million to 6.6 million, state spending per primary student rose by 130%, while secondary-level spending increased by 200%. In comparison, public spending per university student fell by 30%.

Table 10.4: Education Sector Expenditure 1997/1998–2005/2006 (%)

EDUCATION SUB-SECTOR	1997/1998	1998/1999	1999/2000	2000/2001	2001/2002	2002/2003	2003/2004	2004/2005	2005/2006	Average
University	12%	10%	10%	8%	8%	8%	9%	9%	10%	9%
Other tertiary institutions	0%	0%	2%	2%	2%	3%	2%	3%	4%	2%
MoES incl. Primary	18%	24%	24%	22%	19%	20%	15%	14%	14%	19%
Primary (Exclusive)	56%	51%	53%	57%	58%	56%	59%	58%	57%	56%
Others (Secondary + ESC)	14%	14%	12%	11%	12%	13%	15%	15%	15%	14%

Source: National Budget estimates 1997/1998 to 2005/2006

Sources of Funds

The education reforms have led to three sources of financing for higher education. These are: the government (public); private (tuition and other fees) and donor. Although both private and donor funds played a relatively minor role, in recent years these two sources of funding have come to be crucial in the provision of higher education, so much so that in their absence, higher education in Uganda would be in a terrible crisis. While public and donor funds are to be found in both public and private institutions, public funds for higher education are only allocated to public institutions.

Patterns of State Financing in Public Higher Education Institutions

The amount that is allocated to the higher education sub-sector through the ESIP arrangement is subsequently sub-divided among four public universities and the more than 40 other tertiary institutions. Regrettably, there are no clear guidelines shaping allocations within the sub-sector. Instead there is (i) what is referred to as government subvention; (ii) line item funding; and (iii) project financing for newly established universities. These public financing modes run alongside the dual track system of tuition fees.

Public funds are disbursed to institutions through four distinctive channels: (i) directly from the Ministry of Finance; (ii) through Ministry of Education and Sports departments of Higher Education Department, Business, Technical and Vocational Education Training Institutions (BTVET), and the Teacher Education Department; (iii) through the district; and (iv) through other line ministries.

Public Universities

Public universities (Makerere, Mbarara, Kyambogo and Gulu) are required to submit a budget to Parliament. Nonetheless, parliamentary allocations are hardly influenced in a substantive way by these submitted budgets. Instead allocations are based on the institution's historical allocations, its size and needs, although not in a consistent manner.

Government funds are disbursed to universities in two blocks: recurrent and development budgets. For the recurrent budget, each public university receives a block grant or 'subvention'. The amount of the subvention is purportedly calculated using the number of government-sponsored students and the 'unit cost' which the Ministry thinks and feels is 'reasonable' for that particular institution.

Unit costs have ranged from UGS 1.5 million at Kyambogo University to UGS 16.1 million at Mbarara University of Science and Technology. Ministry personnel in charge of budgeting insist that the government 'unit cost' is calculated slightly higher, often more than twice the amount of the annual fee paid by a private fee-paying student, because it is inclusive of the student's welfare costs. For instance, in the financial year 2005/2006, Makerere University received a subvention of UGS 35 billion calculated at about 7 000 students with a unit cost of UGS 4 million per student.

Universities have some discretion on how they allocate the block grants. Almost exclusively, public universities pay their regular staff out of this subvention grant. The development budget fluctuates significantly from year to year. Although there is a popular belief that the development budget tends to favour Makerere University, it receives a mere UGS 140 000 for all its development budget needs.

Other Tertiary Institutions in the BTVET Category
These institutions receive recurrent budget support as a capitation grant based on the number of state-sponsored students. In addition to salaries paid directly for staff recruited through the Ministry of Public Service, these institutions also receive a development budget, especially through donor funding. Nonetheless, the availability and disbursement of this budget fluctuates much more than those to the universities. The fluctuation is so high that it is difficult for these institutions to count on the Ministry for this support.

National Teacher Colleges (NTCs)
All NTCs receive both a recurrent and development budget from the Ministry. For recurrent expenditure, wages and non-wage budgets are separated. As with those in the BTVET category, the wage subsidy is based on the public posts in

the institution (staff pay roll), and the recurrent budget is estimated based on the number of government-sponsored students.

District Tertiary Institution

Education is one of the decentralised services under the decentralisation policy adopted by the Government of Uganda in 1993. In addition to the jurisdiction that Districts have over primary and secondary schools, funds for the district-based other tertiary institutions are channelled through the respective districts. Similar to the BTVET and NTCs, funds are in the form of capitation grants based on the number of students and salaries are paid directly to staff recruited through the Ministry of Public Service. This category of institutions has a bigger financial challenge than the other three precisely because release of funds to the districts is intermittent and the districts have limited sources of funds since the central government curtailed their tax base several years ago.

Distribution of Education Expenditure

The main categories of education expenditure are the following: District Primary 57%; District Secondary 15%; Universities 10%; MoES plus primary 14%; and District Tertiary 3.5%.

Private Higher Education

Ownership and Enrolment

Although the bulk of private (that is, fee-paying) university students are found in public universities, Uganda is witnessing an upsurge of private universities from one in 1988 to more than 20 by 2005. This represents 82% of the total number of universities in Uganda.

Only one private university, Kampala International University, is regarded as a for-profit institution. With the exception of the Islamic University in Uganda which was founded by an international body – the Organisation of Islamic Conference (OIC) – private universities in Uganda fall into three main categories: (i) religious founded (local); (ii) community founded; or (iii) evolved from other tertiary. These institutions depend mainly on tuition fees paid by students and donations made by the founding bodies.

All private universities offer undergraduate degrees predominantly in the humanities, with a few institutions offering postgraduate programmes in the humanities and soft sciences. Despite the increase in number, private universities enrolment by 2004/2005 was around 21 500 representing only 32% of the total university enrolment. Although there is increased private participation through private ownership, most of the institutions are relatively small, accommodating only a limited number of students.

Interestingly, while 25% of Ugandan students are enrolled at the private universities, 70% of the 2 528 international students in Uganda are enrolled in these institutions. The large percentage of international students is a pointer to the nature of private institutions which have tended to have a more aggressive marketing strategy outside the country especially within the East Africa region compared to the public institutions. Moreover, both private and public universities charge the same fees for Ugandan and international students. Additionally there is a tendency for Ugandan students to prefer education at public institutions and they will in many cases go to private institutions only after they have failed to gain admission to the public institutions.

Table 10.5: Enrolment Composition of Private and Public Universities

University Status	UGANDAN		INTERNATIONAL		Total
	Female	Male	Female	Male	
Public	19 325	26 463	290	488	46 566
Private	5 308	6 982	559	1 020	18 154
Private Unlicensed	1 127	2 061	75	96	3 359
Total	25 760	35 506	924	1 604	68 079
% Private	25%	25%	69%	70%	32%

Source: National Council for Higher Education 2005

The situation is further aggravated by the fact that by the 2006/2007 academic year, the private universities charged higher rates than their public counterparts for the same courses. For example, Makerere and Mbarara Universities charge UGS 1 000 000 ($\cong$ US$ 600) and UGS 1 200 000 ($\cong$ US$ 700) respectively for the Bachelor of Development Studies qualification. In comparison, Nkumba University charged UGS 1 800 000 ($\cong$ US$ 1 100), Uganda Christian University Mukono, UGS 2 000 000 ($\cong$ US$ 1 200), and Uganda Martyrs University Nkozi. UGS 2 879 100 ($\cong$ US$ 1 750).

Ability to pay is thus a major factor in determining students' access to private university education.

For the 'Other Tertiary Institutions' sub-sector, private institutions are mainly the Colleges of Commerce, Management Institutes, Communication Institutions and Theological Colleges with very few, if any, Health, Teacher Training, Agricultural, Tourism and the Technical Colleges (NCHE 2005). While this may largely be due to the substantial financial and physical facilities required to set up these institutions, it can also be partly explained by the popularisation of business education, and the perceived demand and marketability of business education graduates.

Per Capita Financing: The Case of Makerere University

Financing of higher education in Uganda is input based, with minimal attention paid to the process and the outputs that accrue out of institutional activities. The primary driver of financing seems to be enrolment. Assessment of institutional performance is mainly based on the number of students admitted and registered per institution.

A study of 15 institutions by the Makerere University Institute of Social Research (2003) revealed that 72% of the total funding in higher education went to Makerere University, compared to its 75% enrolment share. Despite the large share of higher education funding going to Makerere University, budget performance has been recorded at an average of 69% (Table 10.6). The contribution to the budget from public funds declined from 71% in 1996/1997 to 40% by 2005/2006.

Enrolment at Makerere University grew by 250% from 9 861 in 1995/1996 to 34 488 in 2005/2006. Nonetheless, government support to the university grew by only 87% over the same period while average public spending per enrolled student reduced by 62% from UGS 1.4 million in 1995/1996 to UGS 566 040 in 2005/2006. This is despite the other economic variables such as double-digit inflation and the depreciating value of the Ugandan shilling.

The decrease in government funding to Makerere University has been compensated for by a large inflow of private funds. This has, in turn, led to drastic changes in the enrolment structure from a predominantly government-funded student body in 1995/1996 to a predominantly private enrolment in 2005/2006. This change is highlighted in Table 10.7. This table also shows the discrepancy between the public and the overall unit costs. When only government-supported students are considered the average unit contribution per student shows an increase from UGS 2.6 million (equivalent to US$ 1 520) to UGS 5 million (equivalent to US$ 3 000) in 2005/2006.

Table 10.6: Makerere University – Funding and Budget Performance (UGS)

YEAR	PROPOSED BUDGET	GOVT RECURRENT FUNDING	PRIVATE FUNDING	BUDGET PERFORMANCE
1995/1996	33 849 073 330	18 753 017 054	-	55%
1996/1997	37 669 082 257	19 255 308 734	7 627 496 665	71%
1997/1998	47 987 101 561	20 338 131 413	8 799 261 213	61%
1998/1999	48 678 378 791	23 685 889 876	13 663 196 178	77%
1999/2000	51 326 220 765	24 926 134 852	13 808 902 933	75%
2000/2001	61 423 143 234	23 228 971 654	14 014 545 258	61%
2001/2002	70 728 530 956	27 542 569 313	19 030 438 782	66%
2002/2003	73 529 739 120	27 526 750 819	29 438 099 323	77%
2003/2004	78 000 000 000	26 590 262 050	31 915 900 197	75%
2004/2005	103 000 000 000	36 653 142 917	37 411 816 460	72%
2005/2006	127 065 491 821	35 102 426 787	53 589 637 625	70%

Source: Makerere University Planning and Development Department and Finance Department

Table 10.7: Makerere University Enrolment by Category and Public Support

YEAR	GOVERNMENT STUDENTS	PRIVATE STUDENTS	TOTAL GOVERNMENT FUNDING	FUNDING PER GOVT STUDENT	PUBLIC SUPPORT PER ENROLLED STUDENT
1995/1996	7 089	2 772	18 753 017 054	2 645 368	1 484 447
1996/1997	6 710	7 902	19 255 308 734	2 869 644	855 259
1997/1998	6 890	7 477	20 338 131 413	2 951 833	931 063
1998/1999	6 545	11 474	23 685 889 876	3 618 929	803 102
1999/2000	6 103	14 507	24 926 134 852	4 084 243	709 803
2000/2001	6 074	20 034	23 228 971 654	3 824 329	503 424
2001/2002	7 340	22 886	27 542 569 313	3 752 394	518 575
2002/2003	7 932	23 100	27 526 750 819	3 470 342	508 512
2003/2004	7 772	24 664	26 590 262 050	3 421 290	465 679
2004/2005	6 799	26 759	36 653 142 917	5 390 961	607 675
2005/2006	6 948	27 533	35 102 426 787	5 052 163	566 040

Source: Makerere University Planning and Development Department

Conversely and regardless of the increase in fee-paying students, the enrolment composition in public universities does not tally with the resource inflow. The low tuition and other fee levels have meant that the percentage increase in the number of students is higher than the percentage increase in resources from the private sector. The figures can be read to imply that irrespective of the efficiency measures put in place, and the dictum of economies of scale, funding is inadequate to provide quality education.

Declining quality has manifested itself in increased staff–student ratios; limited research; a reduced ratio of student to library books; high student-space ratios; and the obsolescence and decline in science laboratories. In summary, funding has not kept up with enrolments leading to declining quality.

On the other hand, Table 10.8 shows the trend in government expenditure from the period when the Institute of Teacher Education was merged with two other institutions to form the Kyambogo University (the third public University). Expenditure per government-sponsored student is bigger in comparison to Makerere University (the first and Uganda's premier university). Kyambogo's unit expenditure ranged from UGS 3.4 million in 2003/2004 to UGS 8.3 million in 2005/2006 in comparison to Makerere University's range of UGS 3.4 million to UGS 5.2 million in the same time period. On the other hand, government unit expenditure per enrolled student ranges from UGS 1.4 million in 2004/2005 to UGS 0.9 million in 2006/2007 (Table 10.8). Note that the UGS 1.36 million registered in 2005/2006 is above the computed national average of UGS 1.1 million public expenditure per enrolled student in public universities.

Table 10.8: Government Support to Kyambogo University 2002/2003–2006/2007

YEAR	ACTUAL GOVT EXPENDITURE	PRIVATE	GOVERNMENT	UNIT EXP PER GOVT STUDENT	UNIT EXP PER ENROLLED STUDENT
2002/2003	5 814 624 364	3 835	1 066	5 454 619	1 186 416
2003/2004	7 590 234 666	4 965	2 230	3 403 693	1 054 932
2004/2005	10 378 033 000	5 100	2 158	4 809 098	1 429 875
2005/2006	13 079 048 880	8 005	1 561	8 378 635	1 367 243
2006/2007	13 044 478 000	11 435	2 488	5 242 957	936 901

Source: Kyambogo University Department of Planning and Finance

At the national level, Makerere University used to have the largest share of the higher education budget; this has been declining from 77% in 1997/1998 to 39% in 2005/2006. On the other hand, district tertiary institutions have increased from 0% in 1997/1998 to 24% by 2005/2006. Other public universities such as Mbarara University of Science and Technology (MUST) and Makerere University Business School (MUBS) have maintained their percentage share of public funds (see Table 10.9). The implication of these figures is that there has been a clear shift in emphasis by government away from Makerere University.

Thus Uganda's premier public university is increasingly being delivered to the private sector as the country's emphasis shifts from public provision to increasingly private provision for university education.

Table 10.9: Percentage Share of Public Higher Education Funds 1997/1998–2005/2006

INSTITUTION	1997/1998	1998/1999	1999/2000	2000/2001	2001/2002	2002/2003	2003/2004	2004/2005	2005/2006
Makerere	77%	77%	61%	58%	57%	50%	46%	41%	39%
UMI	2%	1%	1%	1%	1%	1%	1%	1%	0.4%
MUST	12%	12%	13%	12%	10%	11%	13%	12%	10%
ITEK	10%	10%	7%	8%	7%	6%	11%	12%	14%
MUBS					5%	5%	5%	5%	5%
Gulu University							2%	5%	5%
District Tertiary			17%	18%	16%	24%	19%	17%	24%
District Health Training Inst.				3%	4%	3%	3%	7%	4%
Total Education Sector Spending	25.7	27.5	37.6	38	47.4	56.3	58	75	90.9

Source: Derived from the National Budget Estimate 1997/1998–2005/2006

Unit Costs

Although the average fee in Makerere is UGS 1.3 million, fees range from UGS 810 000 per annum in the School of Education to UGS 1.9 million per annum in the Faculty of Medicine. The mean percentage fees paid in relation to unit cost is 48%.

Private and Household Expenditure on Higher Education

According to the National Household Survey 2002/2003, expenditure on education constituted 7% of the total monthly expenditure. Considering that average monthly expenditure per household was UGS 139 000 and the average per capita expenditure was UGS 30 000, the average household would have approximately UGS 10 000 per month to spend on education irrespective of the level. According to Appleton (2001), the average direct cost of primary education per adult wage year is only 4%. In comparison to primary education, households spend seven times more on secondary education but they spend far less per student at university level in comparison to secondary education.

While Appleton's calculations might have been applicable in the early 1990s the scenario has since changed. With the introduction of private sponsorship in public institutions and the emergence of private and in some cases 'for profit' higher education providers the household cost of university education has increased substantially.

The cost of higher education has a bearing on what programme a student is likely to take. Students choose programmes according to their ability to pay as opposed to their academic capability or a rational choice based on labour market analysis.

Private versus Public Support to Higher Education

Over the past ten years, the phenomenon of public–private partnerships has manifested itself in the enrolment structure and in the resource inflow to public universities as part of tuition and other fees paid by students. The percentage share of private resources in public institutions has overtaken government support. At Makerere University, for example, funds from private sources contributed 60% to total recurrent expenditure in 2005/2006 up from 28% in 1996/1997. Kyambogo University had 51% of the recurrent budget from private sources in 2005/2006. Mbarara University of Science and Technology, which has a better public funding arrangement than Makerere University, raised only 22% of its total support in the same financial year from private sources.

However, the increase in private resources both at Makerere and Kyambogo Universities is considerably lower than the growth in private student numbers. For example, at Makerere University private students constitute 80% of the total enrolment compared to the resource contribution of 60%. Likewise, in Kyambogo University private students constitute 82% of the total enrolment compared to the 51% contribution to the budget. Considered in this light, students in these institutions are subsidised by government resources with a higher subsidy registered at Kyambogo compared to Makerere. This confirms the earlier observation that the unit government contribution at Kyambogo is much higher than at Makerere. It also highlights the fact that private students do not pay the true cost of the higher education they receive.

Moreover, on average a mere 17% of the students in public universities are government-supported with all costs including tuition, accommodation and welfare costs borne by the state.

Student Financing Schemes

To date, there is no clearly defined student financing scheme in Uganda as is the case in Kenya. Student financing takes the form of direct public or private support.

Public
Public support for higher education is reserved for a few students admitted to public institutions based on academic merit. For universities, students receive a 'full' government scholarship. The scholarship, which is a block grant that universities receive, covers tuition, accommodation, scholastic materials and an allowance for field attachments in programmes with this provision. Government-sponsored students, however, are categorised into resident and non-resident students.

Resident students are accommodated in the halls of residence. This provision is by and large reserved for the top scholars in the various fields. These students receive support in kind apart from the faculty allowance (for scholastic materials) and a field attachment/internship allowance. For the non-resident students, an allowance is given to cover accommodation, food and transport in addition to similar financial support that is given to resident students for scholastic studies and internships.

Public support for the other tertiary institutions' students covers tuition and accommodation. In addition the institutions receive a capitation grant per enrolled student. This grant is expected to cover all the running costs that accrue to the student including meals. The NTCs and the BTVET institutions receive a field allowance on behalf of the government-sponsored students to cover internships.

Private
Tuition and other related fees paid by students form the largest share of non-government resources for higher education. Both public and private universities advertise available programmes and the contingent fees. Neither the institutions nor government have established financing schemes for this category of students. The contributions therefore come from households (students, parents and guardians), non-governmental organisations, church-based organisations and donor funds in the form of tuition fees specifically for the disadvantaged groups and for postgraduate studies. There have been limited cases of sponsorship from government ministries and other agencies for employees who wish to further their education or take advanced degrees. Ironically, there is a category of private students who are directly supported by the President's Office through the State House Scholarship Fund. Selection of this category of students is not transparent

and modalities for choosing who benefits from this scheme are not known to the general public.

Direct External Investments in Higher Education

Until the enactment of the Universities and Other Tertiary Institutions Act 2001, public universities were not allowed to borrow from commercial agencies and/or banks for any development projects. As a new source for resource diversification this avenue has not been explored by the universities. There are, however, isolated cases which are not loan- and interest-based but rather, upfront payments for services. These sources provide the universities with a lump sum to enable them to undertake infrastructure development. One case in point is the recent trend to hire commercial banks for purposes of establishing branches on university campuses.

Private Sector Contribution through Provision of Student Accommodation

Private sector support to public institutions has also come in through the erection and provision of student hostels and accommodation facilities at institutions. While this cannot be taken as direct income to the institution, the availability of affordable accommodation facilitates enrolment growth levels. For example, at Makerere University, student halls of residence can accommodate a maximum of only 5 000 (15%) of the student enrolment. The university is therefore reliant on the private sector to provide accommodation for more than 25 000 students. Some operators of these facilities also provide transport to and from the university as well as recreation facilities.

Donor Funding

Both private and public resources go towards recurrent expenditure, with limited contributions toward research and other capital costs such as physical infrastructure and equipment. This gap has been filled by philanthropic and bilateral support.

Donor support to higher education is largely institution-solicited and commissioned. Institutions have taken the lead to identify donors to support their various activities. Nonetheless, donor support is task specific, with limited room for flexibility. Reliance on donor funds for core university activities is problematic, unreliable and unsustainable since the support is mainly dependent on the interests and policies of the donor agency.

Private Sector Support to Public Universities

Private sector resources are used to supplement salaries in various ways. Universities have adopted internal sharing mechanisms of the privately generated resources. For instance, at Kyambogo University, resources from private students on the regular day-programmes are centrally utilised while resources from the evening programmes are allocated according to the budgetary requirements of the generating unit. Makerere University and Mbarara University of Science and Technology, on the other hand, have worked out varying percentage distributions between the centre and the generating unit designated for the various expenditure categories depending on whether the programme is in a day, evening, external or postgraduate programme. Like the public funds, more than 50% of the private resources are utilised for staff costs, more specifically salaries.

At Makerere University, the governing Council has agreed to a division formula between the centre and the income-generating units, whereby units retain 49% of the tuition on undergraduate private students from day programmes, 51% from undergraduate evening students, 75% of the postgraduate tuition and 87% from the external degree programmes. Faculties with the largest number of students have the highest percentage share of disposable income from the private programmes. For instance, in 2006/2007, the Faculty of Computing and Information Technology retained a total of UGS 7 billion (12% of the total revenue generated by the university) while the Faculty of Arts retained UGS 4 billion (7% of the total revenue generated). In the laboratory-based units, the Faculty of Technology which ranks highest retained UGS 1.1 billion (only 2% of the total revenue generated in Makerere University).

There is no deliberate effort to fund units outside of the monies they generate, apart from the percentage of funds that go to the centre from the various programmes for central management. Centrally managed private resources are utilised to subsidise the general staff salaries and other communal expenditures such as utilities.

Private programmes within public universities were instituted to complement public resources with the view that the state has an obligation to provide higher education as a public good. However, as state funding declines, faculties that cannot accommodate private students in large numbers have also stagnated financially. Yet these are the capital-intensive faculties that require more equipment and infrastructure. Faculty members in these units have responded by putting their energies into generating resources for research and have thus published more than the income- generating units. The result has been reduced teaching activity in these faculties. Faculties such as Medicine and Agriculture have become more inclined towards heavy donor-dependent research as the predominant academic activity.

Generally, science-based faculties have a higher staff–student ratio requirement. They also have more departments and therefore more staff in posts than the humanities. Since approximately 60% of the centrally managed income is utilised for staff pay, the laboratory-based faculties take a substantial share of private resources from the university.

Options for Financing Higher Education

It is evident from the preceding sections that financing higher education poses numerous challenges. In this section financing options are suggested taking into consideration the Ugandan context. The options are investigated at four levels: the state; the private sector; the tertiary institutions; and the donor community.

A clear demarcation of the roles and responsibilities between the public and private sectors undoubtedly will enable institutions to develop long-term, viable and sustainable financing arrangements.

The Role of the State
In tabling the options which the state can consider in financing higher education in Uganda, the following facts have been considered:

- With a country average per capita income of US$ 300 and an average household education expenditure level of 7%, the private household contribution to higher education through tuition fees is likely to be limited;
- The ability of households to pay for higher education at the true cost is hampered by the prevailing socio-economic conditions; and
- At the same time quality higher education requires considerable investments in terms of human resources, facilities and consumables.

Given the above, the state can play a key role in five areas:

1. Regulation of higher education provision, creating a policy environment that favours the autonomy of institutions' resource mobilisation and management planning;
2. Ensuring equitable access to higher education through financial assistance programmes;
3. Maximising economies of scale through the differentiation of public institutions;
4. Provision of central facilities that are accessible by various higher education institutions; and
5. Instituting a deliberate policy to promote the export of higher education through internationalisation.

Regulation of Higher Education Provision

The situation that led to the intensification of private higher education institutions is deeply rooted in the neoliberal philosophy with its unquestioning belief in the role of the market. Leaving higher education to market forces has led to uneven growth, increased inequity, erosion of quality and exploitation of consumers particularly at institutions that fall in the 'for-profit' category.

Before the emergence of the NCHE, the role of the state in higher education provision and regulation was limited to the 'state'-funded institutions. To address the imbalances in the new situation the state has to strengthen its role in higher education provision and financing. The regulatory framework has to ensure value for money. In this case, the NCHE will have to be strengthened and empowered beyond its current levels.

Formula/Performance-based Financing

Currently there is no scientific basis to government financing of similar programmes within the system. Take for instance, the funding of medical students in the two government institutions of Makerere and Mbarara University of Science and Technology, where the government pays a unit cost of UGS 3 million for a medical student in the former institution, and UGS 16 million at the latter institution.

A formula-based funding framework that is responsive to the concerns around equity, efficiency and effectiveness must be put in place as a matter of urgency. Such a framework must take into account both input (student numbers) and output (e.g. success rates) factors.

Differentiation

Related to formula-based financing is the concept of differentiation which can only be effective through an aggressive promotion by the public sector. Currently in Uganda all universities almost offer the same programmes. While there is a perceived 'demand' for these disciplines, the offerings are largely influenced by the low input requirements. Targeted subsidisation of programmes and/or institutions will develop the under-subscribed disciplines necessary for the country's economic development. Differentiation of the various institutions into teaching versus research institutions will meet both the research needs of country as well as the social demand for higher education.

Internationalisation and Market Segmentation

As the world becomes increasingly knowledge-based and a global village with disappearing geographical barriers, Uganda should start to seriously consider higher education as an export product. The prospects in this direction are promising, for instance, the quantifiable value of resources from foreign students undertaking education in 2004/2005 was UGS 40.4 billion of which UGS 11.2 billion was from universities. The ability to attract international staff and students remains a viable option for generating resources to finance higher education in the country.

Financial Assistance Programmes (Loans and Grants)
Financial assistance through grants and loans has been on the table for quite some time in Uganda. The ability to implement cost sharing at realistic unit costs is, to a large extent, dependent upon the operationalisation of a successful loan scheme. The scheme is likely to promote access for students from lower socio-economic households. Experiences from countries where it has been successfully implemented provide several options that could be adopted in Uganda. These options include grants, interest-free loans, subsidised interest loans and commercial-rate loans.

In developing financial assistance programmes based on a loan system, mechanisms will have to be put in place to facilitate greater access not only to public higher education institutions as is the case now, but also to the private higher education institutions.

The Private Sector
Private sector involvement options for higher education financing are envisaged at three levels: (i) direct engagement by the institutions through consultancies and sale of services, business ventures and engagement of industry through contract research; (ii) donations in the form of corporate donations and alumni contributions; and (iii) students' contributions in the form of tuition and other fees.

Consultancy Services
In Uganda, university involvement with the business sector has been limited to consultancy services mainly on an individual basis by staff from the universities. Although it has augmented staff remuneration it has not had a direct monetary benefit for the institutions. Institutionalising consultancy services with a strong unit mandated with the solicitation, management and execution of consultancy services not only to the business sector but with the public sector, non-governmental organisations and international bodies should be considered as a source of income for the institution. The advantage with this option is that it is policy orientated and does not require massive investments or start-up capital.

Direct Business Ventures
Universities in Uganda are known to be among the largest land owners in prime locations in the country. These land holdings have not been optimally utilised for resource mobilisation. In the majority of cases they have been left as wasteland and/or with non-commercial activities such as staff housing at non-commercial rates. Additionally, while Uganda's tertiary institutions have affiliated establishments that could be operated on a commercial basis such as university farms, hospitals and guest houses, these have not been undertaken.

Creating a business arm of institutions either directly or through joint ventures with the private sector will reduce the overreliance on state funds and tuition fees.

Build Own and Transfer (BOT)
The limited facilities and burgeoning student numbers require innovative engagements with the private sector. Increased student enrolments require expansion of higher education facilities particularly in the areas of recreation, accommodation and other facilities that enhance the learning environment. Since Uganda's institutions are financially constrained and their ability to secure loans on a commercial basis are curtailed by the availability of collateral and amortisation potential for the acquired loans, the Build Own and Transfer concept would be a viable option. The advantage with this arrangement is that the institutions are resource rich in terms of the basic land requirement and operationalisation requires limited capitalisation from these institutions, whereas there is a ready market and business potential for the private sector that invests in the institutions.

Donations from Alumni and the Private Sector
Institutions that have been in existence for more than 20 years should cultivate a culture of alumni giving back to their alma mater. Institutions should establish structures that will ensure contributions from future alumni. The old boy's/old girl's network is well established in the secondary school system in Uganda. These networks which largely operate as development oversight committees have an endowment type of operation which targets specific structural or financial achievements. Sadly this culture is non-existent in the universities and other higher education institutions.

Cost-sharing (Tuition Fees)
There are three drawbacks to the current arrangement of tuition fees: (i) it is not equitable and is not paid by all students in the public institutions; (ii) the fees

charged are lower than the true cost of the education; and (iii) private institutions with the exception of one, charge fees set within the ranges of those in the public institutions. These ranges have not changed since the onset of the dual track system and are far below realistic unit costs.

Given these drawbacks, the financial base of both the private and public higher education can be strengthened if these institutions were able to charge realistic or higher than current levels of tuition fees. As in the Indian model, tuition fees could be selectively increased to equal costs while at the same time establishing a mechanism for providing free or subsidised higher education to the most needy students in what has been referred to as the dual track system.

In the absence of income contingent assessments of student support in Uganda, the following should be put in place:

- Institutions should be empowered to mobilise a greater share of the necessary financing from students because higher education is equally a private good and a public good. Moreover, some students come from families with the means to contribute to the costs of education;
- Cost sharing should be pursued through tuition fees and equitable subsidies relative to institutional costs;
- Government should permit public institutions to establish their own tuition and fees without interference. This will facilitate effective private sector contribution to higher education;
- There is a need to work on the mindset of higher education consumers. Sensitisation packages on the value and the cost of higher education need to be developed; and
- Institutions need to establish the true costs of the service they provide, eliminating non-core activities, and highlighting hidden costs as well as curbing wastage.

Contract Research

Contract research can be a good source of revenue for institutions, albeit at a limited level given the size of private sector development in Uganda. Universities have to go out and study the requirements of the market, with a deliberate effort to develop ideas that will attract the private sector through either an incubation arrangement or direct involvement with the private sector from the outset. The private sector should be encouraged to engage the universities for product development and/or improvement and to utilise local expertise to enhance production.

Donors and Endowment Funds
Long-term investments have not featured as a source of income for higher education institutions although they have a potential to be utilised. The Islamic University in Uganda (IUIU) is the only university in the country that has utilised this mechanism with some level of success. IUIU received an endowment from King Fahd of Saudi Arabia. The fund has enabled the institution to finance its activities by up to US$ 100 000 per annum. For both the public and private higher education institutions in the country endowment funds could be explored as an alternative mechanism for resource mobilisation. Since endowments are donor-dependent, its operationalisation in the short run is likely to be more effective in religion-based institutions than in public institutions. Another option would be to cultivate endowment-based donations not only from outside donors but also from the alumni.

Higher education in Uganda is faced with the dual pressures of an increased social demand and receding public support. While the former is a worldwide global phenomenon, the latter is driven by the mounting negative perception that questions the long-treasured and the historically deep-rooted role of the state in higher education. This viewpoint, which is most prevalent in government, articulates higher education not as a public good, nor a social merit good, but as a highly individualised private good.

During the recent past, higher education in Uganda has been characterised by reduced public support and increased demand. Amidst economic trends that characterise a developing country like Uganda, the sub-sector has witnessed a decline in per capita student spending and increased inequity for the few students who are able to access state scholarships. Although the private sector has played an increasingly significant role, it is an inadequate substitute for the declined public support. Higher education is both capital and labour intensive and is operating within the changed global environment of knowledge-based economies. This chapter has shown that fee-paying students usually pay less than the true cost of their education and as a result of inadequate resources from both the private and the public sectors, institutions have been forced to limit expenditures and reduce inputs.

Viable options have been suggested here that the different stakeholders can take in order to better finance higher education in Uganda. These options have been suggested at four levels of the state, the private sector, tertiary institutions and the donor community. The current financing situation will have to be reviewed and addressed at all these levels if the system is to offer equitable and quality Hhigher education to its citizens.

Chapter 11

GOOD PRACTICES, POSSIBLE LESSONS AND REMAINING CHALLENGES

Pundy Pillay[1]

Funding mechanisms are especially important in shaping higher education outcomes in areas such as quality, efficiency, equity and system responsiveness.

Salmi and Hauptman (2006) for instance, identify three goals that countries seek to achieve through the funding of tertiary education:

1. Increasing access to, and equity in tertiary education as measured by:
    - increasing overall participation rates for students of a traditional enrolment age who enter a tertiary education institution in the year following their graduation from secondary school;
    - expanding the number and range of lifelong learning opportunities particularly for older students and other non-traditional groups of students including distance learners;
    - reducing disparities in participation rates between students from low and high family backgrounds as well as other important dimensions of equity such as gender and racial/ethnic group;
    - increasing private sector investment and activity in the provision and support of tertiary education activities.

2. Increasing the external efficiency of tertiary education systems by improving both:
    - the quality of education provided; and
    - the relevance of programmes and of graduates in meeting societal and labour market needs.

---

[1] Note: This chapter is reproduced largely from Pillay 2008.

3. Improving the internal efficiency and sustainability of tertiary education systems by:
   - reducing or moderating the growth over time of costs per student and improving how resources are allocated, both among institutions and within institutions; and
   - decreasing repetition and raising the rates of degree completion.

This volume has attempted to assess the structure and pattern of higher education financing and their implications for access and equity in a comparative study of nine African countries.

African higher education is characterised by extremely low participation rates. With the exception of Mauritius and South Africa, this is true also for the countries considered in this study. Moreover, three key determinants – gender, socio-economic status and region – act to skew the already low participation rates in favour of males, richer families and urban households.

Access and equity in higher education are fundamentally determined by access to and the quality of secondary education. In most African countries, access to secondary schooling is extremely limited and often of poor quality.

Public spending on higher education as a proportion of the education budget varies substantially amongst countries considered in this study. In the case of Lesotho, Mozambique, Namibia and South Africa, higher education spending is relatively high as a percentage of the education budget.

Some Common Themes

It is evident that higher education financing in the countries considered in this study is often inadequate, and almost everywhere inequitable and inefficient.

Even though participation rates remain low in the context of a growing population, enrolments are growing everywhere in absolute terms, in several cases quite dramatically. In the face of serious financial resource constraints for higher education, education ministries have responded mainly in two ways. First, there has been a clear shift towards some form of cost sharing in the form of tuition fees, for example, in Namibia and the East African countries. In the latter group, this has taken the form of a dual-track system where a fee-paying system co-exists with a free, government-sponsored scheme for some students. Second, governments in virtually all countries have permitted the introduction and subsequent expansion of the private higher education sector.

While the cost-sharing and private sector strategies have enabled governments to address to some extent the issue of inadequate public sector funding of higher education, it has almost everywhere resulted in greater inequity. In Kenya and Uganda, for instance, cost sharing unlike in Namibia and South Africa where everyone pays tuition fees, is only for those who cannot access government sponsorships. These scholarships invariably go to those students from more affluent households who are able to access the best schools.

Furthermore, private higher education in Africa, unlike in the industrialised world, appears to be where many of the poor seek access. However, in countries such as Mozambique and Tanzania, many of the private higher education institutions are of questionable quality. Moreover, the situation is not helped by the absence of an effective regulatory framework for private higher education in most countries. Furthermore, in most African countries, private higher education institutions, again unlike in the industrialised world, are for-profit institutions.

A further dimension of the private sector expansion is the entry of overseas providers of higher education in several countries. While these providers may help to address capacity gaps in higher education provision, many of the countries in which they are operating lack the necessary regulatory capacity to effectively monitor quality.

In the countries under consideration here, such as for example, Mozambique, Namibia and Tanzania, higher education financing is extremely inefficient. This is due partly to the fact that higher education financing is largely ad hoc and is not based on any attempt to develop a closer link between sectoral planning and budgeting. In some cases budgeting is done on a purely incremental basis and in other others solely on inputs (student numbers).

Inadequacy of funding for higher education is often a consequence of weak departments of higher education within Ministries of Education. In several countries, there is a an inability and/or unwillingness to make the case for more funding of higher education in the face of politically stronger schooling and other departments within the ministry.

There is moreover, a widespread lack of planning and oversight capacity in these departments of higher education.

Inefficiency of higher education expenditure has been exacerbated by the absence in most countries of a systematic funding mechanism such as a funding formula. Most countries rely on incremental budgeting processes (for example, increases linked to inflation) rather than developing a funding formula that would be able to ensure greater predictability in the budgeting process and 'certainty of revenue' for higher education institutions. Such predictability would be enhanced also by the development of closer links between education planning and the budgetary process, the latter ideally comprising a three-year Medium Term

Expenditure Framework. Very few countries, with South Africa being a notable exception, have established the necessary planning capacity for higher education in the Ministry of Education, and/or appropriate budgetary frameworks for the country as a whole.

A major aspect of inefficiency in expenditure relates to the manner in which so-called loan schemes operate in several countries. In Botswana, Lesotho and Tanzania, for instance, governments operate loan schemes for higher education students. In practice, however, these have been scholarships for study in both local and foreign institutions, as no serious efforts have been made to collect such loans. In practice, therefore, higher education has been free. It has also been inequitable as the students who access these 'loans' are often from the most affluent households.

In the small countries, especially Botswana, Lesotho and Mauritius, limited capacity has resulted in substantial resources being spent on education outside the country. In Mauritius, the costs of overseas study are borne by private households. In Botswana and Lesotho, however, the costs have been carried largely by the state. While there are clearly high private returns to individuals, the social benefits to Botswana and Lesotho more broadly (through, for example, returning graduates, remittances) have not been quantified but the cost to the taxpayers has been high.

Internal efficiency (as reflected in high drop-out and repetition rates, and poor quality of outputs) characterises all systems and is partly a consequence of poor academic salaries resulting in poor quality of teaching and/or poorly motivated staff.

In several countries (Lesotho, Tanzania and Mozambique), there is significant external donor involvement in higher education financing. The long-term implications of this for the government are quite serious.

Good Practices

It is evident that the overall picture of higher education financing, with a few notable exceptions, is characterised by inadequacy, inefficiency and inequity. Nevertheless, there are several examples of 'good practice' that other African countries may want to study and possibly emulate.

Financing practices that address the inadequacy of public expenditure
1. **Private–Public Partnerships:** To address the issue of scarce public resources, Botswana has established a new university on a private–public partnership basis.

In this model, the state provided substantial funding for capital expenditure while the private sector will be responsible for operational expenditure.

2. **The differentiated government funding model in Mauritius**: In Mauritius, all public institutions are not funded in the same way. Where there are seen to be high private returns (e.g. the University of Technology) the state provides proportionally lower funds as opposed to institutions providing higher education with greater social returns (e.g. teacher education).

3. **Cost sharing**: Several countries have recently introduced cost sharing in the form of tuition fees to address the inadequacy of institutional revenue. This is particularly so in Namibia, Mauritius and Tanzania. South Africa has always had a system of fee paying in higher education. However, not all countries apply cost sharing equitably because of the dual-track tuition programmes (Kenya, Uganda).

Financing Policies that Address Equity
1. **Provincial scholarships**: Mozambique provides scholarships to poor students from rural areas.

2. **Loans to students in private higher education institutions** – e.g. Botswana and Tanzania – in both cases (in Tanzania until 2007/2008 when cost recovery began) these are effectively grants but they enhance equity because the proportion of students going to private education are often from the lower socio-economic groups.

3. **Loan schemes to address access and equity**: South Africa's national student loan scheme is designed to attract larger numbers of historically disadvantaged students into higher education. Although there is some controversy about how 'disadvantage' is defined, the scheme attracts a high level of funding from government, operates at a high level of efficiency in terms of cost recovery, and uses 'means-testing' to ensure that loans go to those who are at the lower end of the socio-economic spectrum. Similarly, Kenya has developed a loan scheme that works relatively well in terms of addressing equity in the public higher education system.

Financing Polices that Address Efficiency
1. **Linking higher education planning to budgeting** – e.g. South Africa. In South Africa, as reported earlier, there is a close link between planning (at both

the institutional and system levels) and funding. higher education institutions are required to submit three-year 'rolling plans' to the government as part of the state's planning and Medium Term Expenditure Framework budgeting process. Such planning and budgeting instruments can serve to enhance efficiency in the utilisation of limited public resources.

2. **Funding to improve quality of educational provision**: Mozambique provides a funding facility, the Quality Enhancement and Innovative Facility – an initiative to reward both public and private institutions and individuals for the development of quality-enhancement programmes.

Some Possible Lessons

It is inevitable, given serious public resource constraints, that the higher education sector must look at alternative mechanisms for generating funding to enhance access and equity. Among the funding mechanisms that need to be considered are some form of cost sharing and the development of loan schemes that promote access and equity and are efficient in terms of cost recovery. A third issue relates to the development of a funding formula for higher education that can promote the more effective utilisation of scarce financial resources and enable governments to achieve broader objectives of the higher education system (e.g. appropriate human resource development).

Cost Recovery
Cost sharing can take a number of forms:

- The introduction of tuition fees where those did not exist;
- A rise in the level of tuition fees where those already existed;
- The creation of a special tuition-paying track for a proportion of students;
- The imposition of 'user charges' (e.g. registration fees) for recovering the expenses of some previously heavily subsidised institutional services (such as meals and accommodation);
- The reduction of student grants or scholarships;
- An increase in the effective cost recovery on student loans (e.g. through a reduction of the subsidies on student loans);
- The limitation of capacity in the highly subsidised public sector together with the official encouragement of a tuition-dependent private tertiary education sector (OECD 2008).

The case for cost sharing can be made on several grounds. There are several rationales for students and families to share the costs of tertiary education with tax payers. The arguments often used to make the case for cost sharing are:

- Public money available for tertiary education is lacking in light of enrolment growth and competing priorities for public funds;
- Those who benefit should contribute to the costs of tertiary education;
- Public savings from individual contributions can be channelled to improve equity of access; and
- Tuition fees introduce the virtues of price as a market mechanism (OECD 2008).

However, there may be a number of technical aspects which make the realisation of cost sharing in developing/poor countries more challenging. This is essentially related to two aspects. First, the split of the cost (i.e. the share that each of government and the students/families should pay) is difficult to establish in any precise way because the magnitude of tertiary education externalities is very difficult to measure (OECD 2008). On the other hand, cost sharing, to be compatible with access and equality of opportunities, must be accompanied by measures which remove financial barriers to enter tertiary education at the time of the enrolment decision, especially for the more disadvantaged groups. This requires robust student financial aid systems typically formed of need-based grants and loan schemes and possibly other programmes to compensate for unequal educational opportunities at the secondary level (OECD 2008).

However, the implementation of student assistance programmes is hindered by aspects such as:

- Difficulties in determining the extent of need of students (or families);
- Problems of recovering costs from graduates in the form of loan repayments;
- The need for a substantial initial investment to launch a loan system based on public funds;
- The absence or limitations of private capital markets for student loans to complement the limited amounts of student lending available from public schemes;
- In a number of countries, the absence of a sufficiently affluent middle class that can afford tuition fees would require substantial investments in financial assistance to students (and families), often not readily available from the public budget.

A third dimension includes arguments of a strategic nature. It broadly relates to the assumption that the political acceptance of cost-sharing disadvantages tertiary education relative to competing claims on public money. The two main arguments are as follows:

1. Assuming that tertiary education has greater ability to supplement its public revenue with private revenues (not necessarily limited to cost sharing) places it at a great disadvantage relative to other social areas (such as basic education, health or welfare) and makes the reduction of dedicated public funds politically easier.
2. While a policy of cost sharing combined with student financial aid might target resources better, politicians might give lower priority to the development of the student aid system than to the expansion of cost sharing (e.g. higher tuition).

Clarifying what government wants from its funding is likely to be of great consequence. The question of what the government wants for its funding support is fundamental to the whole endeavour, yet in many countries there is no clear reasoning behind any particular level of funding other than the most general social, economic and tax equity rationales. Often too little attention is paid to using funding processes to address concerns about the relevance of tertiary education, including meeting the emerging societal and economic needs.

Developing an Efficient and Equitable Loan Scheme
Important lessons can be drawn from the South African and Kenyan experiences with regard to designing and implementing an effective student loan scheme. It is encouraging to see Namibia moving towards developing a loan scheme. The South African and Kenyan schemes are specifically designed to address issues of equity even through there is criticism of the Kenyan scheme because it does not provide adequate loans to poor students in the private sector.

Developing a Higher Education Funding Formula to Promote more Effective Utilisation of Financial Resources and Attaining Higher Education Objectives
As reported in Chapter 8, the funding framework developed in South Africa in the post-apartheid era re-conceptualised the relationship between institutional costs and government expenditure on higher education. This framework is seen as a distributive mechanism, that is, a way of allocating government funds to individual institutions in accordance both with the budget made available by government and with government's policy priorities.

The funding framework developed for higher education in South Africa has a number of important implications for equity and efficiency, including ensuring certainty of revenue for institutions, and promoting institutional autonomy and equity.

Given the South African experience, key practical actions that other African countries adopting a funding formula should take note of are the following:

- Simplicity: Design a formula that is simple and can be understood by the broadest section as possible of the higher education community.
- Promote understanding and acceptance of the formula by institutions through designing appropriate consultative mechanisms and undertaking training programmes.
- Develop effective data management systems at both the institutional and government levels to ensure that the formula (particularly with respect to the input and output elements) can be implemented effectively.
- Higher education-labour market linkages: Design an effective system to monitor the outputs and outcomes of the higher education system in relation to the needs of the labour market and economy (Pillay 2006).

Remaining Challenges

In conclusion, the challenges for African policymakers with respect to higher education financing are numerous and can be captured in a series of questions:

1. How do Ministries of Education and higher education institutions make the best possible (most efficient) use of current, limited resources?
2. How can Ministries of Education develop a strong case to Ministries of Finance about the importance of higher education for economic and broader social development?
3. What alternative funding mechanisms (loans, cost sharing, etc.) are possible in poor African states?
4. If cost sharing is to be considered as a possible funding mechanism, how can it ensure greater equity?
5. With cost sharing, is it possible to re-direct current resources being expended in poor quality private systems towards expanding public sector capacity?
6. If a loan scheme is being planned, are necessary pre-conditions in place (e.g. effective tax administration system; ability of employers to play a role

in cost recovery; institutional infrastructure for means testing)?
7. Is a higher education planning and budgeting framework necessary to enhance the case for more funding and to promote more effective utilisation of current funding, and if so, what institutional arrangements are needed to promote systemic and institutional planning?
8. Can higher education financing be used to 'steer' the system to obtain governments' objectives, e.g. in human resource development?

ABOUT THE AUTHORS

Jonathan Adongo is a Researcher at the Namibian Economic Policy Research Unit in Windhoek

Arlindo Chilundo is Professor of Education at Eduardo Mondlane University and an adviser to the Government of Mozambique

Johnson Ishengoma is Senior Lecturer in Education at the University of Dar es Salaam

Florence Mayega is an Academic Planner at Makerere University in Uganda

Praveen Mohadeb is Chief Executive Officer of the Tertiary Education Commission in Mauritius

Nakanyike Musisi is Director of the Makerere Institute for Social Research, Uganda

Wycliffe Otieno is a Kenyan economist and consultant working on education

Pundy Pillay is a South African economist and consultant working on education and other social sector issues

Happy Siphambe is Associate Professor in Economics at the University of Botswana

References

Chapter 1: Introduction

Adedeji, S & Pillay, P (2009) *Tertiary Education Financing in Nigeria*. Unpublished paper, Partnership for Higher Education in Africa, New York.

Organisation for Economic Cooperation and Development (OECD) (2006) *African Outlook 2005-2006*. Paris.

Pillay, P (2008) *Higher Education Funding Frameworks in SADC*. SARUA, Johannesburg.

UNDP (2009) *Human Development Report*. New York: Oxford University Press.

UNESCO (2008) *Education for All Global Monitoring Report 2007*. Paris.

Chapter 2: Botswana

Akanbi, O (2007) *Measuring the Determinants of Education Spending in Africa*. Unpublished paper, University of Pretoria, Pretoria.

Bray, M (1998) Financing Education in Developing Asia: Themes, Tensions and Policies. *International Journal of Educational Research*, 29(7), 627–642.

Colclough, C & S McCarthy (1980) *The Political Economy of Botswana: A Study of Growth and Distribution*. London: Oxford University Press.

CSO (2008) *Botswana Statistical Yearbook 2006*. Gaborone: Government Printer.

Harvey, C & S R Lewis (1990) *Policy Choice and Development in Botswana*. London: Macmillan.

Ministry of Education (2004) Department of Student Placement and Welfare. *The Grant/Loan Scheme*. Gaborone.

Ministry of Finance and Development Planning (MFDP) (2006) *National Human Resource Development Planning*. Gaborone.

Republic of Botswana (1991) *National development Plan 7*. Gaborone: Government Printer.

Republic of Botswana (1993) *Report of the National Commission on Education 1993*. Gaborone: Government Printer.

Republic of Botswana/United Nations (2004) *Millennium Development Goals Status Report 2004: Achievements, Future Challenges and Choices*. Gaborone.

Shantakumar, M (1992) *Loan Financing of University Education in India*. Unpublished paper.

Siphambe, H K (2008). Rates of return to education in Botswana: Results from the 2002/03 HIES data set. *South African Journal of Economics* June.

Tertiary Education Commission (TEC) (2006). *Towards a Knowledge Society: A Proposal for a Tertiary Education Policy for Botswana*. Gaborone.

University of Botswana (2004) *Shaping Our Future: UB's Strategic Priorities and Actions to 2009 and Beyond*. Gaborone: University of Botswana.

University of Botswana (2007) *UB Calendar 2007–2008*. Gaborone.

University of Botswana (2006) *Fact Book*. Gaborone.

University of Botswana (2008) *UB Strategic Plan*. Gaborone.

World Bank (1994) *World Development Report 1994: Infrastructure for Development*. New York: Oxford University Press.

Chapter 3: Kenya

Abagi, O (1997) *Public and Private Investment in Primary Education in Kenya: An Agenda for Action*. Discussion Paper No. DP/005/97. Nairobi: Institute of Policy Analysis and Research (IPAR).

Aduol, F (2001) *Financing Universities in Kenya: A Model Based on Rationalized Student Unit Costs and Staffing*. International Conference on Transformation of Higher Education Management and Leadership Efficacy, Nairobi.

Altbach, P G (ed.) (1999) *Private Prometheus: Private Higher Education and Development in the 21st Century*, Centre for International Higher Education, School of Education, Boston College, Boston MA.

Bogonko, S N (1992) *Reflections on Education in East Africa*. Oxford University Press, Nairobi.

Currie, J & L Vidovich (2001) Privatization and Competition Policies for Australian Universities, *ASHE Reader on Finance in Higher Education*, pp 687–702. Boston, MA: Pearson.

Johnstone B & P Marcucci (2007) *Worldwide Trends in Higher Education Finance: Cost Sharing, Student Loans and the Support of Academic Research*. The International Comparative Higher Education and Finance Project (ICHEAFP). Paper prepared for UNESCO, New York.

Kenya, Republic of (1985) *The Universities Act*. Nairobi: Government Printer.

Kenya, Republic of (1996) *Economic Reforms for 1996–1998: The Policy Framework Paper*. Nairobi: Government Printer.

Kenya, Republic of (2005a) *Sessional Paper No. 1 of 2005 on 'Policy Framework for Education, Training and Research'*. Nairobi: Government Printer.

Kenya, Republic of (2005b) *Kenya Education Sector Support Program (KESSP)*. Ministry of Education, Science and Technology, Nairobi.

Kenya, Republic of (2007) *Ministerial Public Expenditure Review (MPER)*. Ministry of Education, Nairobi.

Kiamba, C (2003) *The Experience of Privately-Sponsored Studentship and Other Income Generating Activities at the University of Nairobi*. Paper presented at a conference on Improving Tertiary Education in Sub-Saharan Africa:Things that Work!, Accra.

Kimalu, P, N Nafula, G Manda, G Mwabu & M S Kimenyi (2002) *A Situational Analysis of Poverty in Kenya. Kenya Institute of Public Policy Research and Analysis* (KIPPRA) Discussion Paper No.6, Nairobi.

Otieno, W (2004) Student Loans in Kenya: Past Experiences, Current Hurdles and Opportunities for the Future, *Journal of Higher Education in Africa*, 2(2): 75–99.

Otieno, W (2005) *Improving Institutional Efficiency and Student Choice in Higher Education: The Prospects of Educational Vouchers in Kenya's University Education*. Unpublished PhD Thesis.

UNESCO (2007) Education for All Global Monitoring Report *2006*. Paris.

Wagacha, M & R Ngugi (1999) Macroeconomic Structure and Outlook, in P Kimuyu, M Wagacha & O Abagi (eds) *Kenya's Strategic Policies:Macroeconomic and Sectoral Choices*. Nairobi: IPAR.

Weidman, J C (2000) *Diversifying Finance of Higher Education Systems in the Third World: the Cases of*

Kenya and Mongolia. Available at: www.pitt.edu/~weidman

Wesonga, P (2003) *Private Provision of Higher Education in Kenya: An Analysis of Trends and Issues in Four Select Universities.* Report to the Ford Foundation Office for Eastern Africa, Nairobi.

Wongosothorn, T-I & Y Wang (eds) (1997) *Private Higher Education in Asia and the Pacific.* Bangkok: UNESCO.

Chapter 4: Lesotho

Ministry of Education and Training (2005) *Education Sector Strategic Plan 2005–2015.* Maseru.

Ministry of Finance and Development Planning (2005) *Report on the Restructuring of the National Manpower Development Council Secretariat and Revolving Fund.* Maseru.

UNESCO (2009) *Education for All Global Monitoring Report 2008.* Paris.

World Bank (2005) *Report on Tertiary Education in Lesotho.* Washington, DC.

Chapter 5: Mauritius

Bunwaree, S S (1994) *Mauritian Education in a Global Economy.* Rose Hill: Editions de L'Océan Indien.

Financial Statements of MIE, MCA, UOM, MGI and TEC, Various Years.

Glover, V (1985) *Tertiary Education: Report of the study Panel on Tertiary Education.* Reduit: Mauritius Institute of Education.

Ministry of Education and Human Resources (1991) *Master Plan for Education.*

Ministry of Education and Scientific Research. *'Education Cards' Statistics.* Various Years. Mauritius: Phoenix.

Ministry of Education and Scientific Research (2000) *White Paper on Tertiary Education.* Mauritius: Phoenix.

Ministry of Education and Scientific Research (2001) *Ending the Rat Race in Primary Education and Breaking the Admission Bottleneck at Secondary Level – The Way Forward.* Mauritius: Phoenix.

Morisson, T R (1997) *The Children of Modernisation: Adolescence and the Development of Mauritius.* Port Louis: Bahadoor Printing.

Suddhoo, A (2001) *The Financing and Cost of Education in Mauritius.* Dakar: CODESRIA.

Tertiary Education Commission (TEC) (1999) *Biennial Report on Tertiary Education 1997/1998.* Port Louis: TEC.

Tertiary Education Commission (2000) Survey on Private Provision of Post Secondary Education in Mauritius. Port Louis: TEC.

Tertiary Education Commission (2007) *Participation in Tertiary Education.* Port Louis: TEC.

Chapter 6: Mozambique

Chilundo, A (2002) *The State of Higher Education in Mozambique,* Paper presented at the UNESCO Africa Regional Conference on Progress and Future Directions of Higher Education in Africa, Abuja, Nigeria, June.

Chilundo, A (2004) Presentation on: *Preface and Introduction of 'Indicadores de Ciencia e technologia em Mozambique 2002-2003* published by Ministry of Education, Science and Technology (MESCT), and *Economist Intelligence Unit Country Profile 2004 and Country Report of January 2004, Balance of Activities*. Meeting of International Partners hosted by MESCT.

Government of Mozambique (2003) *Action Plan for the Reduction of Absolute Poverty (PARPA)*, Maputo.

Government of Mozambique (2000) *Strategic Plan of Higher Education in Mozambique 2000-2010*, Maputo.

Merisotis, J, J Welman, M Mario, F Lichucha & M Malate (2003) Determining Unit Cost Analysis for Higher Education in Mozambique: a Pilot Study, Ministry of Higher Education, Science and Technology and Universidade Eduardo Mondlane, Maputo (unpublished).

Ministry of Education (2000) *Strategic Plan for Education in Mozambique 2000–2010*, Maputo.

Chapter 7: Namibia

Adams, A V (2005) 'Foreword' in M T Marope *Namibia: Human Capital and Knowledge Development for Economic Growth with Equity*. Africa Region Human Development Working Paper No. 84. Washington, DC: World Bank.

Central Bureau of Statistics (2007) *Namibia Household Income and Expenditure Survey Dataset*. Windhoek.

Eduloan. www.eduloan.co.za

Education and Training Sector Improvement Programme (ETSIP) (2005) *Education and Training Sector Improvement Programme: Planning for a learning nation. Programme document: Phase 1 (2006–2011)*, Working draft, November, Namibia.

Godana, T & J M Ashipala (2006) *The Impact of Education Quality on Rates of Return to Education in Namibia*, Working Paper No. 4. Dakar: Secretariat for Institutional Support for Economic Research in Africa (SISERA).

Godana, T & K Ogawa (2003) *Cost and Financing of Education Study In Namibia, Report 06/05/03 of the ESW-P078682*, Human Capital Development for Economic Growth with Equity. Washington, DC: World Bank.

Gwartney, J D, R L Stroup, R S Sobel & D A MacPherson (2003) *Economies: Private and Public Choice*, 10th Edition. Ohio: Thomas/South Western Press.

Johanson, R & R Kukler (2003) *Vocational Skills Development in Namibia: Background Report 03/05/03 of the ESW-P078682*, Human Capital Development for Economic Growth with Equity. Washington, DC: World Bank.

Marope, M T (2005) *Namibian Human Capital and Knowledge Development for Economic Growth with Equity*, Africa Region Human Development Working Paper No. 84. Washington, DC: World Bank.

Ministry of Education and Culture (1993) *Education; National Vision and Strategic Plan*. Windhoek.

Ministry of Finance (2005) *Medium Term Expenditure Framework for 2005/06-2007/08 and Revenue, Income and Expenditure Estimates for the Financial Year 2005/06*, presented to Parliament, Windhoek, Namibia.

Mutorwa, J (2004) *Access to Education: 1990–2000*. Johannesburg: Gamsberg, Macmillan.

Office of the Auditor General (2003) *Report of the Auditor-General on the accounts of the Social Security Commission, Employees' Compensation Fund and Materntiy Leave, Sick Leave and Death Benefit Fund*. Windhoek.

Polytechnic of Namibia (1996–2002) *Annual Reports*. Windhoek.

State Revenue Fund (2002–2007) *Estimates of Revenue and Expenditure for the (Respective) Financial Years, April-March*. Windhoek: Ministry of Finance.

University of Namibia (1996–2002) *Annual Reports*. Windhoek.

Chapter 8: South Africa

Bunting, I (2002) 'Funding' in *Transformation in Higher Education: Global Pressures and Local Realities in South Africa*. Pretoria: Centre for Higher Education Transformation in South Africa (CHET).

Department of Education (DoE) (1997) *Education White Paper 3: A Programme for the Transformation of Higher Education*. General Notice 1196 of 1997. Pretoria.

DoE (2001) *National Plan for Higher Education*. Pretoria.

DoE (2007a) *Information on the State Budget of Higher Education*. Pretoria

DoE (2007b) Student Tuition Fees and the Resourcing of Public Higher Education. Presentation by Ian Bunting to HESA Task Team on Tuition Fees, 15 May.

Duncan, J (2009) *Third Stream Income at South African Universities*. Grahamstown: Centre for Higher Education Research, Teaching and Learning, Rhodes University.

Le Roux, P & M Breier (2007) *Steering from a Distance: Funding Mechanisms, Student Access and Success in higher education in South Africa*, Paper prepared for the First Annual SANORD Centre Conference: Higher Education and Development: Shifting Challenges and Opportunities University of the Western Cape, Bellville, South Africa.

Ministry of Education (2001) *National Plan for Higher Education*. Pretoria.

Ministry of Education (2002) *Funding of Public Higher Education: A New Funding (Revised)*, November, Pretoria.

Ministry of Education (2003) *Schedule – Funding of Public Higher Education*, November. Pretoria.

Ministry of Education (2004) *Statement on Higher Education Funding: 2004/05 to 2006/07*, February. Pretoria.

National Treasury (2009) *MTEF 2009/10–2011/12*. Pretoria.

Wangenge-Ouma, G & N Cloete (2008) Financing Higher Education in South Africa: Public Funding, Non-government Revenue and Tuition Fees, *South African Journal of Higher Education* 22(4): 906-919.

Pillay, P (2006) The South African Experience with Developing and Implementing a Funding Formula for Tertiary Education, *Journal of Higher Education in Africa* 3(4).

Chapter 9: Tanzania

Bloom, D, D Canning & K Chan (2005) *Higher Education and Economic Development in Africa*. Boston: Harvard University Press.

REFERENCES

Carol, B (2004) *Dual Tuition Policy in Uganda*. Research report prepared for the International Comparative Higher Education Finance and Accessibility Project, Centre for Comparative and Global Studies in Education, State University of New York at Buffalo.

Castro-Leal, F (1999) Public Spending in Africa: Do the Poor Benefit? *Research Observer* 14(1): 49–72.

Chuta, E J (1998) New Dimensions in Educational Financing: The Nigerian Education Bank, *Higher Education* 35: 423–433.

Galabawa, J C J (1991) Funding, Selected Issues and Trends in Tanzanian Higher Education, *Higher Education* 21: 54.

Higher Education Accreditation Council (HEAC) (2005) *Guide to Higher Education in Tanzania*, 2005. Dar es Salaam.

Ishengoma, J M (2004) Cost Sharing and Participation in Higher Education in sub-Saharan Africa: the Case of Tanzania, Unpublished doctoral dissertation, State University of New York at Buffalo.

Ishengoma, J M (2005) Cost Sharing and Equity in Higher Education in Tanzania, Paper presented at the Regional Conference on Financing of Higher Education: The Role of the Student Loan Scheme, Nairobi, October.

Ishengoma, J M (2006a) Student Background, Higher Education Costs and Attitudes towards Cost Sharing in Higher Education in Tanzania: Case Study of the University of Dar es Salaam and St Augustine University of Tanzania, Research report prepared for the International Comparative Higher Education Finance and Accessibility Project, Centre for Comparative and Global Studies in Education, State University of New York at Buffalo.

Ishengoma, J M (2006b) Socio-economic Backgrounds and Participation in Private Higher Education in Tanzania: Implications for Equity in Higher Education, Research report presented at the 11th Research on Poverty Alleviation Program (REPOA) Annual Research Workshop, Dar es Salaam, April.

Johnstone, B D (2006) Higher Education Cost Sharing, Dual Track Tuition Policies, and Higher Educational Access: the East African Experience, Paper presented at the IREDU Conference on Economics of Education, Dijon, France, June.

Johnstone, B D (2003a) Cost Sharing and Equity in Higher Education: Implications for Income Contingent Loans, Paper presented at the Douro III Seminar, Portugal, October.

Johnstone, B D (2003b) Cost Sharing in Higher Education: Tuition, Financial Assitance and Accessibility in a Comparative Perspective, *Czech Sociological Review* 39(3):351–374.

Lamptey, A S (1994) *Financing Higher Education in Africa: a Marketing Perspective*, UNESCO, Dakar, BREDA Series No. 5.

Morley, L, F Leach & R Lugg (2007) Democratizing Higher Education in Ghana and Tanzania: Opportunity, Structures and Capacity Changes. www.sussex.ac.uk//education/wideningparticipation.

National Bureau of Statistics (NBS) (2002) *Household Budget Survey 2000/2001*. Dar es Salaam.

Oketch, M O (2003) Market Model of Financing Higher Education in sub-Saharan Africa: examples from Kenya, *Higher Education* 16(3): 313–332.

Omari, I (1994) Cost Sharing and Student Loans in Higher Education in Tanzania, *Papers in Education and Development*, No. 15.

Omari, I & G Mjema (2007) Towards Pro-Poor Spending in Education in Tanzania, Paper presented at the 12th REPOA Annual Research Workshop, Dar es Salaam, March.

Tanganyika African National Union (TANU) (1967) *The Arusha Declaration and TANU's Policy on Socialism and Self-Reliance*. Dar es Salaam: NUTA Press.

United Republic of Tanzania (URT) (1995) *National Education and Training Policy*. Dar es Salaam.

URT (1998) *Financial Sustainability of Higher Education in Tanzania, A Report of the Task Force*. Dar es Salaam: Ministry for Science, Technology and Higher Education (MSTHE).

URT (1999) *National Higher Education Policy*. Dar es Salaam: MSTHE.

URT (2002) *An Evaluation of the First and Second Phases of Cost Sharing in Higher Education in Tanzania*. Dar es Salaam: MSTHE.

URT (2003a) *Methodology for Determination and Updating of Student Unit Costs in Higher Education Institutions in Tanzania*. Dar es Salaam: MHEST.

URT (2003b) *Higher and Technical Education Sub-master Plan*. Dar es Salaam: MSTHE.

URT (2005) *Review of Financial Sustainability in Financing Higher Education in Tanzania*. Dar es Salaam: MHEST.

URT (2006a) *2006/2007 Budget Speech by the Minister for Higher Education, Science and Technology*. Dar es Salaam: MHEST.

URT (2006b) *Basic Education Statistics in Tanzania (BEST) 2002–2006 National Data*. Dar es Salaam: Ministry of Education and Vocational Training.

URT (2006c) *Basic Statistics on Higher Education, Science and Technology*. Dar es Salaam: MHEST.

URT (2006d) *The Economic Survey 2005*. Dar es Salaam: Ministry of Planning, Economy and Empowerment.

URT (2007) *Education Sector Public Expenditure Review (PER) 2005 2nd Draft*. Dar es Salaam.

University of Dar es Salaam (UDSM) (2004) *Facts and Figures 2003/2004*. Dar es Salaam.

UDSM (2006) *Facts and Figures 2005/2006*. Dar es Salaam.

World Bank (1995) *Tanzania Social Sector Review*. Washington, D.C.

Chapter 10: Uganda

Appleton, S (2001) *Education, Incomes and poverty in Uganda in the 1990s*. Centre for Research in Economic Development and International Trade, University of Nottingham.

Ashby, E (1966) *Universities: British, Indian and African. A Study in the Ecology of Higher Education*. Cambridge University Press.

Coleman, J S (1983) The Idea of the Development University. In J Heltand *Universities and National Development*. Stockholm: Almqvist and Wiksell International.

Girdwood, A (1992) The Function and Financing of African Universitie: A Review of Selected Policy Statements 1933–1988. *Occasional Paper 36*. Centre of African Studies, Edinburgh University.

Kasozi A B K, N B Musisi, F Nakayiwa, A Balihuta & S Katunguka (2003) *The Uganda Tertiary/Higher Education Unit Cost study*. Makerere Institute of Social Research.

Liang, X (2004) *Uganda Tertiary Education Sector Report*. Africa Region Human Development Working Paper Series.

Makerere Institute of Social Research (2006) *Graduate Tracer and Employers Expectation*. A study Conducted for and on behalf of the National Council for Higher Education in partnership with the Center for Higher Education Policy Studies (CHEPS) of the University of Twente.

Makerere University Planning and Development Department (2007) *Physical Planning and Space Audit: Final Report on the Study of Existing Situations*.

Mayanja, M K (1998) The Social Background of Makerere University Students and the Potential for Cost Sharing. *Higher Education* 36: 21–41.

Ministry of Finance and Economic Planning (2005) *National Budget Estimates, 1997/1998–2005/2006*. Kampala.

National Council for Higher Education (2004) The State of Higher Education in Uganda, Report of a Survey of Uganda's Institutions of Higher Learning. Kampala

National Council for Higher Education (NCHE) (2005) *State of Higher Education in Uganda*. Kampala.

Uganda National Bureau of Statistics (2003) *Uganda National Household Survey: Report on the Labour Force Survey*. Entebbe.

UNDP (2006) *Human Development Report, Beyod Scarcity: Power, Poverty and the global crisis*. New York: Oxford University Press.

World Bank (1974) *Education Sector Policy Paper*. Washington DC: The World Bank.

World Bank (1988) *Education in Sub Saharan Africa*. Washington DC: The World Bank.

Chapter 11: Conclusion

OECD (2008) *Tertiary Education for the Knowledge Society – Thematic Review of Tertiary Education*, Vol. 1. Paris: OECD.

Pillay, P (2006) The South African Experience with Developing and Implementing a Funding Formula for Tertiary Education, *Journal of Higher Education in Africa* 3(4).

Pillay, P (2008) Higher Education Funding Frameworks in SADC. In P Kotecha (ed.) *Towards a Common Future: Higher Education in the SADC Region Research Findings from Four SARUA Studies*. Johannesburg: SARUA.

Salmi, J & A Hauptman (2006). *Innovations in Tertiary Education Financing: A Comparative Evaluation of Allocation Mechanisms*. World Bank forthcoming (cited in OECD, 2008).

www.ingramcontent.com/pod-product-compliance
Lightning Source LLC
Chambersburg PA
CBHW081152290426
44108CB00018B/2524